THE NATURE OF THE MIND

"This book is excellent, certainly a deserving addition to the existing texts in the philosophy of mind. It is also distinctive both in the topics it covers and in its approach to those topics."

Curtis Brown, *Trinity University, USA*

The Nature of the Mind is a comprehensive and lucid introduction to major themes in the philosophy of mind. It carefully explores the conflicting positions that have arisen within the debate and locates the arguments within their context. It is designed for newcomers to the subject and assumes no previous knowledge of the philosophy of mind.

Clearly written and rigorously presented, this book is ideal for use in undergraduate courses in the philosophy of mind.

Main topics covered include:

- the problem of other minds,
- the dualist/physicalist debate,
- the nature of personal identity and survival,
- mental-state concepts.

The book closes with a number of pointers towards more advanced work in the subject. Study questions and suggestions for further reading are provided at the end of each chapter.

The Nature of the Mind is based on Peter Carruthers' book, *Introducing Persons*, also published by Routledge (1986).

Peter Carruthers is Professor and Chair of Philosophy at the University of Maryland. His recent books include *Phenomenal Consciousness* (2000), *The Philosophy of Psychology* (1999) and *Language, Thought and Consciousness* (1996).

THE NATURE OF THE MIND

An Introduction

Peter Carruthers

Routledge
Taylor & Francis Group

NEW YORK AND LONDON

First published 2004

Simultaneously published in the UK, USA and Canada by
Routledge
29 West 35th Street, New York, NY 10001
and
Routledge
11 New Fetter Lane, London EC4P 4EE

Routledge is an imprint of the Taylor & Francis Group

© 2004 Peter Carruthers

Typeset in Sabon by Wearset Ltd, Boldon, Tyne and Wear, UK
Printed and bound in Great Britain by MPG Books Ltd, Bodmin

Library of Congress Cataloging in Publication Data
A catalog record for this book has been requested

British Library Cataloguing in Publication Data
A catalogue record for this book is available from the British Library

ISBN 0-415-29994-2 (hbk)
ISBN 0-415-29995-0 (pbk)

This book, like its ancestor, is lovingly dedicated to my parents
– Micky and Maureen Carruthers –
each of whom died bravely and with dignity fighting cancer
and each of whom believed firmly in the existence of the soul

Contents

List of figures

Preface

This book is a descendant of an earlier book of mine, *Introducing Persons*, which was published by Croom Helm (London) and SUNY Press (New York) in 1986. (It was then reprinted by Routledge in 1988.) Some material has been passed down into the present book from its ancestor, with some sections being reproduced here virtually unchanged. But much has been rewritten; a good deal of the old material has been cut; and much new material has been added.

The original book was written while I was still partially influenced by the philosophy of Ludwig Wittgenstein, having completed my DPhil thesis on his work at the University of Oxford in 1979; and it therefore included a chapter on the so-called private language argument. That chapter was always too hard for the intended level of difficulty of the book as a whole, however, and wasn't really necessary to make sense of the remainder. (When I taught from the book myself, I found that I always tended to skip it, and advised others to skip it), and the argument didn't really work anyway. Accordingly, that topic has now been dropped altogether.

In the years following the completion of that first book, I came to see that the issues concerning the metaphysics of the self couldn't be presented independently of debates between Rationalists and Empiricists in the theory of knowledge (as I had previously attempted to do); and I also became a convinced theory-theorist about the manner in which we conceive of the mental states of ourselves and others. (Some of the material in Chapter 4 on the former topic is drawn from my book *Human Knowledge and Human Nature*, published by Oxford University Press in 1992; and some of the material in Chapter 7 on the latter topic comes from *The Philosophy of Psychology*, co-authored with George Botterill and published by Cambridge University Press in 1999; I am grateful to the publishers, and to my co-author, for permission to make use of it.) These changes have led to some major restructuring and a good deal of new writing in the present book.

The main focus of this book, however – as of its ancestor – remains the metaphysics of the self. Do we have non-physical (and perhaps immortal) souls, with which we ourselves should be identified? Or are we purely physical creatures, consisting of nothing more than a particular body and brain? The overall goal of the book remains the same, too: to bring the reader to an appreciation of the main foundational issues and theories in contemporary philosophy of mind. The book now closes with a pointer towards some more advanced debates, concerning recent reductive accounts of intentionality and consciousness, for example.

I am grateful to generations of students at the Universities of St Andrews, Queen's Belfast, Essex, Michigan, Sheffield, and Maryland for helping me to get clear about the issues covered in this book. (I have found that teaching, for me, is always a co-operative enterprise, in which I stand to learn almost as much as my students do.) I should mention especially, from among recent cohorts of students: Steve Bell, Tim Bernard, David Didion, Tim Foley, Ramsey Haver-Dieter, Robert Kummerer, Christopher McLaughlin, Keely Owens, Anna Ribeiro, Heidi Schoen, Paul Shaklan, Jared Smith and Adam Spier. I am also grateful to my family for putting up with my occasional absences and preoccupations while this book was being written.

Introduction

This book is about the fundamental nature of ourselves, and the metaphysical character of our minds. (*Metaphysical* questions are questions concerning the most general structure of reality.) Many people throughout the course of human history, across all human cultures, have believed themselves to be distinct from their physical bodies, and have used this belief to ground a hope for some form of life after death. They have believed that they themselves are non-physical spirits or souls, who are connected with a particular body during life, somewhat as a captain is connected with his ship – it is via the effects of the world upon that body that the self is caused to undergo experiences of the world, and it is via the effects of its intentions and decisions upon that body that the self is able to move about in, and have an effect upon, the world in turn. Such people have hoped that when they die, they themselves (i.e., their souls) will continue to exist, perhaps subject to other forms of experience and other capacities for agency.

Such beliefs are no longer popular among philosophers. Few are now prepared to defend a dualism of soul and body. Most are now physicalists of one sort or another, believing that both the self and its mental states are physical in nature. In consequence, it is common for introductory books on philosophy of mind to deal quite briskly with the dualist position, moving swiftly on to physicalism, functionalism, and issues of contemporary debate. In consequence, I believe, many students of the subject feel short-changed. They think that their initial beliefs have not been taken sufficiently seriously, and they feel bullied into accepting the physicalist framework. Although I, too, am a physicalist, I shall take dualism extremely seriously in this book. I present, and carefully analyze and discuss, the strongest arguments in support of a dualism of self

1

and body, as well as displaying the latter's major weaknesses. Also, the various objections and obstacles to physicalism, too, are carefully analyzed in turn.

The book begins, however, with a discussion of the traditional *problem of other minds*. The question is: how do I know that the people around me are subject to thoughts and feelings, and how do I know what they are thinking or feeling on particular occasions? Various proposed solutions to the problem are discussed and criticized, and the assumptions which give rise to the problem are isolated and defended. One of these assumptions is metaphysical, namely the belief that conscious states are quite unlike anything else that we find in the natural world. At the end of the chapter the problem of other minds remains, to be unpicked gradually in later chapters of the book.

Chapter 2 then turns to concentrate on matters metaphysical. It first develops and defends a purported proof of the existence of the soul, before replying to some of the traditional criticisms of body/soul dualism. One of the assumptions of the proof is that thoughts require a thinker (and more generally that mental states require a subject or self). This assumption is challenged by the so-called bundle theory of the self, which forms the topic of the second half of the chapter. The bundle theory is argued to be untenable, leaving the argument for the existence of the soul still standing.

Chapter 3 investigates the identity-conditions for a non-physical soul or self. It asks what would fundamentally make it the case that an earlier and a later soul are different stages in the existence of the very same self. It then asks what fundamentally makes it the case that different souls are distinct from one another at one and the same time. This latter question builds into a purported proof of the *non*-existence of the soul, arguing that the available criteria for individuating souls would conflict with our considered beliefs about the distinctness of different selves. Accordingly, we have a paradox: a seeming-proof (from Chapter 2) of the existence of the soul; and now a seeming-proof of its non-existence. The final section of the chapter revisits the argument of Chapter 2, and succeeds in discovering a non-obvious fallacy within it.

Chapter 4 locates the arguments from the previous two chapters within the Rationalist tradition in philosophy, in that they attempt to generate knowledge of substantive matters of fact (such as the existence or non-existence of non-physical souls) through the use of reason alone, unaided by experience. The contrasting Empiricist tradition is explained and defended. Then in the second half of the chapter the alleged empirical evidence for the existence of the soul is examined and discussed (including near-death experiences, remembrance of past lives, and messages from the spirit-world). The upshot is that neither Rationalism nor Empiricism supports the existence of the soul.

Chapter 5 develops the main (empirical) arguments for physicalism, which is the doctrine that both selves and their mental states are physical in character. Distinctions between different versions of physicalism are drawn, and a partial solution to the problem of other minds is arrived at. But then the second half of the chapter is concerned to examine the myriad objections which have been mounted against physicalism, arguing that none is obviously successful.

Chapter 6 confronts the main non-philosophical argument for the existence of the soul, namely that belief in life after death – grounded in some form of religious faith – requires it. The chapter argues, on the contrary, that physicalism is consistent with after-life through resurrection of the body, and also with various forms of reincarnation, before arguing that we should conceptualize our own survival in terms that don't require identity. The upshot, then, by this stage of the book, is that there are no convincing arguments *against* physicalism or *for* the existence of the soul, whereas there exist powerful arguments *for* physicalism; which leaves physicalism as the most rationally believable metaphysical position overall.

Chapter 7 returns to the question of how we conceptualize mental states, challenging another assumption made in Chapter 1, namely that the meaning of mental terms is exhausted by a capacity to recognize the "feel" of the corresponding mental state. This assumption is criticized, before the reader is taken through a brisk tour of behaviorism and functionalism, finally lighting on so-called theory-theory as the most plausible account. (Theory-theorists hold that mentalistic concepts are embedded in a substantive theory of the causal workings of the mind.) Reasons are adduced for thinking that the theory in question is *innate*, before this idea is put to work in generating a finally satisfying solution to the problem of other minds.

In conclusion, in Chapter 8, various outstanding problems and prospects for physicalism are briefly outlined and discussed. The chapter is intended to provide a pointer towards more advanced work in the subject. Topics discussed include artificial intelligence, free will, the prospects for reductive theories of intentionality (or the *content* of beliefs and desires) and consciousness.

Although this book is designed as an introduction to issues in the philosophy of mind, it is not an introduction to philosophy. On the contrary, it presupposes some familiarity with philosophical methods, and with some of the basic philosophical concepts, such as valid/invalid, logically possible/impossible, and so on. While I do try to explain any such terminology briefly on the first occasion of use (see the concept box below for some initial examples), students new to the subject should probably take a little time working with one or other of the many excellent philosophical dictionaries and encyclopedias whenever a concept which is new to them first occurs.

I should also emphasize that the book warms up a good deal as it goes along, and that readers are likely to find the chapters in the middle and later part of the book more intuitive and appealing than those at the beginning. This is largely a result of the Rationalist framework which governs the arguments of the opening chapters, making them seem somewhat dry and narrowly philosophical. Purported proofs from reason alone are apt to seem less interesting than discussions of empirical evidence – and rightly so if, as I

Some philosophical terminology

A possible world – a way things could be, or could have been;
  – (some say: a possible world is a conceivable world).

X is logically possible – there is some possible world in which X is so;
  – X could be or could have been the case;
  – (some say: X can be conceived to be the case).

X is logically necessary – there is no possible world in which X isn't so;
  – X couldn't have been otherwise;
  – (some say: X can't be conceived to be otherwise).

A valid argument – there is no possible world in which the premises are true but the conclusion false;
    – it is impossible for the premises to be true but the conclusion false;
    – if the premises are/were true, the truth of the conclusion is/would be guaranteed;
    – (some say: it isn't conceivable that the premises should be true while the conclusion is false).

4

believe, Empiricism is the correct framework within which to conduct enquiry. I can only urge the reader to be patient, and to give each of the arguments careful consideration on its own merits.

Each chapter closes with some questions for discussion, and with some suggestions for further reading. Many of the latter are classic books and articles, which any student of the subject should be acquainted with; but I do also include some contemporary readings (especially in later chapters); and whenever I refer to an author in the text, a relevant item is always then included among the suggested readings.

Philosophy of mind is one of the most vibrant and exciting areas of contemporary philosophical research. Indeed, it has been *the* growth area of the subject over the last couple of decades, and many people now regard it as the very core of philosophy – in something like the way that philosophy of language used to be regarded as central to philosophy in the 1960s and 70s. I hope that readers working through this book will go away fired up, wanting to do further work in philosophy of mind and philosophy of psychology. In any case, and above all else: *enjoy!*

1

⟨⟨⟩⟩

The problem of other minds

This chapter begins with a skeptical problem, concerning the extent of our knowledge of other minds besides or own. The argument which gives rise to the problem is outlined, and its underlying assumptions are discussed. This will serve to introduce a number of themes which will recur and be addressed in later chapters. For questions concerning our *knowledge* of the mind are quite intimately related to the question of the *nature* of the mind, which forms the main focus of this book.

1 The problem

The problem of other minds is this: there is an argument which seems to show that we can have no knowledge of any other mental states besides our own. If the conclusion of the argument were correct, then I could not be said to know that the human beings around me are, in the strict sense, persons. Although I should see them walking and talking, laughing and crying, I should not be able to know that they have thoughts, have feelings, are amused or upset, and so on. All I should be able to know is that there are certain living organisms which physically resemble myself, which move around and behave in characteristic ways, and which are the source of complicated patterns of sound which I call speech. Since the conclusion of this argument conflicts powerfully with our everyday beliefs, we have a problem – either to find some fault with the argument itself, or to give up an important element of our commonsense attitudes towards one another.

Many will be inclined to dismiss the problem out of hand. Since they are completely certain that other minds do exist, they will insist that there must be something wrong with an argument which makes our knowledge of them seem problematic. Either one of the premises must be false, or the conclusion must fail to follow logically from the premises (i.e., the argument itself must be *invalid*). But notice that there have been many periods throughout history when people would have been equally dismissive of any argument suggesting that we can't have knowledge of the existence of God. They, too, would have insisted that since they are completely certain of God's existence (Everybody knows it!) there must be something wrong with the argument somewhere. Yet many of us would now think that they were wrong.

The general point is that it is possible to be subjectively certain of a belief without actually having any adequate reason for holding it. One's certainty may have causes but no justification. For example, there may have been causal explanations of people's certainty about the existence of God, either of a sociological sort (People believe what others around them believe) or of a psycho-analytical sort (People need to believe in a father-figure). Similarly, our certainty about the existence of other minds may serve some biological or evolutionary function, without any of us really having adequate reason for believing in any mental states besides our own. It is no good people beating the table shouting, "But of course I know!" – if they think they know, then they should take up the challenge presented by the problem of other minds, and show us *how* they know.

It is no good complaining, either, that the whole attempt to raise a problem about the existence of other minds must be self-defeating, because of the use made of the terms "our" and "we" in the above exposition. It is true that the use of these terms does strictly presuppose the existence of other minds besides my own. But then it is not really necessary that I should make use of them. The whole argument giving rise to the problem of other minds can be expressed in the first-person singular throughout. I can present this argument to myself, and you (if there really *are* any of you!) can present it to yourselves. At no point does it need to be presupposed that there really are a plurality of us.

There is another reason for taking the problem of other minds seriously, even if we could reasonably be confident in advance that the conclusion is false. This is because examination of such arguments – which begin from seemingly-undeniable premises and lead by means of seemingly-obvious steps to an unacceptable conclusion – can be valuable in so far as they require us to examine our background assumptions. Some of these assumptions will be responsible for the apparent force of the argument; but some will need to be rejected if the conclusion is to be avoided. (One way of looking at paradoxical arguments in general – which lead to obviously-false conclusions – is that they are tools for uncovering some of the false assumptions within our ordinary mind-set.) This will be one of our tasks in later chapters, in fact.

1.1 A preliminary statement of the problem

As a way into the problem of other minds, ask yourself the question, "How do I know that what I see when I look at a red object is the same as what anyone else sees when they look at a red object?" That is: how do I know that our experiences are the same? Perhaps what I see when I look at a red object is what you see when you look at a green object, and vice versa. The point is: we naturally assume that we call objects by the same names (red, green, and so on) in virtue of having the same experiences when we look at those objects; but it could equally well be the case that we have different experiences, but the differences never emerge because we call those *experiences* by different names.

So how do you know that the situation is not as follows: what I see when I look at a red object (e.g., a tomato) is what you see when you look at a green one (e.g., a leaf) and vice versa; but because the experience which causes me to say "red" is the experience which causes you to say "green", and vice versa, we always describe the colors of the objects in the same way. This can be represented diagrammatically, as in Figure 1.1. When I look at the red tomato I have an experience of red which leads me to refer to the tomato as "red" and which I describe as "an experience of red"; but when you look at the red tomato you have an experience of *green*, which causes you, too, to refer to the tomato as "red", and which you also describe as "an experience of red". So our behaviors will match, despite the differences in our experiences.

In order to get yourself into the feel of what is going on here, stare intently at a brightly colored object, immersing yourself in its color, and ask: "How do I know that any other person has *this*?" referring not to the color of the object itself, but to your immediate experience of the color. Doesn't it seem that it would only be possible for you to know that another person has *this* sort of experience if you could look into their minds, thus in some sense having, or being aware of, their experience? But this is impossible. I

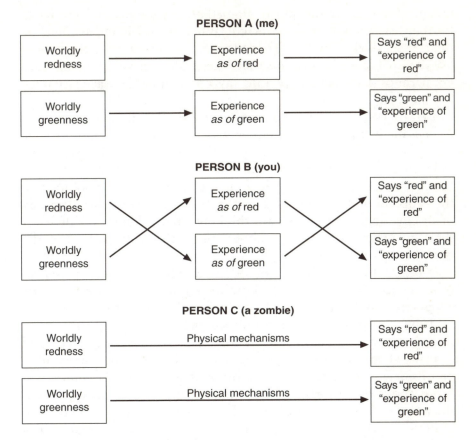

Figure 1.1 Cases of inverted or absent experience.

cannot be aware of your experiences, because anything which I am immediately aware of is, almost by definition, my own experience. Even if two Siamese twins feel pain in exactly the same place (the place where they join) they don't feel one another's pain. On the contrary, each feels her own pain. So it appears impossible that I should ever know whether or not anyone else has the sort of experience which I have when I look at a red object.

(Let me make a remark about telepathy, or direct mind-reading, here. If such a thing can occur, then there would be a sense in which it is possible to have awareness of the thoughts, if not the experiences, of another person. For I might then be able to know what you are thinking, while you are thinking it, without having to ask you, or otherwise infer it from your behavior. All the same I should not be able to have the sort of immediate awareness of your act of thinking which you have yourself. What would happen might be this: I suddenly think, "That person is considering a summer holiday in France", and find that I generally get such things right. Or perhaps a thought pops into my mind unbidden, accompanied by the belief that my act of thinking this thought is somehow caused by your act of thinking an exactly similar thought; and again I generally get it right. But either way, telepathy can only provide me with knowledge of other people's thoughts if I have some independent way of checking my intuitive, telepathically induced, beliefs. So telepathy, even if it occurs, cannot provide a solution to the problem of other minds. For it is only if I have some *other* way of discovering what people are thinking, that I could ever discover that my telepathic beliefs about their thoughts are generally correct.)

It begins to seem that I cannot know what *sorts* of experiences other people have. But now: how do I know that they have *any* experiences at all? How do I know, when they utter the word "red" on being confronted with a red object, that there is really *any* intervening experience? How do I know, when other people cry and scream when they are injured, that there is really any intervening pain? For why cannot the light entering their eyes, or the injury, just bring about those sorts of behaviors directly? Other people would then be zombies (of the philosophical as opposed to the voodoo-induced variety; see person C in Figure 1.1) – namely, human beings who are physically just like me, and who behave just like me, but who lack any experiences at all.

The point is: all that I ever see, or have direct knowledge of, are other people's circumstances and behavior. I can observe the input (injury), and observe the output (crying). But what entitles me to infer that there exists any intervening experience? It would seem that the inference cannot be a valid one. The conclusion cannot follow logically from the premises. For as everyone admits, there is always the possibility of pretence. Since it is possible to writhe and scream (and even have a genuine injury) without actually feeling any pain, the inference from the former to the latter cannot be a valid one.

There is an obvious objection to make at this point, however: namely, that pretence is itself a mental state. To pretend to be in pain is to act as if you were in pain *while believing that you are not*. In which case the argument cannot show that we lack knowledge of other minds altogether. It looks as if I can know for sure *either* that others feel pain *or* that they are pretending; and either way, they possess mental states.

There are two points to make by way of reply to this objection. First, to know that others have mental states of some sort or another (to know that they have minds in general) is not at all the same as saying that we can sometimes know what specific mental states they have on particular occasions. Yet we do ordinarily take ourselves to possess knowledge of the latter sort as well as of the former. If I see someone with an obviously broken leg writhing and screaming, I don't just take myself to know that there is *something* mental going on in them; on the contrary, I take myself to know that they are in pain, and this hasn't yet been accounted for.

The second point is that we don't need to appeal to the possibility of pretence (a mental state) in order to show that the inference from circumstances and behavior, on the one hand, to specific mental states, on the other, must be invalid. For the logical possibility of zombies can serve the same purpose. If it is conceivable that other people could be zombies – physical systems which behave as I do but without undergoing any experiences at all – then the inference from others' behavior to the existence of other minds looks like it can't be a valid one. For it will always be possible that the premises of the argument should be true – people are behaving thus and so – while the conclusion that they have minds is false. (Note that the shift from what is *conceivable* to what is *logically possible*, which has just been made here in this argument, is one whose validity can be challenged. For discussion, see Chapter 3:4 below.)

As expounded thus far, the argument giving rise to the problem of other minds might be summarized as follows:

(1)   It is impossible to have direct awareness of the mental states of another human being.
(C1) So our knowledge of such states (if it exists) must be based upon inference from observable physical and/or behavioral states.
(2)   Because of the ever-present possibility of pretence and/or because of the conceivability of zombies, no such inference can ever be valid.
(C2) So (from (C1) and (2)) it cannot be reasonable to believe in the mental states of other human beings.

11

Premise (1) seems obviously true. I surely cannot experience another person's experiences. I cannot, as it were, look into their minds. I can only, in that sense, look into my own, by introspection. Premise (2) also seems true. No matter what behavior a human being exhibits, there are possible circumstances in which they exhibit such behavior without possessing any conscious experiences. So everything appears to turn on the validity of the two steps, from (1) to conclusion 1 (C1) on the one hand, and from (C1) and (2) to conclusion 2 (C2), on the other.

(Let me make an aside, here, about the value of laying out arguments so explicitly, in the form of numbered premises and conclusions like this – a practice which may be unfamiliar to some readers. One motive is convenience: it enables one to refer to specific points in the argument, as I have just done in the previous paragraph. But much more importantly, it forces one to be explicit about one's assumptions. Often when trying to write down an argument in this sort of form one will realize that some of one's assumptions are obviously missing, and should be stated, or are in need of further defense.)

1.2 Perceptual knowledge

The validity of the move to (C1) might certainly be challenged. For it depends upon the suppressed premise that there are only two modes of knowledge, namely immediate awareness and inference. But this is false. There is a third mode of knowledge, namely observation (or perception). When there is a tomato on the plate in front of me, I obviously don't have the kind of immediate awareness of it which I have of my pains, when I have them; for the tomato is not itself an experience of mine. But then neither do I have to infer that the tomato is there on the basis of anything else. Rather I observe that it is there: I see it. Now we do, in fact, very often say such things as, "I saw that she was in pain, so I called the doctor". So perhaps our knowledge of the existence of other minds isn't knowledge by inference, nor knowledge by immediate awareness, but knowledge by perception.

It might be acceptable to say that we sometimes know of other people's mental states by observation, *if* there were no problem of other minds, or if we had somehow solved that problem. It will be possible to perceive that someone is in pain if, but only if, one already knows on other grounds what sorts of behavior generally have pains as their cause. For although we do not, in ordinary life, normally infer – deduce, or reason out – that someone is in pain on the basis of their behavior, our claim to observe that they are suffering will only be justified given a particular background of empirical assumptions, among which will be the claim that behavior of that sort is regularly correlated with pain.

The general point is that what you perceive is partly a function of what you have reason to believe. As it is sometimes said: perception is theory-laden. Thus if you have previous experience with tomatoes, and the ways in which color and texture tend to correlate with ripeness, then you might truly be able to say, "I saw that the tomato was a ripe one", without having to make any inferences. But even given that you have seen plenty of tomatoes before, if you have never had occasion to taste some, and have never been told that red tomatoes are ripe, then you will be in no position to see the ripeness. Similarly, an experienced engineer might truly be able to say, "I saw that the bridge was in danger of collapsing", whereas an ordinary person could only say, "I saw that the bridge was sagging in the middle".

Thus it will only be possible to perceive the mental states of other persons if we already possess a certain amount of background knowledge: for example, that injury followed by screaming is regularly correlated with pain. But now, how are we supposed to have discovered that these correlations exist? We discovered that the redness of a tomato is correlated with ripeness by observing the color and then tasting the fruit. But this required us to have independent access to the states of the two kinds: observing the redness is one thing, tasting the ripeness is quite another, and each can be done independently of the other. But as we noted above we do not, and cannot, have any direct access to the mental states of other people, independently of our access to their behavior.

It seems that we can only perceive the mental states of other people if we can know such general truths as that writhing and screaming are regularly correlated with pain. But since these general truths themselves can't be known on the basis of perception, it cannot be perception of the mental states of others which provides the solution to the problem of other minds.

1.3 Reliabilism

In fact there is a conception of knowledge according to which perception can give rise to knowledge, even in the absence of background belief. This is a view of knowledge as *reliably acquired* true belief, as opposed to the more traditional concept of knowledge as *justified* true belief. (Both views agree that you cannot know something which isn't true; and that you can't know something without at least believing it.) The resulting view of knowledge is known as "reliabilism", as opposed to the more traditional doctrine which is known as "justificationalism".

According to reliabilists, you can count as knowing something provided that (a) your belief in it is actually true, and (b) your belief was acquired by some reliable process, the sort of process which usually issues in true beliefs. Then provided that our beliefs in the mental states of other people are (a) sometimes true, and (b), when those beliefs are true, they are formed in a way which is in fact reliable, we can count as sometimes knowing the mental states of others.

Although there is much that could be said in support of reliabilist conceptions of knowledge, in fact this maneuver leaves the problem of other minds as outlined above untouched. For the conclusion of the problematic argument was that we have *no reason* to believe in the mental states of others, not just that we *lack knowledge* of the mental states of others. Our common-sense attitude isn't just that we have true beliefs about the mental states of others which have *in fact* been reliably acquired (whether or not we have any reason to believe in the reliability of the acquisition process) – it is that we have *good reason to think that* others have mental states, and that on some occasions we can have good reason to think that another person has one sort of mental state rather than another.

The argument as far as (C1) has thus been sustained: if we have knowledge of the mental states of others (in the sense of justified true beliefs concerning those states), then such knowledge must ultimately be based upon inference from observable physical states.

1.4 Knowledge by analogy

The move from (C1) and (2) to (C2) is also invalid as it stands. From the fact that no description of someone's behavior can ever validly entail a description of their mental state, it doesn't follow that the one can't provide good reason to believe the other. There are two possibilities here.

First, such arguments may contain a suppressed premise. For instance, if we put together a description of someone's behavior with the claim that behavior of that sort is regularly correlated with pain, then these do now entail that the person in question is (very likely) in pain. But this is where we were a moment ago: how could we ever have discovered that there are general correlations between certain kinds of behavior and certain kinds of mental state? For we never have direct access to other people's mental states.

It might be replied that there is at least one case in which I have direct access to both behavioral and mental states, and that is my own. So why can't I discover the empirical correlations in my own case first, and then reason outwards to the case of other people? This would be a form of inductive (as opposed to deductive) argument. This now gives us our second possibility: although an argument from descriptions of behavior to descriptions of mental states may not be deductively valid, it may nevertheless be a reasonable inductive step, founded upon my knowledge of the correlations which exist in my own case.

So the proposal before us is this: first of all I discover in my own case that when I am physically injured this often causes me pain, which in turn causes me to cry out. I then reason inductively that since other people, too, can be injured, and since when they are they generally display similar behavior to my own, that there is very likely a similar intervening cause – a pain. But the trouble with this is that it attempts to argue inductively to a general conclusion on the basis of one case only (namely my own). It is rather as if the first person ever to discover an oyster had opened it up and found a pearl inside, and had then reasoned that all other oysters will similarly contain pearls. On the basis of this one case they were surely entitled to reach no conclusions whatever about oysters in general.

It is important to note, at this point, that the problem of other minds doesn't arise out of any especially strong constraints being placed on the concepts of knowledge or justification. For the conclusion of the above argument isn't merely that I cannot be *absolutely certain* of the mental states of any other human being besides myself, or anything like that. It is, rather, that I have only the very *slightest reason* to believe in them. For my knowledge of other minds would have to be based upon an inductive argument from one case only. So I appear to have just as little reason to believe in other minds as I would have for believing in the redness of all the balls in a large sack, having blindly selected just one of them and found it to be red.

1.5 Summary

We may now summarize the full argument giving rise to the problem of other minds as follows below. (An alternative summary of the argument is provided in Figure 1.2, where the bracketed numbers correspond to the premises below, and the crosses represent that a possibility has been closed off.)

(1)   There are three sources of reasons for belief: (a) immediate awareness, (b) perception, (c) inference from either (a) or (b).
(2)   It is impossible to have immediate awareness of the mental states of another person.
(3)   I can only have perceptual knowledge of the mental states of another if I already know of general correlations between mental and physical states.
(C1)   So (from (1), (2) and (3)) if I have knowledge of the mental states of others, it must ultimately be based upon inference from observable physical states.
(4)   Such an inference must either be deductive or inductive.
(5)   Because of the ever-present possibility of pretence and/or because of the conceivability of zombies, the inference cannot be deductively valid.
(6)   Because it is based upon one case only (my own), the inference cannot be a reasonable inductive step.
(C2)   So (from (4), (5) and (6)) the observed physical states of others fails to provide me with any reason to believe in their mental states.
(C3)   So (from (C1) and (C2)) I cannot have good reasons for belief in the mental states of any other human being besides myself.

This argument gives every appearance of being conclusive. I shall take it that premises (1) through (4) are true, and that the argument itself is valid. It would appear that if there is a weakness anywhere, it must lie either with premise (5) or premise (6). Premise (6) will be challenged, and defended, in the next section. Then in section 3, I shall argue for the conception of the nature of mental states which makes it seem plausible. Finally, in section 4, I shall explain and argue for a conception of the meaning of terms referring to our mental states which makes premise (5) seem especially plausible.

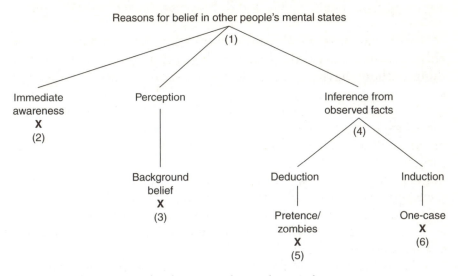

Figure 1.2 The argument for skepticism about other minds.

2   Attempted solutions to the problem

I shall discuss two different ways in which it might be argued that we can reason inductively to the existence of other mental states besides our own. At this stage our conclusion will be that neither is successful. (We will return to re-examine the first of these proposals in a fresh light in Chapter 7:4.)

2.1   *Scientific theory*

Our first attempted solution takes issue with the problem of independent access, raised by the redness–ripeness example in the last section. It was claimed, you will recall, that we cannot establish correlations between two different kinds of thing unless we can have independent access to both of them. (We can establish the ripeness of a tomato independently of observing its redness.) It was then claimed that since we can never have direct access to the mental states of other persons, we could never have discovered that behavior of a certain sort is a sign, e.g., of pain. We attempted to reply to this difficulty by pointing out that there is at least one case in which we have independent access to both behavioral and mental states, namely our own; and this then launched us into the

17

argument from analogy. We could, however, have replied in quite a different way.

Notice that there is at least one sort of case where we can reasonably believe in a general correlation between two different kinds of thing without having independent access to instances of the two kinds. This is where one of the kinds is a theoretical entity, postulated to explain occurrences of the other kind. Thus we postulate the existence of electrons and neutrinos in order to explain such phenomena as tracks across photographic plates in certain laboratory conditions. Of course it is reasonable to believe in electrons, despite the fact that we have no access to them independently of their supposed effects. Similarly then, mightn't it be reasonable to believe in the mental states of other people if postulating the existence of such states provides us with the best available explanation of their observed behavior?

What is being proposed is that our belief in other people's mental states has the status of a scientific theory. Observing the behavior of other human beings, we naturally seek some systematic way of explaining it. We then postulate an elaborate and complex structure of mental states, which are related causally in various ways to one another and to the behavior we observe. Then in the absence of any competing theory to explain that behavior, the inference to the existence of other minds will be an inference to the best available explanation of the observed phenomena. (Just as, in the absence of any suitable competition to explain the tracks on our photographic plates, the inference to the existence of electrons is an inference to the best available explanation.)

Obviously crucial to what we might call "the mentalistic scheme of explanation" will be attributions of suitable beliefs and desires to other people, in terms of which one may rationalize, and to some extent predict, their behavior. Such a scheme can often meet with a fair degree of success. Not only can we make sense of much of the behavior of the people around us in terms of what we take to be their beliefs and desires, we can also predict on that basis much of what they will do. For instance, by attributing to you the desire to survive, and the belief that the ice on a particular pond is thin, I can predict that you will not go skating there. Indeed, it is not merely the behavior of other human beings which is susceptible of explanation and prediction in terms of the mentalistic scheme. We also meet with a fair degree of success in connection with non-human animals. We postulate desires suitably related to the creature's known biological needs, and beliefs suitably related to its sensory apparatus and present and past environment, and in those terms we find that we can make sense of, and predict, much of its behavior.

There are at least two problems for this approach, however (we will return to the issue in Chapter 7). One is that our attitude to the existence of other minds appears to be quite unlike our attitude towards a scientific theory. For we know that scientific theories are apt to be replaced by better theories, and we hold ourselves prepared to see any such theory modified or replaced in the course of scientific enquiry. But this isn't the attitude which we actually take towards the mental states of other people. Our belief isn't tentative and subject to revision in the way that this account would predict. In which case it seems that our *actual* reason for believing in other minds isn't that the postulation of such minds forms the best available explanatory theory for other people's behavior.

The second problem for this approach is to show how our knowledge of our own mental states can be integrated with the sort of knowledge which is postulated for the mental states of others. For I surely don't have knowledge of my own mental states in the manner of knowledge of theoretical entities in science. My knowledge of my own states seems immediate and non-inferential. In which case mental states *in general* cannot be theoretically-postulated entities. Then there is a puzzle as to how it can be the same kinds of states which are theoretically-postulated in the case of other people, but of which I have immediate awareness in my own case.

2.2   *Causal analogies*

We may do rather better if we look once again at the argument by analogy with my own case. Our objection to this was that it was like someone arguing by analogy from the existence of a pearl in their first oyster to the existence of pearls in all oysters. But notice that one very important difference between my knowledge of my own mental states and the case of the pearl in the oyster is this: I know of many causal connections between my mental states and overt physical events; whereas the pearl, on the other hand, just sits there in the oyster, apparently inert. For instance, I know that I speak in order to express my thoughts; that my decision to pick up my drink will normally cause my arm to move; that a pin driven into my flesh will normally cause me to feel a sensation of pain; and so on and so forth.

In fact it appears that I may be able to argue by analogy to the existence of other minds as follows:

(1)   I observe in the world physical bodies which appear, in many respects, to be like my own.
(2)   These bodies go in for the sorts of behavior which I have found, in my own case, to be causally connected with various mental states.
(C)   So these bodies, too, possess mental states.

Of course this argument neither is, nor purports to be, strictly valid. It is rather a species of inductive argument. However, it is being proposed that the argument is rationally convincing – despite the fact that the induction is based upon only one case – in virtue of the myriad causal connections mentioned in premise (2).

It can often be reasonable to allow oneself to be convinced by an argument from analogy which is based upon only one case. Imagine that you are walking on the sea-shore one day, and discover a great many black boxes washed up on the beach by the tide. They all have an array of colored buttons and lights, and you discover that they behave in a similar manner: pressing a red button causes a red light to flash, pressing a green button causes a green light to flash, and so on. Now you open up one of the boxes and discover its internal mechanism of wires and levers. Surely you are entitled to conclude that all the other boxes will have the same internal mechanism (even if, for some reason, you are unable to get them open).

Yet reflect for a moment upon what justifies you in drawing such a conclusion. It is not merely your knowledge, in this one case, of the causal connections between the internal mechanism and the external appearance and behavior of the box; this by itself is insufficient. You must also be taking for granted (surely reasonably, in our era of mass production) that the boxes will all have been constructed according to a common pattern. For it is easy to think of some different assumptions, which wouldn't warrant the conclusion drawn, which just happen in this case to be rather unlikely: for instance, that all of the boxes have been made by different people as part of a competition to see who can produce a machine fulfilling a given function with the greatest economy of materials.

Consider another example: on discovering a new species of lizard you do a post-mortem and discover a particular internal arrangement of heart, lungs and so on. Surely you are entitled to conclude, from just this one case, that all other members of the new species will have a similar internal distribution of vital organs? But the background assumption here, derived from our knowledge of biology more generally, is that although members of the same species can differ in superficial characteristics (like eye color and skin color in humans), they never differ in their basic anatomy (except through sexual, and occasionally other, kinds of dimorphism).

The important point is that an argument by analogy from just one case can only be rationally convincing given a certain amount of background knowledge, in addition to knowledge of the causal connections involved in the one case investigated. Then the question is whether we do have the appropriate sort of background knowledge to warrant an argument to the existence of other minds.

I shall argue in the next section that our own states of consciousness appear to be radically different from anything else which we find in the natural world. If that is the case, then we shall certainly lack sufficient knowledge to warrant an argument by analogy. Our situation would be essentially similar to the following. We arrive on Mars to discover a rich natural life. Among other plants and animals, we discover a species of carnivore rather like our tigers. They seem to be made of flesh and blood: they bleed when you cut them, and they need to eat other animals in order to survive. However, when we do our first post-mortem on one of them, we discover that instead of a brain of living tissue it has what appears to be a silicon-chip computer inside its head. What are we to say? Can we conclude that all the other Martian tigers will be similarly constructed? I suggest not: for the case is so unlike anything we have ever come across before that any one of a thousand hypotheses is possible. There may be some intelligent being which has given this one beast (or some, or all, of the others) an artificial brain as some sort of experiment. Or there may be some natural way in which a living being (or species of being) can come to have a brain of metal and silicon. Or it may even have sprung into existence by some sort of miracle.

The case of a mind in a body is, I shall suggest, apparently even more extraordinary than the case of the computer-brained tiger. For conscious states appear to be quite unlike physical states, having unique attributes among the other elements of the natural world. But the observable similarities between other human beings and myself, on the other hand, all relate to our existence as physical systems. Indeed, the more I learn about other human beings the more likely it seems that their behavior will ultimately be explicable in purely physical terms. Yet in my own case I am aware of possessing mental states which are, it can be argued, *non-physical states*. Then my situation with respect to the existence of other minds *will* be like that of the person who first opened an oyster and found a pearl, after all. For here was something so extraordinary – a hard smooth translucent object existing inside a living organism – that the person was entitled to come to no conclusion whatever concerning the existence of pearls in other oysters.

3   The uniqueness of consciousness

In this section I shall present three different arguments in support of a doctrine called "weak dualism". (These arguments will be re-visited and re-evaluated in Chapter 5:3.) This doctrine asserts that mental states are non-physical states. It deserves the title "dualist" because it involves a duality of kinds of state: on the one hand physical states, and on the other hand non-physical (mental) states; the two kinds being radically different from one another. But it is only "weak" dualism, because nothing is as yet said about the kinds of thing which possess those states. The weak dualist (about states) may be a monist about things, believing that the only kinds of thing which exist in the natural world are physical things. For they may believe that mental states are non-physical states of a physical thing, namely the living human organism. (Strong dualists, on the other hand, believe that the subject of conscious states is itself a non-physical thing – a non-physical mind or soul. Arguments for strong dualism will be considered in Chapters 2 and 4.) Note that if weak dualism is true, then there can't be a successful argument by analogy to the existence of other minds.

3.1 Phenomenal qualities

Consider what takes place when you perceive a brightly colored object, say a red tomato or a yellow tulip. Light of a certain wavelength enters your eyes, being focused on the retina. There, receptors are stimulated by the impact of the light, and fire off electro-chemical impulses along the optic nerve. These impulses are in turn received in the visual center at the back of the brain, where

22

they cause a further complicated pattern of electro-chemical activity. At this point you are caused to experience a sensation of red. Now here, suddenly, is something quite unlike the other elements in the causal chain. With the advent of a conscious sensation, something radically new has entered the story.

Consider the nature of the events leading up to the sensation of red. They consist of changes in the states of certain living cells in your body, the states in question having to do with the electrical and chemical properties of those cells. Now consider the nature of your experience itself. It is perhaps of a particularly bright, warm, shade of red. It has, indeed, a distinctive phenomenal quality: a qualitative "feel" all of its own. This is surely something quite different from any possible state of your brain; surely nothing electrical or chemical can have a qualitative *feel*. It would seem that no brain cell, or interaction of brain cells, can be either "bright" or "warm". Yet this is an accurate description of your experience.

What is being argued here is that physical states and events, on the one hand, and conscious states and events, on the other, possess quite a different range of attributes or properties. Physical states consist of arrangements of matter possessing electrical or chemical properties. They do not themselves seem to have any qualitative "feel". No physical state is "bright" or "warm" or "piercing" in the senses in which a conscious state can be these things. (The piercingness of a piercing pain is not literally the same as the piercingness of a knife piercing the flesh, though described by analogy with it.) Conscious states, on the other hand, do not possess electrical or chemical properties. It seems straightforwardly nonsensical to say of your sensation of red that it has such-and-such an electrical potential. (As if someone had said, "Your green ideas sleep furiously". Although this is a grammatical sentence – it has a subject, a verb and an object – it appears to have no literal meaning.) What they do have, are characteristic qualitative "feels".

If physical states and conscious states possess quite different kinds of properties, then they must themselves be different kinds of states. For if they did belong to the same kind – if, in particular, each conscious state were a physical state of the brain – then they would have to have the same attributes. Identical things have identical attributes; different things have different attributes. (This point will become clearer in Chapter 3. For the moment, take it on trust.) So the conclusion of this argument is that conscious mental states aren't physical ones.

23

3.2 *Intentionality*

Most mental states – for instance beliefs, desires and perceptions – are intentional: they represent things. (Note that "intentional", here, is a bit of philosopher's jargon. It doesn't mean "on purpose", but rather "possesses representational content".) More importantly, such states represent things in one way rather than another. To make use of a famous fictional example: when the police believe that Mr Hyde is the murderer, their belief contains a representation of a particular man, who is in fact Dr Jekyll. But it does not represent him *as* Dr Jekyll, but only as Mr Hyde. For they do not yet know that "Jekyll" and "Hyde" are associated with representations of one and the same man. Similarly, Oedipus' desire for marriage involves a representation of a particular woman, who is in fact his mother. But it does not represent her *as* being his mother, but rather as "Jocasta", or perhaps as "the woman I have recently come to love". Hence his surprise when he discovers that Jocasta – the woman he loves – is in fact his mother.

Mental states not only represent things in one way rather than another; they can also represent things which don't really exist. Someone looking for the lost city of Atlantis has a desire which represents something which (probably) neither does nor ever has existed. An ancient Greek believing that Zeus has just thrown a thunderbolt possesses a mental state containing a representation of a non-existent God.

The intentionality of mental states provides us with a powerful argument for saying that mental states cannot be physical states. For how is it possible for any merely physical state (e.g., a state of the brain) to represent anything? How could a particular pattern of cellular activity possess the properties of intentionality? It is difficult to understand how any physical arrangement could represent something that exists outside itself, and represent it in one way rather than another. It is even less intelligible how it could represent something which doesn't exist at all.

Of course we know that some physical arrangements can represent things. Think of a portrait-painting, for example, or of a sentence on the printed page. But it is arguable that such forms of representation are derivative from the representative properties of the mind. It is only the intentions of the artist, or the beliefs of the viewer, which make a portrait-painting represent one particular person rather than another. Otherwise the portrait is merely an arrangement of colors on canvas with an appearance similar to that of the subject, but similar also to many other people who physically resemble the subject. Equally, it is only the intentions of speakers of English to use words in particular ways which make the sequence of marks in, "It is raining", to represent anything.

If mental states like intentions and beliefs were themselves physical states, then it would have to be possible for a physical state or arrangement to represent something without doing so via the intentionality of some other state. A physical arrangement would have to be capable of representing something in its own right. But this appears impossible. It seems that no pattern of cellular activity can represent, by itself, the fact that it is raining. So the conclusion of this argument too, is that mental states are non-physical ones.

3.3 Spatial position

Unlike all physical objects and states, many (perhaps all) mental states appear to lack spatial positions. Certainly it seems that *some* mental states possess no spatial position. For instance the question, "Is your mental image of your mother to the right or left of your thought about the weather?" appears utterly nonsensical. (Just as if you had been asked, "Does your thought of your mother weigh less than two kilograms?") Equally nonsensical would be the question, "What is the spatial relation between your anger at the betrayal and your fear of reprisals?" So it seems that neither conscious acts like thinking and imagining, nor emotions like anger and fear, occupy positions in space.

Compare thoughts with numbers. There are many things which it makes no sense to say about a number. For instance, you cannot attribute colors to them, nor spatial locations. The sentences, "The number 7 is green" and, "The number 7 is in London" are both equally nonsensical. The truth is, the number 7 isn't the kind of thing which can either have a color (or be colorless), or have a spatial position. It therefore follows that numbers (if there really are such things) cannot be physical. For it belongs to the very essence (the logical nature) of any physical object or state that it should occupy some position in space. How could there exist a rusty bicycle, for instance, unless both the bicycle and its rust occupy some particular region in space, standing in determinate spatial relations to all other physical objects? So any thing (like a number or a thought) which isn't the sort of thing to have a spatial position, must be a non-physical thing.

It might be conceded that thoughts and emotions lack spatial positions, and are therefore non-physical. But is the same true of all mental states? What of experiences for example? Surely visual experiences, at least, occur in space. For can't I say, "My blue after-image is slightly above and to the left of my red one"? (An after-image is what you experience when you stare intently at a brightly colored light and then look away at a blank wall.)

Now, I can certainly attribute to my visual experiences spatial positions *within my visual field*; that is to say: *in relation to one another*. Yet it is doubtful whether this is to attribute to them genuine (literal) spatial positions; that is to say: positions relative to all physical objects and states. For although you can describe the position of your blue after-image in relation to that of your red one, it would be strange to ask, "Where exactly is your blue after-image in relation to the mole on your left cheek?" It would be equally odd to ask, "Is your blue after-image two inches behind your right eye?"

I suggest that construed literally, "This after-image is to the left of that one", should be understood as saying something like this: this after-image is related to that one in the way in which visual experiences are related to one another, when one is an experience of something which is (in the physical world) positioned to the left of the thing of which the other is an experience. That is to say: they are related spatially to one another within the visual field (within "visual space"), but not literally (not within physical space).

But what of bodily sensations such as pains and tickles? Surely they, at least, occupy genuine spatial positions. For don't I say, for instance, that I have a pain "in my left foot"? Yet in fact we could treat these cases rather in the way that we treated visual experiences: as non-literal ascriptions of position within my "tactile field", and perhaps we *should* treat them like this. For consider the phenomenon of phantom-limb pain. After the amputation of a limb it is common for the patient to continue to feel pains and itches "in" the amputated limb. So if we insist that pains have spatial positions, while allowing that no one can be mistaken about the nature of their own experiences (see section 4 below), we shall have to say that the pain occurs in empty space, or perhaps in the pillow on which the stump is resting. Since this is absurd, it seems better to say that what one is immediately aware of is a pain *felt as emanating from* a foot. That is to say: a pain which feels as a pain normally feels when it is caused by damage to a foot. It would then be nonsensical to ask, "Where – literally – in physical space is your awareness of the 'pain-felt-as-emanating-from-a-foot?'"

So even in the case of pains and tickles it seems coherent, and indeed plausible, to claim that they are not the kinds of thing which can have genuine spatial positions. It will then be plausible to claim that no mental states occupy positions in physical space, and it will follow that no mental states are themselves physical states. So the conclusion of this argument, as of the other two, is that mental states are non-physical ones, and that is sufficient to block any argument to the existence of other minds based on causal analogies.

4   Certainty and meaning

Recall from section 1 that the problem of other minds can be presented as a dilemma: every argument must be either deductive or inductive, and yet neither deduction nor induction can give us knowledge of other minds. Over the last two sections we have been concerned to bolster up the second horn of this dilemma. In section 2 we argued that neither scientific hypotheses nor an argument by analogy are what give us knowledge of the mental states of others. Then in section 3 we defended a conception of the nature of mental states – namely weak dualism – which explains why no argument by analogy from my own case can ever be rationally convincing.

In this section we return to the first horn of the dilemma: that no deductive argument can give us knowledge of the mental states of other people. I shall explain and argue for a particular conception of the meaning of terms referring to mental states which makes this claim seem particularly plausible. I shall call this "the Cartesian conception of the meaning of consciousness-terms", after the French philosopher René Descartes; or "the Cartesian conception" for short. The Cartesian conception is this: that the meanings of terms like "pain" and "experience of red" are wholly a matter of the subjective *feel* of the corresponding states.

It is easy to see how the Cartesian conception would lend support to the view that no arguments from descriptions of physical circumstances and behavior, on the one hand, to descriptions of mental states, on the other, can ever be deductively valid. For if the Cartesian conception is true, then it will always be possible to conceive the premises of such arguments to be true while conceiving the conclusion to be false. (Remember, a valid argument is one where it is *impossible* that the premises should be true while the conclusion is

27

false.) One will be able to think, "All that [circumstances and behavior] might be the case, and still *this* sort of subjective experience might not be present". Since there would exist no conceptual links between our ideas of mental states and our concepts of physical and behavioral phenomena (according to the Cartesian conception), such thoughts will always be conceivable ones. (Note, however, that this argument assumes – controversially – that *conceivability* entails *possibility*. We will return to this point in Chapter 3:4.)

4.1 *An argument from logical independence*

In section 1 we claimed that there can be no deductively valid arguments from descriptions of physical states to descriptions of conscious states. In fact it would be equally plausible to hold the stronger thesis that there can be no deductively valid arguments in either direction. For not only is it possible to display pain behavior (even after genuine injury) without actually feeling any pain; it is also possible to be in pain without this in any way revealing itself in your behavior (think of someone who has been paralyzed, for example). It would thus appear that the appropriate sorts of physical states are neither necessary nor sufficient for the experience of pain to occur. They are not logically necessary, because you can have pain without pain-behavior or injury, and they are not logically sufficient, because you can have the injury and the behavior without the sensation.

The notion of "necessary and sufficient conditions" is an important one in philosophy. This is because many philosophers believe that the meaning of an expression is constituted by the conditions necessary and sufficient for its correct application. (By no means all philosophers accept this, however. This assumption about meaning is a controversial one; but the controversies needn't matter for our purposes here.) Consider the term "bachelor" (to take a hackneyed example). It is clearly necessary to being a bachelor that you be a man, since neither infants nor women can be bachelors. But this is of course not sufficient, since a married man is not a bachelor either. A sufficient condition for being a bachelor is that you are a man who has never been married. Therefore, what is more natural than to think that the word "bachelor" *means* "man who has never been married", thus equating meaning with necessary and sufficient conditions for truth.

(Note that meaning cannot be equated with sufficient conditions alone. It is a sufficient condition for someone to be my uncle that he be my father's brother. But "uncle" does not mean the same as "father's brother", since although this condition is sufficient, it isn't necessary. Someone can be my uncle by being my mother's brother.)

It thus appears that descriptions of physical states can form no part of the meaning of consciousness-terms. Since the behavior and physical injury which are characteristic of pain are neither logically necessary nor logically sufficient for the occurrence of the feeling of pain, they cannot form any part of our concept of that state. Then the Cartesian conception is the only remaining alternative: the meanings of such terms must be wholly concerned with the subjective qualitative feel of the states they describe. The condition necessary and sufficient for the occurrence of pain is that there should occur a sensation with the characteristic feel of pain.

4.2 An argument from certainty

Another argument for the Cartesian conception is based on the premise that I can be absolutely certain of my own conscious states. (As it is sometimes said: my knowledge of them is "incorrigible" or uncorrectable.) By the phrase "absolutely certain" here, I mean that it is logically impossible that I might turn out to be mistaken: if I sincerely believe myself to be in pain, then is it inconceivable that I might turn out to be not really having that experience. If this were correct, then the Cartesian conception would appear to provide the only plausible explanation of it. The explanation would be that I am, in my own case, immediately presented with the conditions necessary and sufficient for the correct application of the terms I am using, namely a particular qualitative feel. I cannot be mistaken about being in pain because there is no "gap" between what I mean when I judge that I am in pain – the state of affairs I am describing – and the awareness on whose basis I judge. On the contrary, what I am judging about (the condition necessary and sufficient for truth) is itself a particular state of awareness: a feeling.

In connection with any belief about the external physical world it is always at least logically possible that I might turn out to be wrong. This is because in such cases there always is a "gap" between what is represented by my belief (a state of affairs in the physical world) and the awareness on which my belief is based (my experience of that world). For example, while delivering a lecture I believe myself to be faced with a room full of people. But of course

I could be hallucinating (someone might have slipped something into my coffee without me knowing). Or they could all be cleverly designed robots, and so on. So it would seem that, in possible contrast with beliefs about my own experiences, "Are you sure?"–questions will always make sense (be intelligible) in connection with any belief about the physical world (even beliefs about my own body).

Suppose, then, that the Cartesian conception of the meaning of consciousness-terms were wrong. For instance, suppose that some physical state were logically necessary to the state of being in pain. Then it would seem to be possible for me to be mistaken in thinking that I am in pain, e.g., by hallucinating the presence of that necessary physical state. So if my awareness of my pain is incorrigible, as suggested above, then the Cartesian conception must apparently represent the true picture of the meaning of the corresponding term. It is therefore a matter of some importance to establish whether or not I really can be absolutely certain about my own states of consciousness.

4.3   The certainty-thesis

It needs to be conceded straight away that there are some kinds of mistakes which it is possible to make about one's own experiences. Firstly, it is possible to be mistaken about the true cause of an experience, as with the phenomenon of "referred pain". Thus I might go to my doctor complaining of a pain in my back, but after examining me she might say "It is not your back which hurts, it is your stomach". This is a loose way of saying that the pain I feel in my back is in fact caused by a disturbance in my stomach. Secondly, one can be mistaken about the relations which pertain between a current experience and one's past or future experiences. Thus I might be mistaken in claiming that my current headache is more intense than the one which I had yesterday. Thirdly, it is possible to be mistaken about anything which involves some sort of intellectual operation upon a current experience. I might claim to have an eight-sided after-image but then later, after a recount, realize that in fact it has nine sides. Then finally, there will of course be the usual sorts of mistakes due to such things as slips of the tongue, or to linguistic ignorance. As when I misdescribe a tickle as "a pain" because I am under the mistaken impression that that is what "pain" means.

In the light of the above, our thesis (the certainty-thesis) will have to be this: *that it is impossible to be mistaken in simple judgments*

30

of recognition of one's own experiences; where the terms of those judgments do not bring in anything extraneous to current experience, such as causes, earlier times, or numbers; and where the judging subjects adequately understand the terms involved in the judgment, and use the terms which they intend to use.

For example, although I cannot be absolutely certain that I see (really see) a room full of people, I can surely be certain that I at least *seem* to see a room full of people. It appears inconceivable that I should turn out to be not really having that experience. Suppose someone were to ask me, "Are you sure that you haven't mistaken the nature of your experience? Are you sure that it is a room full of people that you seem to see, and not a pink elephant climbing the wall?" These questions appear to be nonsensical. Equally unintelligible would be the question, "Are you sure that it is a headache that you have, and not an itchy foot?" To this one should want to expostulate, "Surely I know what I feel!"

Someone might concede that it is impossible to make mistakes of this order of magnitude, but claim that in other more subtle cases it is possible to be in error (or at least uncertain). For example, couldn't I have occasion to say, "I am not sure whether what I am feeling is a pain or an intense tickle"? But in reality this is just like the case where I say that I am uncertain whether a particular object is colored yellow or green. This is merely a loose way of saying something of which I *can* be perfectly certain, namely that the object is yellowish-green. Similarly, can't I be absolutely certain of this: that what I feel is an experience midway between a pain and a tickle?

There are other more interesting cases in which I can apparently misclassify an experience. For example, suppose that I am being played a tape of various bird-calls, and am asked to describe my experiences. Might I not say, "At first I thought that I was seeming to hear the call of an Oyster-catcher, but now I realize that I was seeming to hear the call of a Redshank"? Here I have changed my classification of an experience, yet it doesn't appear very plausible to claim that the experience itself changed in the interim; for I am being played exactly the same bit of tape. So wasn't my first judgment a mistake?

In fact I think we ought to say that my experience *has* changed, for a reason which is both interesting and important. This is that experiences are themselves partly interpretative. To change the interpretation (the classification) is to change the experience itself. Thus consider the famous duck–rabbit picture (Figure 1.3) which

31

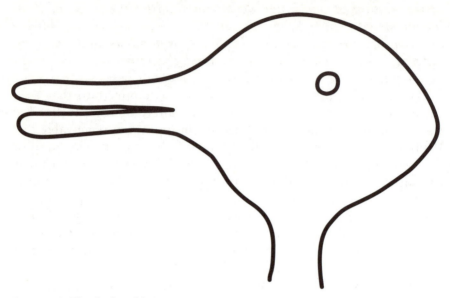

Figure 1.3 The duck–rabbit.

you can see either as a duck or as a rabbit. When you see it one way or the other, what happens is not simply that you have a particular ("neutral") experience accompanied by the belief, "This is a picture of a duck", or "This is a picture of a rabbit". You actually *see* the picture differently. So the correct response to make to the example above is that to hear a sound as the call of an Oyster-catcher, and to hear the same sound as the call of a Redshank, are in fact two different experiences. So neither judgment was false. The only mistake was over the kind of bird which would normally cause such a sound.

It would seem that our thesis has been sustained. The mistakes which it is possible to make about one's own experiences aren't of a kind to threaten the Cartesian conception. Since I can't be mistaken in simple recognition judgments, the content of those judgments (the meanings of the terms employed) must apparently be wholly confined to the immediate contents of consciousness: to the subjective qualitative feel of the states described.

4.4 The scope of the certainty-thesis

It is by no means easy to see exactly how the scope of our thesis should be formulated. For it obviously isn't the case that I can be absolutely certain about the application of literally any mental term. Of course I may be wrong in thinking that I am *intelligent*, in believing that I *understand* the French word "ouvert", or in thinking that I am *generous*. These terms refer to mental capacities or dispositions. That I am capable, on the whole, of solving problems more easily than most (intelligence), that I am able to use a word correctly (understanding), and that I am sufficiently disposed to help those in need (generosity), are not things which I can be immediately conscious of. What might be suggested is that I at least can't be mistaken about the (first-person, present tense) application of any mental term which refers to a sensation or experience ("seem to see", "seem to hear", "am in pain", etc.), nor any term which refers to a mental action ("think", "imagine", "wonder whether", etc.).

But what of emotions, like anger and fear, as well as beliefs and desires? Do they fall within the scope of the certainty-thesis? Should the Cartesian conception be extended to them? Now, what is distinctive about such states – as opposed to states of thinking and feeling – is that someone can possess them without being currently aware of them. For instance, it may truly be said of someone who is asleep, "She believes she has been betrayed, is angry at it, and wants revenge". In contrast, it couldn't be said of the sleeper that she is in pain, or thinking about the weather. If someone isn't aware of any pain, then she is not in pain. As it is sometimes said: pains and thoughts are "self-intimating" (to have them is to be aware of them), whereas beliefs and desires are not.

The fact that they are not self-intimating needn't *by itself* prevent us from bringing emotions, beliefs and desires within the scope of the certainty-thesis. Although they can continue to exist while the subject isn't currently aware of them, it might be said that they are nevertheless always infallibly *available* to consciousness. So if someone thinks that they have a particular emotion, or belief, or desire, then so they do; and if they think that they don't, then they don't. All that is possible, is that they may have emotions, beliefs or desires which they aren't currently thinking about.

This response might be problematic, however, if we are prepared to allow the existence of *unconscious* emotions, beliefs and desires – that is, states of these kinds which *aren't* available to consciousness. For the moment, I propose simply to leave this issue unresolved, returning to it again in later chapters. It appears that we can at least conclude that the Cartesian conception is plausible in respect of the meaning of *a great many* mental state terms; which in turn will support the claim that there can't be deductively valid arguments linking mental states with physical states.

Conclusion

This now completes our preliminary discussion of the problem of other minds. In this chapter we have outlined the problem, and have explained and argued for the views – weak dualism, and the Cartesian conception of the meaning of mental-state terms – which apparently underlie it. If weak dualism is true, then my own mental states are quite unlike anything else that I know of in the world, and no argument from analogy can be successful. If the meanings of my mental-state terms are exhausted by the way the states feel to me on the inside, as the Cartesian conception maintains, then no argument from the behavior of other people to their states of mind can apparently be valid. (In that case nor, of course, can mental states be regarded as theoretical quasi-scientific entities, somewhat like electrons.) So it seems that neither inductive nor deductive arguments can give us reason to believe in the existence of other minds.

We shall be returning to various aspects of the problem of other minds at different points throughout the remainder of this book (especially in Chapters 5 and 7). But for the moment, we shall be leaving the problem to one side. We turn from the question of how we *know of* other minds, to consider the question what minds themselves really *are* (already begun in section 3 above), or to consider the question of the *nature* of the mind.

Questions for discussion

1. How do you know that the human beings around you aren't *zombies*? – i.e. physical systems which behave just as if they had minds like yours, but are really mindless.
2. Is our belief in other minds the best available scientific explanation of other people's observable behavior?
3. Are there enough similarities between yourself and other humans to warrant an argument by analogy to the existence of other minds?
4. How convincing do you find the arguments for saying that mental states aren't physical ones? Can you think of any arguments in the contrary direction?

5. Is it possible to be mistaken about one's own conscious mental states? How is this question connected with the problem of other minds?

Further reading

Ayer, A. J. (1953) "One's knowledge of other minds", *Theoria*, vol. 19. Also reprinted in Ayer, A. J. (1954) *Philosophical Essays*, London: Macmillan, and in Gustafson, D. (ed.) (1964), *Essays on Philosophical Psychology* London: Macmillan.

Ayer, A. J. (1959) "Privacy", *Proceedings of the British Academy*, Oxford: Oxford University Press. Also reprinted in Ayer, A. J. (1963) *The Concept of a Person*, London: Macmillan.

Churchland, P. (1979) *Scientific Realism and the Plasticity of Mind*, Chapter 4. Cambridge: Cambridge University Press.

Churchland, P. (1984) *Matter and Consciousness*, Chapter 4, Cambridge, MA: MIT Press.

Descartes, R. (1641), *Meditations on First Philosophy*, 1 & 2. (Many translations available.)

Malcolm, N. (1958) "Knowledge of other minds", *Journal of Philosophy*, vol. 55 (1958). Also reprinted in Chappell, V. (ed.), (1962) *The Philosophy of Mind*, Harlow: Prentice Hall; in Gustafson, D. (ed.) (1964) *Essays on Philosophical Psychology*, London: Macmillan; and in Pitcher, G. (1966) (ed.) *Wittgenstein*, London: Macmillan.

2

Strong dualism: body and soul

Our topic in this chapter is none other than the fundamental nature of ourselves. Are we non-physical – or "spiritual" – beings, which are linked causally with a particular body during life, but which could possibly survive the destruction of that body? Or are we just living physical organisms of a special sort?

1 Developing an argument for dualism

In the last chapter we offered arguments in support of weak dualism, apparently establishing that people's mental states are non-physical states. Our task in the present section is to see whether we can construct a proof of strong dualism (sometimes called "Cartesian dualism" after the French philosopher René Descartes; more often simply called "dualism"). The strong dualist maintains that the subject of mental states (the person or self) is a non-physical individual thing – a non-physical mind or soul.

I should stress that the subject matter of this section (and indeed of this whole chapter) is among the hardest and most abstract of the book. But the reader is urged to persevere, nevertheless. For it is vital that we should carefully examine the strongest and most historically-influential arguments which have been offered in support of a non-physical soul. (In Chapter 4 we will consider a further set of arguments.) Unfortunately, these arguments aren't easy ones to understand or evaluate.

1.1 Preliminary points

Like the weak dualist, strong dualists believe that there are two radically different kinds of states and events in the world. But they also believe that the world contains two radically different kinds of substance and thing. They believe that there exists matter, which goes to make up physical objects, which must always occupy some position in space. They also believe that there exists consciousness, which goes to make up minds or souls, which are non-physical and non-spatial. On the strong dualist view it is the soul which is the bearer of conscious mental states. It is the soul, not the body or brain, which thinks, feels, imagines and undergoes experiences.

Note that weak dualism doesn't by itself entail strong dualism. Indeed, it doesn't even follow that it is logically possible for strong dualism to be true. Even if weak dualism is true, it may still be a necessary truth that conscious states are non-physical states of a physical thing. An analogy may help show this. The state of being married is not a physical state, since marriage is a conventional rather than a physical relation. Yet only a physical being can be in that state, at least if one takes the traditional view that marriage requires consummation in order to be genuine. For the sexual act is necessarily a physical act. So it may be that something similar holds true in the case of conscious states also: although they aren't them-selves physical states, there may nevertheless be some reason why only a physical being can possess such states.

A word about terminology before we proceed further. From now on I shall reserve the term "soul" for use in referring to the non-physical thing which is, according to the strong dualist, the bearer of our conscious states. So to deny the truth of strong dualism would be to deny that souls exist. However, I shall continue to use the term "mind" neutrally, to mean the collection of mental states, whether they be states of a physical or of a non-physical thing, and whether those states themselves are physical or non-physical. So to deny the truth of either form of dualism wouldn't be to deny that minds exist. Since we shall be concerned with strong dualism throughout the remainder of this chapter and the two chapters following, I shall often for brevity speak simply of "dualism". We will return to consider possible criticisms of weak dualism in Chapter 5.

What should dualists say about the person or self? Should they *identify* people with their souls? Or should dualists say that a person is a union, or combination, of a soul and a body? I can see no reason why they should say the latter. For after all, it is the soul which is said to be the bearer of thoughts and experiences. So if it were to prove possible for my soul to survive the destruction of my body, why should I regard *myself* as having been destroyed? For I should presumably still be able to go on thinking, remembering and feeling. I might even be able to go on experiencing, since it is possible for experiences to be caused in some other way than by stimulation of the various bodily organs (think of hallucinations and dreams, for instance). Why should my body be so important to me that I ought to regard myself as ceasing to exist without it, if my mental life could continue relatively unchanged? (Similarly if it were to prove possible for my soul to become attached to a different body: surely the only reasonable way to describe this would be to say that I myself had changed bodies, in the way that a truck driver may change from one vehicle to another.)

Strong dualists hold that the person, or self, should be identified with the soul. The body should be relegated to the status of mere vehicle, providing the focus for the soul's causal intercourse with the rest of the natural world. (It is this body which I can cause to move around by making decisions, and it is things happening to this body which cause most of my experiences.) This doctrine is important. For what it is at issue is nothing less than the fundamental nature of ourselves. Moreover, dualism does at least hold out the possibility of some sort of life after death. For to say that the self is distinct from the body is to say that it is possible that it should continue to exist even when the body has been destroyed or decomposed.

As I remarked at the outset of this book, almost all human beings throughout all of human history, across all human cultures, have been strong dualists. Belief in the soul has a powerful claim to being a cultural "universal", in fact, along with pointing, body-decoration, possession of language, systems for making and enforcing contracts, and so forth. Moreover, developmental psychologists have discovered that young children will spontaneously start to draw a contrast between mind and body at around the age of three or four, suggesting that belief in weak dualism, at least, is well neigh inevitable. Why do such beliefs come so naturally to us? In part, perhaps, it is just because mind and body *seem* so different from one another. Also, wishful thinking may have an important role to play, too – for of course we would very much *like* to believe in the possibility of life after physical death. Our task in the present section, however, is to see whether we can construct some more powerful *argument* in support of strong dualism, avoiding the main fallacies which have traditionally been alleged in such arguments.

1.2 The initial argument – Descartes' doubts

Let us now see how strongly we can argue for the truth of dualism. Descartes famously argued as follows:

(1)   I can doubt whether my body and brain exist.
(2)   I cannot doubt whether *I* exist.
(C)   Therefore I am not my body and/or brain – I am a non-physical thing.

We need not bother to discuss the truth of the two premises. (Each can actually be made to seem quite plausible, at least.) For the argument itself is invalid – the conclusion just doesn't follow. (Even supposing that the premises are true, the conclusion could still be false.) In order to see this point, suppose that Oedipus is ever so certain that Jocasta exists – after all, he may be holding her in his arms! But having left his home many years before, he no longer knows whether or not his mother is alive. He might then be tempted to reason in parallel with Descartes, as follows:

(1)   I can doubt whether my mother still exists.
(2)   I cannot doubt whether Jocasta now exists.
(C)   Therefore Jocasta is not my mother.

Since, as we know, the conclusion would be false although the premises may well be true, this form of argument must be invalid.

The problem arises because, as we saw in Chapter 1:3, properties like *doubt*, *belief*, and so on are *intentional* ones. They *represent* things in one way or another. What it is possible for you to doubt, of a given thing, may depend on how that thing is being conceived of or represented by you. When Oedipus represents the woman he loves as "Jocasta", he cannot doubt that she is real; but when he represents what is (unknown to him) the very same woman as "my mother", he *can* doubt whether she still exists. Similarly, then, in respect of myself – conceiving of myself as an object of outer perception (a physical body) I may be able to doubt whether that thing exists; but conceiving of myself on the basis of introspection *as* myself, perhaps I can't doubt that I exist. But it just doesn't follow that I am not in fact my physical body.

Although Descartes' most explicit statement of his argument for the existence of the soul is a failure, it may be that we can rescue it. Perhaps, in particular, when Descartes talks of whether something can or can't be *doubted*, he really means to get at the question of whether it can or can't be *conceived to be otherwise* – whether or not it is logically possible that it should be false.

1.3 *Replacing doubt with logical possibility*

A good place to begin our reconstruction is with the conceivability of disembodied thought and experience. I can imagine dropping dead in the middle of a train of thought, my thoughts continuing uninterrupted. Or I can imagine hearing the doctors pronounce me dead, and thinking to myself, "Well this is not so bad as I feared!" I can then imagine a sequence of experiences which do not in any way involve the experience of having a body. I can imagine perceiving physical objects without there being any visible hands, feet, out-of-focus nose, etc., especially closely connected with my visual field. Indeed, I can imagine my visual field shifting away from the body which I now regard as mine, so that I look back on that body from a separate point of view. (Many people have actually reported having just such experiences; we shall return to consider the empirical evidence for the existence of the soul in Chapter 4.) I can then imagine the experience of moving through the physical world, but in such a way that my progress is unimpeded by any physical obstacle (e.g., I am able to move through walls and so on).

All of this seems sufficient to establish that it is logically possible for there to occur thoughts and experiences which are not the thoughts or experiences of any physical organism. There are possible worlds in which my conscious states occur in the absence of any physical subject of those states. However, there is surely no possible world in which my conscious states occur in the absence of any conscious subject whatever. Thoughts and experiences surely cannot occur in the absence of any thinking experiencing thing: thoughts require a thinker, experiences require an experiencer. It therefore follows that there can exist conscious things (persons) which aren't physical things. (Or to put it in other ways: I – the thinker – am not an essentially physical thing; physicality isn't an attribute which I necessarily *have to* possess.)

Thus far, our reconstruction of the argument can be summarized thus:

(1)   It is logically possible that thinking (or experiencing) should occur while no physical thinker exists.

(2)   It isn't logically possible that thinking (or experiencing) should occur while no thinking thing exists.

(C1) So it is logically possible that thinking things aren't physical things.

Note that it has not yet been established that I am not, in fact, a physical thing. From the fact that I am not essentially (necessarily) physical, it doesn't follow that I am not in fact physical. To see this, compare the following. Physical things aren't essentially colored things (think of a pane of glass, or an electron). But it obviously cannot follow from this that physical things are not colored, since many of them are in fact colored. Yet it is the stronger conclusion – that I am *not* a physical thing – which we need to establish if we are to establish the truth of dualism. For the dualist believes that I (the thinker) am, in fact, a non-physical thing. It is not as if we had made no progress at all, however. On the contrary, if the argument above is as convincing as it appears, then we have proved that it is logically possible for dualism to be true, and this is already more than many philosophers would be prepared to admit.

What could justify the move from, "I am not an essentially physical thing" to, "I am not in fact a physical thing"? It would apparently be sufficient if we could show that any object which is *in fact* a physical thing is an *essentially* physical thing. For in that case, anything which was not essentially physical would not be physical at all. So we could then continue our reconstructed argument as follows:

(C1) It is logically possible that thinking things aren't physical things.

(3)   All physical things are such that their physicality is a logically necessary attribute of them.

(C2) So (from (C1) and (3)) thinking things aren't physical things.

Now the claim expressed in (3) can be made to seem extremely plausible. For it would seem that the physicality of any physical thing must always form an essential part of our conception of that thing. (In contrast: the coloredness of any particular colored thing – e.g., a pane of glass – need not form an essential part of our conception of that thing.)

The argument for thinking that all physical things are essentially physical is as follows. Firstly, we can make no sense of the idea that

41

any particular physical object might not have been physical. We cannot conceive of any possible circumstances in which that object might have existed, only without being physical. Look at a particular chair, for instance, and try to think the thought, "This chair might have existed without being physical". Can you do it? The best you can achieve is to imagine, say, a holograph of a chair, which would present you with a similar three-dimensional appearance of a chair without there really being anything physical there. But then of course a holograph of a chair isn't a genuine chair. (In contrast, you can look at a particular piece of colored glass and think, "This piece of glass might not have been colored". You just have to imagine the glass-maker forgetting to put in the dye when he made it.)

Secondly, we can make no sense of the idea that a particular physical object might cease to be physical without ceasing to exist. It cannot be intelligible that a particular chair might cease to be physical without ceasing to exist, because we have no conception of what, in that case, would make it true that there still exists that very same chair. (In contrast, a physical object can cease to have a color without ceasing to exist. Think of a piece of colored glass whose color fades away. Here we have a clear conception of the conditions under which we should still be left with the very same piece of glass, rather than a substitute.)

It thus appears that the move from "X isn't *essentially* colored" to "X *isn't* colored" (which is, as we saw, obviously invalid) is really quite different from the move from "X isn't essentially physical" to "X isn't physical". The latter move now appears to be justified, because the physicality of any physical thing must always form an essential part of our conception of the existence of that thing. So it would appear that we have now done enough to establish dualism. We appear to have shown that I – the thinker – am not a physical thing.

1.4 Essentially thinking things

Indeed, we may go further. (Note that the material in this subsection isn't especially important as regards the case for strong dualism: that has already been laid out above. But it may be useful in seeing how Descartes could have reached his actual conclusion, namely that minds or souls are *essentially thinking*, or essentially conscious, non-physical entities.)

Suppose we had reason to believe that everything has an essence: suppose that for every kind of thing there must be some property, or range of properties, which it possesses necessarily. Then it would be reasonable to conclude that I am an essentially thinking (or at least an essentially conscious) thing. For if I am not a physical thing, then I possess no physical attributes. In which case my essential attributes obviously cannot be physical ones. Then the only remaining candidates would be attributes of consciousness. This is just what Descartes himself asserts: I am an essentially conscious thing, in exactly the sense in which a particular chair is an essentially physical – that is to say "space-occupying" – thing. I thus could not have existed without being conscious, and I cannot wholly cease to be conscious without ceasing to exist. Then we could complete our argument as follows:

(C2) Thinking things aren't physical things.
(4) Every kind of thing must possess some essential (logically necessary) attributes.
(C3) So (from (C2) and (4)) thinking things are essentially thinking, or conscious, non-physical entities.

Is it true, then, that everything must have an essence? It would certainly appear so. For if there were some thing, every one of whose properties were contingent (non-necessary), then there would be possible worlds in which that thing exists without having *any* of those properties; and it would be logically possible that all those properties might change at once without the object ceasing to exist. But neither of these ideas seems intelligible.

Suppose that there were to exist an object X which possessed, contingently, just three properties: *F*, *G* and *H*. Now consider the possible world in which X is supposed to exist having only the properties *I*, *J* and *K*. What could make it true that it is X, rather than some quite different object, which exists in that world? No answer can be given. Similarly if we are told that X might instantaneously change from having the properties *F*, *G* and *H* to having the properties *I*, *J* and *K*. What could make it true that X would here have changed, rather than ceased to exist and been replaced by some quite different object? Again, no answer can be given.

(To get the feel of these suggestions, consider what sense can be made of the propositions, "I might have been a poached egg", or, "I might in future become a poached egg". Despite the fact that physicality isn't lost in these imagined transformations, even these thoughts seem doubtfully coherent.)

We shall return to some of these ideas in greater detail in Chapter 3. But for the moment the moral of the story appears to be this: it is an essential part of our concept of an individual thing, that we should have an idea of what distinguishes one individual thing from others, and of what constitutes the continued existence of any one particular thing over time; and such conceptions would not be possible in connection with individual things which possessed no essential attributes. So it follows that all individual things must have an essence.

1.5 Interim summary

To summarize, then, the full version of our reconstructed argument for strong dualism runs as follows:

(1)   It is logically possible that thinking (or experiencing) should occur while no physical thinker exists.
(2)   It isn't logically possible that thinking (or experiencing) should occur while no thinking thing exists.
(C1)   So it is logically possible that thinking things aren't physical things.
(3)   All physical things are such that their physicality is a logically necessary attribute of them.
(C2)   So (from (C1) and (3)) thinking things *aren't* physical things.
(4)   Every kind of thing must possess some essential (logically necessary) attributes.
(C3)   So (from (C2) and (4)) thinking things are essentially thinking, or conscious, non-physical entities.
       That is to say: souls exist, and persons are souls.

Premise (1) is established by the conceivability of disembodied thought and experience. Premise (2) appears intuitively obvious: how could there be thoughts which aren't entertained by any thinker, or experiences which aren't experienced by any experiencer? (We shall return in section 3 below to see how, despite its apparent obviousness, this premise *might* be challenged.) Premise (3) was established by considering what is required for the existence of a particular chair. Premise (4) is the thesis for which we have just been arguing. Then if the whole argument is valid, as it appears to be, we have constructed a proof of the existence of the soul.

1.6 A fallacy exposed

The step from (C1) and (3) to (C2) is in fact invalid as it stands, involving a fallacy sometimes called by philosophers "a modal shift". (Modal terms are terms such as "necessary", "possible" and "impossible".) But in order to see how the premises (C1) and (3) can be true, while conclusion (C2) is false – i.e. in order to see how the argument is invalid – we need to investigate a phenomenon known to philosophers as "scope".

It can make all the difference to the truth or falsity of a judgment involving a modal term such as "necessary", what the scope of the necessity is. What will often be crucial, is whether it is the whole sentence which falls within the scope of what is being judged to be necessary, or only part of it. On the first alternative, let us say that the necessity has "wide-scope", and on the second alternative, that it has "narrow-scope". Then I shall claim that the argument above is invalid because the possibility in (C1) is wide-scope, whereas the necessity in (3) is narrow-scope.

Consider, for example, the sentence, "The thing of which Mary is thinking is, necessarily, physical". This is ambiguous, depending upon whether we read it as saying: "It is a necessary truth that the thing of which Mary is thinking is physical" (wide-scope); or rather as saying: "The thing of which Mary is, in fact, thinking is necessarily-physical" (narrow-scope). Taken with wide-scope the judgment is false. For it comes to the same as saying: "Mary can – as a matter of logic – think only of physical things". This is obviously false, since Mary may think of the number 9, or the Greenwich Meridian. But taken with narrow-scope the judgment may be true. For if Mary is in fact thinking of the chair on which she is sitting, then that thing is necessarily-physical. For as we saw above, we can make no sense of the idea that a particular chair might not have been physical, nor of the idea that it might cease to be physical while continuing to exist.

The difference between wide and narrow scope can be represented most clearly in terms of possible worlds. Suppose that we are dealing with a judgments of the form, "X is physical". Then a judgment of wide-scope necessity will say: "It is a truth about all possible worlds that if X exists in that world, it is physical". Further, a judgment of wide-scope possibility will say: "It is a truth about some possible world that X exists in that world and is physical." On the other hand, a judgment of narrow-scope necessity will say:

"The thing which is X in our world, is physical in all possible worlds in which it occurs". Also, a judgment of narrow-scope possibility will say: "The thing which is X in our world, is physical in some possible world in which it occurs".

In general, a judgment of the wide-scope necessity of "X is physical" will only be true if the description "X" describes the thing in such a way as to imply its physicality. Thus if "X" is, "The chair on which Mary is sitting", then the wide-scope judgments will be true. It is a truth about all possible worlds that if there is a chair on which Mary is sitting, then it is physical. But if "X" is, "The thing of which Mary is thinking", then the wide-scope judgment will be false. For even if Mary is in fact thinking of the chair, that thing is not described in such a way as to imply its physicality. It is not a truth about all possible worlds that if Mary is thinking about something in that world, then it is physical.

In general, a judgment of the narrow-scope necessity of "X is physical" will only be true if the thing which is described by the term "X" in the actual world belongs to one of those sorts of thing for which the criteria of identity and individuation involve physical attributes. Thus if "X" is, "The thing of which Mary is thinking", and Mary is in fact thinking of the chair, then the narrow-scope judgment will be true. For the chair is physical in all possible worlds in which it exists. But if Mary is in fact thinking of the Greenwich Meridian, then the narrow-scope judgment will be false. For the thing of which Mary is thinking (the Greenwich Meridian) is not physical in all possible worlds in which it occurs (in particular, it is not physical in the actual world).

Armed now with the distinction between wide- and narrow-scope, we can return to the crucial step in the argument for dualism. Since the possibility in (C1) is wide-scope, it should properly be represented thus:

(C1$_w$) It is a truth about some possible world that there exist thinkers in that world who aren't physical.

But since the necessity in (3) is narrow-scope, it should properly be represented thus:

(3$_n$) All things which are in fact physical in the actual world, are physical in all other possible worlds in which they exist.

Now from these two premises together it simply doesn't follow that thinking things aren't in fact physical things.

To see this, suppose that conclusion (C2) is actually false. Suppose that the things which are, in the actual world, the thinking things, are all of them physical things. For example, suppose that they are, in fact, physical brains. Yet it is still possible for $(C1_w)$ to be true. It may be that in some other possible world thinking things are non-physical souls. Thus, it is equally possible for (3_n) to be true. We merely have to conclude that the things which do the thinking in this world (brains) are physical in all other possible worlds in which *they* exist. Then since it is possible for the premises to be true while the conclusion is false, the argument from $(C1_w)$ and (3_n) to (C2) is invalid.

1.7 *Avoiding the fallacy*

The strong dualist has a reply to the above criticism. It is that the arguments originally given in support of (C1), could equally well have been used to support a narrow-scope version of it, namely:

$(C1_n)$ The things which are, in the actual world, the thinking things, are non-physical in some possible worlds in which they occur.

Then this really could be put together with (3_n) to entail that thinking things are not in fact physical things. In brief, the argument would then be as follows:

$(C1_n)$ Thinking things aren't essentially physical.
(3_n) All physical things *are* essentially physical.
(C2) So thinking things are not in fact physical things.

This argument is certainly valid: it commits no modal fallacy. Replacing "essentially physical" by the dummy predicate "property F" will help to show this. For in that case it can be seen that the argument has the following valid form:

(1) No thinking thing has property F.
(2) All physical things have property F.
(C) So no thinking thing is a physical thing.

(Compare: No whales have gills. All fish have gills. So no whales are fish.) To show that the argument is valid, let us see if we can have the conclusion (C) false while the two premises are true. So, contrary to (C), suppose that some particular thinking thing is actually a physical thing. For the sake of concreteness, suppose that it is I who am identical with my brain. Then by premise (2), since all physical things have property F (are essentially physical), I too must have property F. But now there is no way to hold on to the truth of premise (1) – if I have property F, then of course it can't be true that *no* thinking thing has property F.

So it is impossible for the two premises to be true while the conclusion is false – the argument is valid. The only issue then outstanding is whether the dualist can indeed provide adequate support for premise $(C1_n)$, the claim that no thinking thing has the property of being essentially-physical.

Recall the crucial role played, in the argument to (C1), by the apparent conceivability of disembodied thought and experience. It seems that I can imagine what it would be like to die, and cease to be embodied, but continue having thoughts and experiences. Indeed it seems that I can imagine what it might have been like had I never been embodied. We took this, at the time, to establish the truth of premise (1), that it is logically possible for thoughts and experiences to occur in the absence of any physical thinker or experiencer. But it seems we could equally well have taken it to establish the stronger thesis that I, myself, am not an essentially physical thing. If it is conceivable that I might continue to exist without being physical, and conceivable that I might have existed without ever being physical, then I myself am not an essentially physical thing. It will follow that the thing which is me (the thinker) in the actual world, is non-physical in some possible worlds in which it occurs. Then if the disembodied existence of other actual thinkers is similarly conceivable, we shall have done enough to establish $(C1_n)$.

We seem to be able to show that I (the thinker) cannot really be a body or brain (nor indeed any other physical thing). For it is conceivable that I might continue to exist without being physical; but it is surely *in*conceivable that a particular brain might continue to exist without being physical. Then if we have our premise that it is impossible for thoughts and experiences to occur in the absence of some thinking experiencing thing, it follows that I am myself a non-physical thing. The argument for strong dualism can thus go through without committing any modal fallacy.

1.8 Immortality?

If dualism is true then it is logically possible that I (my soul, my self) might survive the destruction of my body. So the argument above can be taken as a proof of the *possibility* of disembodied after-life. It is worth considering whether the argument can be strengthened still further. Is it possible for us to go on to prove that I shall *in fact* survive the destruction of my body? Can we develop the argument for dualism into a proof of the immortality of the soul? Some philosophers have thought so (including Descartes). They have believed that they could show that the soul is *simple* (not made up of parts), and that it follows from this that it must be *indestructible*. But neither of these claims can be adequately defended, in fact.

Firstly, how are we supposed to establish that the soul is a simple (non-complex) entity? This certainly doesn't follow from the fact that it is a non-physical thing, and so is not (of course) made up out of physical parts. It is true that when we use the phrase "composite object" in ordinary life, we naturally tend to think of such things as tables and chairs, which are made up out of physical parts standing in various spatial relations to one another. But "composite" surely does not *mean* the same as "made up of physical parts". It simply means: "made up of objects which could exist separately, but which presently stand in some sort of relation to one another". So who knows? Perhaps a non-physical soul is made up of some arrangement of non-physical entities, in such a way that the dissolution of that arrangement would mean that the soul ceases to exist as such. There is certainly no way of ruling out such a possibility merely by reflecting on the concepts of "soul" and of "composite object".

Secondly, even if souls were simple, why should it be supposed to follow from this that they must be immortal? For why should it be thought that the only possible way for an object to cease to exist is for it to be broken up into parts? The ideas of "creation out of nothing" and "destruction into nothing" are perfectly intelligible (not self-contradictory), even if a trifle mysterious. (Some physicists have hypothesized that there are places in the universe where hydrogen atoms are created out of nothing, for example.) It is surely conceivable that God might have the ability to point his finger at any physical object (even a simple atom, if there are such things) pronouncing the words, "Away with you!", whereupon that object would cease to exist. Then it would cease to exist, not by being destroyed into its parts (for it may have no parts), but simply by disappearing out of existence. If this is conceivable, then it is logically possible for non-composite things to cease to exist. In which case even if the soul were simple it wouldn't follow that it is immortal. If it is true that the soul is immortal, then it will only be possible to know that it is on the basis of some sort of empirical evidence (an issue we return to in Chapter 4), or perhaps on the basis of religious revelation.

2   Difficulties for strong dualism

In this section I shall consider some of the traditional objections to dualism. If they were accepted, then we should be forced to look again at the argument of section 1. (It is impossible to have a proof of a false conclusion. So if dualism were false, then there would have to be something wrong with the argument: either one of the premises must be false, or the argument itself must somehow be invalid.) But in fact I shall show that these objections are less than conclusive. They may make dualism hard to believe, but they don't refute it.

2.1   *The soul asleep*

One traditional objection has been this: if it is of the essence of the soul to be conscious, then what are we to say about sleep? If conscious attributes are necessary to the existence of the soul, in the way that physical and spatial attributes are necessary to the existence of the body, then what is to become of the soul during sleep? For we all believe that, although sleep may contain periods of dreaming, it also contains a number of periods of unconsciousness. If I (my self) am a soul (an essentially conscious thing), then how is it possible for me to exist in a state of complete unconsciousness?

There are at least three possible lines of reply that dualists can take. Firstly, they might reject the claim that people are ever really unconscious. They may insist that the soul (the person) is always in fact thinking or experiencing throughout its existence, maintaining that appearances to the contrary arise merely from the fact that some periods of consciousness are much easier to remember than others. On this view, what we call "sleep" or "unconsciousness" are really periods in consciousness about which nothing can later be remembered, or which can only be remembered imperfectly (what we call "dreams").

This view is certainly a possible one. Moreover, it is exceedingly difficult to refute. If you think you know that you are sometimes unconscious, then reflect for a moment upon whether you could convince someone who believes otherwise. Certainly there are periods of your life – some of them fairly recent – about which you now remember nothing. But how do you know that this is because there really was nothing to remember (you were unconscious) rather than that you have merely forgotten it? It seems that your memory (or lack of it) is not by itself sufficient proof that you are ever unconscious. But then neither can you directly verify that you are ever unconscious. For of course if you really *are* unconscious, then you are in no position to verify anything.

In fact we all do believe, for whatever reason, that we are sometimes completely unconscious. But if dualists choose to believe otherwise, then it is hard to see how we can prove them wrong. Moreover, if it came to a straight choice between belief in dualism and belief in periodic unconsciousness, then it seems we should give up the latter, no matter how counter-intuitive this might at first seem. For in support of dualism we have a powerful argument, whereas it isn't obvious that we have anything at all to support our belief in unconscious existence.

A second option would be for dualists to claim that the essential attribute of the soul isn't *conscious* mentality, but just mentality (whether conscious or unconscious). They might say that during sleep people continue to have *unconscious* mental states. Since unconscious mental states are, by definition, states we don't know we are having, and have no (conscious) memory of afterwards, it is only to be expected that we wouldn't know that we have them during sleep or other periods of unconsciousness, either.

Now, ever since the writings of the founder of psychoanalysis early in the 20th Century, Sigmund Freud, the idea that there can be unconscious emotions, unconscious desires and unconscious thoughts has become part of everyone's common-sense conception of the mind. So this response by dualists to the problem of the sleeping soul can certainly seem well-motivated. (Admittedly, they don't really have any positive evidence of continuous unconscious mental activity; but this might reasonably be accepted as a commitment of their dualistic theory.)

Note, however, that the present proposal conflicts with the Cartesian conception of the meaning of mental state terms, which we elaborated and defended in Chapter 1:4. If the meaning of terms like "anger" and "thirst" is wholly exhausted by the introspectible subjective *feel* of the corresponding states, then there is really no room left for the idea of unconscious anger. For what sense can be made of the idea of an unfelt feel? Now, this point is by no means decisive against the present proposal for reconciling dualism with the existence of unconsciousness during sleep; for dualists perhaps don't *have* to be committed to the Cartesian conception. But then they do owe us some account of what should replace it. (We will return to this topic at some length in Chapter 7.)

The third possible line of response for dualists to take (and perhaps the most interesting), would be to allow that periods of unconsciousness do occur, and to allow that during these periods no soul exists. They need only claim that the soul, like some kinds of physical object, can have an existence which is *intermittent* in nature. They can claim that one and the same soul can survive across periods of non-existence. (This is an idea which will be pursued in some depth in Chapter 3:2, and then again, from a somewhat different perspective, in Chapter 6:2.)

An example will make clear what I mean. Suppose that you are the owner of an expensive motorcycle, of which you are hugely fond. Fearing for its theft, when you go on vacation you dismantle it as completely as you can, leaving the parts spread around your attic and garage wrapped in oily rags. Then when you return, you reassemble it again just as it was. Now during the time you are away, there exists no motorcycle. For a collection of unrelated motorcycle parts no more constitutes a motorcycle than a pile of bricks and a bag of cement constitutes a house. Yet when you reassemble the parts, you rebuild your original machine, rather than construct a new one. If you continue your practice for five years, going on vacation each year, then you have owned only one motorcycle during that time, not five.

This is what I mean by intermittent existence: one and the same motorcycle exists at the end of the five-year period as existed at the beginning, although during part of that time no motorcycle has existed at all. It is thus open to dualists to say that the soul, too, has intermittent existence, ceasing to exist during periods of unconsciousness. Once again this conflicts with something which we are all intuitively inclined to believe. We all tend to think that during periods of unconsciousness we continue to exist. But how do we know? For while we are unconscious we are of course in no position to know whether or not we still exist. Then, when we are conscious once again, we seem to lack any positive evidence one way or the other. So here, too, if it came to a straight choice between belief in dualism and our belief in our own continuous existence, it seems that it is the latter which should give way.

2.2   The relation between body and soul

The other main traditional objections to dualism have concerned the kind of relation which is supposed to exist between body and soul. Notice to begin with that the soul cannot literally be *in* the body. For since the soul is non-physical it cannot itself occupy any position is space. Only physical objects (together with spatial lines and points, of course) can occupy spatial positions. Thus consider the number 9, for instance. This object – if there really is such an object – isn't a physical one. As a result it makes no sense to speak of it occupying a particular place (nor indeed all places). Sentences like, "The number 9 is in London" seem obviously nonsensical.

The soul is only metaphorically "in" a particular body. The literal truth, for the strong dualist, is this: I am "in" my body in the sense that it is only via that body that I can engage in causal commerce with the rest of the physical world. As a matter of fact there is only one body (my body) which I can cause to move around the world just by thinking about it: by forming intentions and making decisions. As a matter of fact my experience of the world only comes to me via the effects of the world upon that very same body. So the relationship between my soul and my body is *causal*, not spatial.

2.3   Interactions in principle

Now this is where the difficulties start. For how is it possible for soul and body to have causal effects upon one another? How can a non-physical, non-spatial, soul interact causally with a physical, space-occupying, body? Certainly not by bumping into it. Nor can the soul affect (nor be affected by) the body magnetically, electrically or chemically. For all of these kinds of causal relation can only be entered into by physical objects and states. So how is it supposed to happen? It appears that there must be some kind of radical "quantum leap" between the last event in the causal chain of mental events (a thought causing another thought, causing a decision) and the first event in the causal chain of physical events (one particular brain cell firing off an electro-chemical impulse to another). Many have found it unintelligible how anything could ever bridge this gap, and have concluded that the whole idea of soul–body interaction is unintelligible (i.e., impossible).

Dualists should reply that a causal connection does not have to be intelligible (in the sense of being explicable in terms of some other kind of causal connection) in order to be real. Consider the force of gravity for instance. In the manner of the above objection to dualism, we might demand to know how it is possible for massive bodies to attract one another with a force inversely proportional to the square of the distance between them. It seems we cannot provide a model for this form of causal interaction in terms of anything more basic. (Perhaps physicists now can, I don't know.) Certainly the bodies aren't pulled towards one another by invisible elastic bands! Yet for all that, we are sure that the causal connection exists.

The general point is that at any given stage in the development of science there will always be some kinds of causal connection which have to be treated as basic, being inexplicable in other terms. So it is open to strong dualists to claim that the causal connections between soul and body fall into just this category.

Perhaps all that is really required, in order for there to be a causal connection between two particular events, e and f, is that those events should belong to two event-kinds, E and F, which are governed by the universal law: *whenever an event of type E occurs, then so does an event of type F* (so long as the law is sufficiently strong to warrant counter-factual claims: *if e had not happened, then f would not have happened either*). Thus if we believe that the taking of a cyanide pill caused Mary's death, then we must believe that there is some general description of the first event (the ingestion of such-and-such quantities of cyanide by a person with such-and-such bodily constitution) and some general description of the second event (death), such that events of the first kind are invariably followed by events of the second.

But now this might seem to play into the hands of the opponent of dualism. For the fact is, we just do not possess such general laws when it comes to mind–body interaction. The most plausible candidate for such a law would be this: *whenever someone has decided, all things considered, that doing X right now would be the best thing to do in the circumstances, then they will do X*. Yet this runs up against the familiar phenomenon of weakness of will. It is a dis-

turbing fact of human experience that someone may, after delibera-
tion, decide that the best thing to do in the circumstances would be
X rather than Y, and then go ahead and do Y all the same. I may
decide not to have another chocolate, and then the very next
moment, without apparently changing my mind, reach out and take
one.

Dualists have a reply to this, too. It is that we often have reason
to believe in the existence of a causal relation in a particular case,
prior to the discovery of any general law. For example, this is very
likely our situation in connection with death caused by cyanide. I
very much doubt whether scientists know of any precise law correlating quantities of cyanide and bodily constitution with resulting
death. Yet, for all that, we may be certain, in the particular case,
that Mary's death was caused by cyanide. So dualists may defend
the reasonableness of our belief in the causal connections between
mind and body in particular cases (of course a decision will sometimes cause a bodily movement; and of course a thorn in the flesh
will sometimes cause a sensation of pain), despite our ignorance of
any universal causal laws connecting the two. Perhaps such laws
will one day be discovered.

2.4 Interactions in fact

It appears that attempts to refute strong dualism – by claiming that
causal connections between body and soul are impossible in principle – have failed. A quite different line of objection is to claim that
our beliefs about the physical world give us good reason to think
that such causal connections do not occur *in fact*. This is an argument which will be pursued at some length in Chapter 5, since it
provides one of the main reasons for believing in *physicalism* – for
believing, that is, that both minds and their states are physical.

The argument in question begins, however, from scientific claims
about the physical world in general, and about the operations of
our brains, in particular. It will therefore cut little ice with those
who are tempted by our argument for strong dualism. For this argument purports to be a purely philosophical one; and many have
held that such arguments are prior to, and more basic than, mere
scientific evidence. These issues will become clearer once we have
discussed, in Chapter 4, some elements of the debate between
Rationalists (who maintain that pure thinking can obtain substantive knowledge for us) and Empiricists (who believe that the only

legitimate source of real knowledge is experience, or empirical evidence). For the moment we merely note that strong dualism has thus far survived the attacks of its critics unscathed, although one such attack has been postponed for later consideration. We turn, now, to a different line of criticism, first launched by the Scottish philosopher David Hume.

3   Hume'n bundles

In section 1 above, we constructed what appeared to be a proof of the existence of the soul. Some philosophers have challenged this and similar arguments at precisely the point where they appear most solid, however, namely at the claim that *thoughts require a thinker*. The challenge is, in fact, a challenge to the validity of Descartes' famous argument, "Cogito ergo sum", or, "I think, so I exist", which is perhaps the most famous in all philosophy.

(In order to avoid the appearance of circularity created when the word "I" figures in the premise as well as the conclusion, Descartes' argument is best expressed thus: "*These* thoughts are occurring, so there must be a thinker of these thoughts – call it 'I'." Here the premise can be known with certainty on the basis of introspection, in accordance with the "certainty thesis" defended in Chapter 1:4.)

The objectors have argued that the sense of obviousness which attends this argument derives entirely from our common-sense beliefs about physical human beings: never to our knowledge have thoughts occurred in the absence of a human thinker. But of course this cannot show it to be logically impossible that this should happen. In any case we had better not rely upon our beliefs about physical human beings, if we are trying to prove that the real subject of thoughts and experiences is a non-physical soul.

The foremost exponent of this line of objection to our argument was David Hume. He made two points. First, the most that can be immediately established on the basis of introspection is the existence of conscious states and events themselves. When I "look into" myself, I am aware of thoughts, experiences, and feelings. I am not aware of any self which has or possesses these states. The self is not an item in consciousness. Second, the existence of a thinking, feeling self – an underlying *ego* – cannot be validly deduced from the occurrence of the thoughts and experiences of which we are aware.

The first point may be granted as obvious. It is the second claim which will occupy our attention throughout the remainder of this section. I shall consider three different arguments attempting to prove that conscious thoughts or experiences necessarily require the existence of some conscious thing, which would be the thinker of those thoughts, or the subject of those experiences. Each tries to do this on the basis of the necessity of some more general principle. I shall argue that none is successful.

I should emphasize at the outset, however, that it is only the validity of our argument for *strong* dualism which is under attack, here. The truth of weak dualism is still being taken for granted. Hume, just as much as Descartes, believes that mental states and events are non-physical states and events, and so don't literally occupy positions in space. He only denies that we can know that these mental states and events inhere in some underlying *thing*, a non-physical self or soul.

3.1 Events

Many experiences belong to the category of *event*: they are *happenings*, changes which take place within the contents of consciousness. Then, if we could show that an event must take place in (or to) some subject, we could argue thus:

(1) Experiences are mental events.
(2) It is logically necessary that events occur in (or to) some subject or thing.
(C) So experiences require an experiencer.

Note that premise (1) will state a necessary truth. For all propositions assigning something to its most general category (telling you what basic kind of thing it is) are necessary truths. Compare: red is a color; tables are items of furniture; trees are plants.

Unfortunately for our purposes, premise (2) is false, in fact. Think of a flash of lightning, for example. This is very definitely an event, a happening. But is there any individual thing which is the subject of the event? *Which* thing is it that flashes? The clouds? But they are rather the cause of the flash. The discharge of electricity? But an electrical discharge is itself an event (indeed plausibly the very same event as the flash of lightning). The air or region of space through which the lightning passes? But it sounds strange to speak of either of these as though it were an individual thing like a person or a house or a tree. It seems best to say that a flash of lightning is an event without a subject. In which case it does not follow, from the mere fact that a mental event takes place, that there must exist some subject of that event, some underlying *self* in which that event inheres.

3.2 *Attributes*

Even more fundamental than the category of *event*, are the categories of *property* and *attribute* (I shall treat these as roughly equivalent). An event is, as we said, a change. For a change to take place is for there to be one attribute instantiated at an earlier time, and then for there to be a different attribute at some later time. For example, think of a light going off. At one moment the light has the property of being on, and then at the next moment it is off. But for the light to be either on or off are states or properties of it. They are not themselves changes, although there may be changes underlying them (e.g., the movement of electricity through a filament).

Now, we might wonder whether it isn't a necessary truth that an attribute requires a subject. For what *is* an attribute but a property of some *thing*? We could then argue as follows:

(1) Some mental states are properties, or attributes.
(2) Any attribute must be an attribute of some subject or thing.
(C) So some mental states require the existence of a subject, or self.

But here again, premise (2) is false, in fact (or at least, it is not true in a way which enables us to derive the conclusion). Think of what is being said by a statement like, "It is cloudy". Cloudiness seems definitely to be a property or attribute. It is not itself a change, although there may be changes underlying it (i.e., millions of water droplets traveling across the sky). But what is the cloudiness an attribute *of* ? The only two candidates are: a region of space (e.g., the sky above Los Angeles), or a period of time (e.g., this afternoon). But again it seems strange to think of either of these as if they were some sort of individual thing.

The general point is that properties can figure, not only in genuine subject–predicate statements (The pavement is wet, Mary is tall) but also in discourse which is merely "feature placing" (It is raining, It is cloudy, etc.). So again it does not follow, from the mere fact that there occur mental states, or mental attributes, that there must exist some subject – a self – who possesses them.

Now it is true that, on the face of it, statements attributing mental states to oneself seem to be of genuine subject–predicate form. (Consider: "I am in pain", "I am thinking of my mother".) But here Hume can set us a dilemma, demanding to know what the word "I" is intended to refer to. If (on the one hand) it refers to my body, then the statements will indeed be of genuine subject–predicate form. But they will be useless to figure in an argument for dualism. For the dualist believes that conscious states aren't states of the body, but rather of the soul. If (on the other hand) the word "I" is intended to refer to my soul, then again we shall have a statement of genuine subject–predicate form. But I shan't be in a position to know these statements to be true, until I know that I really do have a soul. Yet that is just what we are trying to prove.

The most that we can be aware of on the basis of introspection is that pains and thoughts are taking place. So perhaps we ought properly to restrict ourselves, in the present context (that is: while attempting to provide a proof of dualism) to statements of the form: "It hurts", and, "A thought of mother is presently occurring". Then these will be genuinely analogous to mere feature-placing discourse.

(Of course, I have no objection if someone wants to insist that a region of space is the subject of the property of being cloudy, or if they want to insist that because cloudiness doesn't have a subject it isn't a genuine attribute. For then it will only follow, either that the "subject" of thoughts and experiences may be something like a region of space – which isn't the kind of thing which we think a conscious soul, or self, should be – or that mental states may not be genuine attributes.)

On Hume's view, the most that we have reason to believe in, on the basis of data available to introspection, is the existence of the stream of consciousness itself. We have no reason to believe in any underlying subject or self in which, or to which, the stream occurs. On the contrary, the mind is to be compared to a thunderstorm. Here is an immensely complicated sequence of events and states: the clouds and the gathering darkness; the rain and the hail; the rolls of thunder and the flashes of lightning. These stand in many complex relations to one another: some occur simultaneously, some at different times; some are near to one another in space, some further apart; some are causes or effects of one another, others are causally independent. But there is no substantial subject, no individual thing, in which or to which the thunderstorm occurs. A thunderstorm doesn't have a subject. All that exists is a particular bundle of

59

meteorological states and events. Similarly, then, the mind is simply a bundle or collection of conscious states and events. This is sometimes called "the no-self view" of the mind, or more simply "the bundle theory".

3.3 Actions

It might seem that we stand a better chance of finding an argument against Hume if we confine ourselves to a particular class of mental events, namely those belonging to the category of *action*. Thinking, imagining and judging all appear to be mental *activities*. Now, how could an *action* occur without an *actor*? For what distinguishes an action (e.g., kicking a ball) from a mere event (e.g., someone turning over in their sleep), if not that an action is an event which is intentionally brought about by an agent? Then it seems we may construct the following argument:

(1) Thinking (or imagining, or judging) is a mental activity.
(2) It is impossible for an action to occur in the absence of an acting subject.
(C) So at least some mental states require the existence of a subject, or self.

Since this argument is valid, everything will turn on the truth of the premises.

Hume might challenge premise (1), demanding how we are to know that thinking is an activity. You may reply that this is just obvious: for what else could it be? But he might say that this sense of obviousness derives entirely from our common-sense beliefs about (physical) human beings. We are accustomed to distinguish between things which happen to a human being ("Mary is injured", "Mary is in pain") and things which a human being does ("Mary is talking", "Mary is kicking a ball"). Of course, we should normally place thinking in the latter category. Yet as before, we had better not rely upon our ordinary beliefs about human beings if our objective is to prove the existence of a non-physical soul. All we should allow ourselves to take for granted is what we can be immediately aware of: the character of our own conscious states.

But now we are in difficulty. For in order to know on the basis of introspection that thinking should be classified as an activity ("a change intentionally brought about by an agent") we should have to be aware, not just of the change, but also of the agent (and perhaps also the *bringing about*). Yet as we saw earlier, the most that we are in fact aware of is that a certain thought takes place. We are not in addition aware of a particular self which has the thought, or which does the thinking. So perhaps the most that we are entitled to believe is that a thought, like the onset of a headache, is a conscious event or change.

Hume might also challenge premise (2). He might deny that actions necessarily require actors, by denying that the concept of an action is the concept of a change intentionally brought about by an agent. He might claim instead, that what distinguishes an action from a mere event is its distinctive causal history in prior mental states. Perhaps an action is an event which is caused by beliefs and desires. Thus what caused the kicking of the ball will have been a particular desire (to win the game) combined with some particular beliefs (that this is the appropriate moment to kick). Whereas what caused the person to turn over in their sleep will not have been any beliefs or desires. If this were correct, then there would be nothing in the concept of an action, as such, to imply the existence of some acting thing or subject.

In fact the proposed definition is inadequate as it stands. First, not everything caused by beliefs and desires is an action. My belief that I am about to be shot, combined with my desire to stay alive, may cause me to have a heart-attack; but the heart-attack is not itself an action of mine. Secondly, not all actions are caused by beliefs and desires. Suppose that I am sitting idly twiddling my thumbs. The twiddling is an intentional activity alright, but it is not being done for any reason. I do not twiddle *for* anything – because I believe this and want that – rather, I just twiddle.

All the same, it is hard to be confident that no adequate analysis of the concept of action can be provided along these lines. There is certainly no easy way of proving that the distinction between actions and mere events cannot be defined in terms of the causal connections between the event which is the action, and other mental states and events: beliefs, desires, thoughts, decisions. In which case there is no easy way of showing, against Hume, that the concept of an action has to bring with it the notion of an acting subject, or agent.

3.4 Conclusion

All our attempts to demonstrate that mental states necessarily require the existence of a substantial self, in terms of the necessity of some more general principle ("an event requires a subject", "an attribute requires a possessor", "an act requires an actor"), have been a failure. So the only remaining possibility is that there is something peculiar to mental states themselves which implies that they cannot exist in the absence of a subject or self. In the next section we shall investigate this possibility, by seeing whether or not we can show the Humean bundle-theory to be a necessary falsehood. If the "no-self view" of consciousness *cannot* be true, then by contrast the "some-self view" *must* be true.

4 Against the bundle theory

If we are to prove the existence of the soul, then we must show that the mind cannot merely be a bundle of mental states and events (in the way that a thunderstorm is in fact a mere bundle of meteorological states and events). We must show, on the contrary, that there must exist some self which is their subject. Since we are trying to prove the existence of a non-physical self, we shouldn't rely upon any of our common-sense beliefs about physical human beings. Rather, we may take for granted only the data immediately available to introspection. In this section I shall present the three main traditional objections to the bundle theory. The first fails, the second is somewhat more troublesome, but the third seems conclusive.

In order to see how these objections to the bundle theory of the mind arise, consider – by way of analogy – a bundle of sticks. If the mind is like a bundle of sticks, then mental states must be able to exist individually, outside of any bundle, in the way that the sticks, too, can exist separately and unbundled. If the mind is like a bundle of sticks, then there must be something to be said about what binds the different mental states together into a single bundle, similar to the string which binds the bundle of sticks. Finally, if the mind is like a bundle of sticks, then the individuation of particular mental states must be prior to the individuation of minds, in something like the way that individual sticks can be picked out and distinguished for the individual things that they are – and counted up – independently of their occurrence in any bundle.

4.1 Singular conscious states

If the mind is merely a bundle of states and events, then it must be logically possible for the various elements of the bundle to exist on their own. It is logically possible for a bolt of lightning to strike out of a clear blue sky, in the absence of any of the other events which normally go to make up a thunderstorm. It is even possible that the universe might have contained nothing except this one event. There is a possible world which consists only of a single flash of lightning. But is it similarly possible for a single pain to occur independently of any mind (i.e., for the Humean, independently of any bundle)? Is it logically possible for all organic life to be extinguished in a nuclear holocaust, and yet a single headache goes on? Is there a possible world which contains nothing whatever except this: a single pain?

We have no difficulty in conceiving of a world which contains nothing except a single flash of lightning. But a world which contains nothing except a single headache seems, on the face of it, to be *in*conceivable. For how could a unitary pain exist all by itself? Yet the Humean may respond that our difficulty only arises because we are trying to imagine the pain, like the lightning, from a standpoint outside it. Of course you don't know what to imagine if you are asked to conceive of someone else's pain existing in the absence of any physical body, and so in the absence of any perceptible manifestation of that pain. But it may be different in the case of one of your own pains.

Consider the following example. You are lying on the dentist's couch, having a tooth worked on without the benefit of an anesthetic. The drill strikes a nerve, causing you intense pain, but the dentist does not stop. In a case like this the pain can come to flood your whole consciousness. Its intensity may leave no room for any other thought or idea. You may cease to be aware of your own body, perhaps even ceasing to be aware of the sound of the drill. There might simply be nothing that you are aware of except this: an intense pain. If you are asked to imagine a world which contains only a single pain, then imagine a pain like this, only without the story about the dentist and the drill. Imagine to yourself a pain which floods the whole of consciousness, unaccompanied by any other conscious states, and frame to yourself the thought, "and nothing else exists besides this".

It seems that a single pain, like a single flash of lightning, really can be imagined to exist on its own. However, the case of many other mental states may be different, particularly those involving the use of concepts, such as beliefs, thoughts and judgments. Could there be a world which contains nothing besides the occurrence of a particular thought, say the thought that money doesn't grow on trees? I suggest not. For what would make it the case that this thought is about money, or about trees? Also, what would give it the structure which it has? (For example, what would make it different from the thought that trees don't grow on money?)

The point will emerge most clearly if we consider a public act of thinking: a public saying. Imagine Tarzan brought up by the apes in the jungle. He never learns a language, but on just one occasion – out of the blue – he utters an English sentence. He says, "Money doesn't grow on trees". So far the story is imaginable, if unlikely. (Just as it is imaginable that an ape tapping randomly at a typewriter might produce the sentences, "To be or not to be? That is the question".) But can we also imagine that Tarzan means what he says? I claim not. For someone can only mean something by uttering a sequence of sounds against a background of linguistic capacities. Only someone who is capable of using the words "money" and "tree" in other contexts and in other combinations, and who is capable of identifying money and trees when he sees them, can mean that money doesn't grow on trees. (This is the reason why a parrot doesn't mean what it says: because it isn't capable of using its words in other combinations, and in application to reality.)

What is true at the level of language is true at the level of thoughts and beliefs as well. Someone can only have the thought, or the belief, that money doesn't grow on trees against a background of conceptual capacities and other beliefs. They must be capable of using those concepts in other thoughts, and must be able to tell the difference between trees and other things. They must believe that money is a conventional means of exchange, that trees are plants, that growth is part of the life-cycle of living organisms, and so on. A thought is only a thought within a conceptual system. A belief is only a belief within a network of other beliefs. Neither thoughts nor beliefs can occur singly, but only in groups.

Hume might concede these points, but deny that it follows that there must be some underlying self who possesses the network of beliefs and thoughts. Consider, by analogy, a move in a game of chess. A particular physical event – e.g., the moving of a pawn forward one space – is only a move in a game against a background of other similar events. If I simply walk up to a chess-board one day and move a pawn, leaving the board forever after untouched, then I have not made a move in a game. Moves in games, like thoughts, cannot occur singly but only in groups. For they only acquire their significance as moves within the wider context in which they occur. But of course it doesn't follow from this that there must be some individual thing ("the game") in which or to which the moves occur. For the game itself is not a thing. It is, like a thunderstorm, merely a complex arrangement of states and events, in which things participate.

Hume could also concede that thoughts and beliefs are only possible against an enduring background of conceptual capacities, but deny that it follows from this that there must be some underlying self who possesses those capacities. He need only say that the mind is a bundle of both conscious and unconscious states and events, where some of the unconscious states are enduring conceptual capacities, which are exercised in acts of thinking. For compare: a weather system, too, may have capacities. At a particular time it may be capable of hailing. That is to say: if certain other things happen (e.g., a drop in temperature) then it will hail. But of course there is no enduring thing in which the capacities of a weather-system reside.

Our first line of objection against the bundle theory has been a failure. Many conscious states can indeed be imagined to exist on their own. There is no obvious objection to the theory arising out of the necessary inter-connectedness of many other conscious states, nor out of the dependence of many of these states upon unconscious capacities.

4.2   The unity of consciousness

What binds together the bundle? What makes it true that a particular thought or experience is a member of one bundle rather than another? There are, in fact, two rather different questions here. One relates to the unity of consciousness *over* time. (That is, what makes my experiences today and my experiences last week part of the same stream of consciousness?) The other relates to the unity of consciousness *at* a time. (That is, what makes my visual experiences now and my auditory experiences now part of the same bundle or mind?) If we can solve the latter problem then I can see no particular difficulty about solving the former. If we can sort mental states

into discrete bundles at any one time, then I can see no real difficulty in keeping track of those bundles over a period of time. (See
Chapter 3:2 for some ideas on how such tracking of bundles might
be done.) I shall thus concentrate upon the latter problem: what
binds together the elements of consciousness at any particular time,
giving it its characteristic unity?

Hume's own account is provided in terms of the notions of
resemblance and causality. On his view it is the resemblance of the
different conscious states to one another, and the causal relations
between them, which binds them together into a single bundle.
Now this might stand some chance of success as an account of the
unity of consciousness *over* time, but is obviously hopeless as an
account of the unity of the mind at any particular time. For there
will often be neither resemblance nor causal connection between the
various elements in consciousness at any given moment.

For example, think of someone whose in-grown toe-nail is
causing them pain at the same time as they listen to a Beethoven
sonata. There is obviously not the slightest resemblance between the
pain and the sound of the sonata. Nor is there any causal relationship between them. On the contrary, both are directly caused by
external physical events, in the one case tissue-damage in the toe, in
the other a physical stimulus to the ear-drums.

Moreover, the use of resemblance as a criterion will bundle
together experiences in quite the wrong way. Imagine two people,
Mary and Joan, each of whom is examining a modern painting.
Mary is looking at a painting whose left half is red, and whose right
half is blue. Joan is looking at a painting which is the reverse: its
right half is red and its left half is blue. Now the experience making
up the left side of Mary's visual field will resemble the experiences
making up the right side of Joan's visual field much more closely
than they resemble the right side of her own visual field. If we were
to rely upon resemblance to bundle together experiences, then we
should have to say that there is one consciousness here containing a
uniform visual field of an experience of red, and another containing
a uniform visual field of an experience of blue, and of course this
would be absurd.

Hume's best response to these difficulties would be to give up his
reliance on resemblance and causality, and to appeal instead to
certain "higher-order" states of consciousness (i.e., states of consciousness which are *about* other states). Thus when Mary looks at
the painting there isn't merely an awareness of red and an aware-

ness of blue. There is also an awareness that there is a simultaneous awareness of both red and blue. Similarly with the suffering sonata-lover: there isn't merely an awareness of pain in the toe and an awareness of the sound of the piano. There is also the higher-order awareness that there is an awareness of pain which is simultaneous with an awareness of sound.

So Hume should say that what binds together the bundle of states of consciousness is: other states of consciousness. For consciousness isn't merely a collection of discrete thoughts and experiences. It also contains higher-order states of consciousness, namely states of awareness of the simultaneous presence of the various first-order states of consciousness. Then what makes an experience X part of the same bundle (the same mind) as a simultaneous experience Y, will be the presence of a third state of consciousness Z, caused by X and Y, which takes the form of an awareness that there is a simultaneous occurrence of X and Y.

Construed in this way, the bundle theory is not altogether implausible. There remains a further objection, however: not all states of consciousness belonging to the same mind are in fact united by higher-order states of awareness. In which case the only remaining explanation of what makes all these states belong to the same mind is that they are all states of the same person or self. What makes consciousness a unity will not be any of the relations existing between the mental states themselves, but rather the fact that they all belong to the same individual thing.

For example, suppose that I am listening to a Beethoven sonata while thinking about the nature of the self. I may be aware of the music, and aware of what I am thinking, without being aware of what I am simultaneously hearing and thinking. I may in fact hear the music reach a crescendo at the same time as I think, "There is a distinction between strong and weak dualism". But I may not be aware that the experience of the crescendo and the thinking of that thought are simultaneous with one another. Looking back afterwards I may recall the sequence of the music, and recall the sequence of my thoughts, without in any way being able to correlate the two sequences. So what is it that makes both the experience and the thought part of the same mind, if not that they are both states possessed by the same underlying person or self? (Note that neither resemblance nor causality can be of any help here. For there is no resemblance, and there is no causal relation.)

Hume's best response is to appeal to the mere *possibility* of second order awareness, at this point. He might say that what binds together the elements of consciousness is the *capacity* for there to be an awareness that all of them are occurring simultaneously. For even if I am not at the moment aware that I currently possess both experience X and thought Y, I *can* be aware of it. This may be sufficient to make both of those experiences part of the same bundle of consciousness. Once again it looks as if Hume can rebut his critics if he allows that the mind isn't just a bundle of *conscious* states, but also of enduring mental capacities of various sorts.

4.3   The particularity of mental states

On the Humean view, minds are *constructs* out of thoughts and experiences, since particular minds are merely bundles of particular mental states. If this is so, then our notion of the particularity of any given individual mental state (i.e., our idea of what makes that state the individual state which it is) must be logically prior to our notion of the particularity of any given particular mind. What makes an individual mind be the individual mind which it is, will be the fact that it is made up out of the individual mental states which make it up. ("Same mental states" implies "same mind"; "different mental states" implies "different mind".)

I shall argue that this order of priority is, in fact, the wrong way round. (It should rather be: "Same mind" implies "same mental states"; and "different mind" implies "different mental states".) We have a concept of people (minds) as distinct individual things, and distinct (though exactly similar) experiences are distinguished precisely because they are the experiences of two distinct people. We do not, and cannot, first establish that we are dealing with two distinct but exactly similar experiences, and then settle the question whether those experiences belong to two distinct minds or only one. On the contrary, the question, "Are there two exactly similar experiences here, or only one?" can only be answered in terms of whether or not the experiences belong to two different experiencing beings, or only one.

Contrast the case of a thunderstorm. The particularity of individual meteorological events really is prior to the particularity of thunderstorms. For example, we can distinguish two simultaneous flashes of lightning from one another – which are otherwise exactly similar – in terms of their distinct spatial positions. We can do this without first having to know how many thunderstorms we are dealing with. We can, in principle, count up all the individual flashes, the rain-drops, the regions of dark cloud and so on, which are in existence at a given time, and *then* go on to ask whether these all belong to one thunderstorm, or to two or more distinct thunderstorms.

Similarly, consider a case where we have two bundles of sticks placed side by side (see Figure 2.1). Suppose that the sticks are glued together rather than tied up with string, so that it isn't immediately obvious that we are dealing with two bundles here, rather than one (or three). Plainly we could set about counting the total number of sticks before we try to settle the question of the number of bundles. This is because each stick occupies its own unique position in space. (In contrast, the unique position in space occupied by each of the bundles is derivative from the positions of the individual sticks which make them up.) So the answer to the question, "How many sticks?" is logically prior to the question, "How many bundles?" But nothing like this seems to be possible in the case of mind. The question, "How many mental states?" can only be answered if we can *first* settle the question, "How many minds?"

Consider, for example, a case where two Siamese twins each feel pain in the place where they join. Suppose that they are joined back-to-back, and that they both feel an exactly similar pain in the center of their back. Now we provide the Humean with a complete list of their thoughts and experiences, demanding that they be

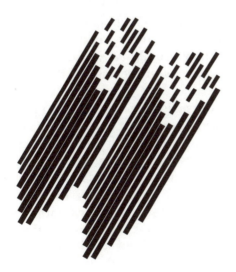

Figure 2.1 Two bundles of sticks.

sorted into bundles. What we want to know is whether the two twins constitute a single mind (a single bundle), or two distinct minds (bundles). (Remember: weak dualism is being assumed here; so the fact that there are two distinct humans in the example isn't directly relevant.)

The list might go something like this: there is a pain in the back, a thought about the weather, an awareness that there is a pain in the back simultaneous with a thought of the weather, a pain in the back, a thought about Mozart, an awareness that there is a pain in the back simultaneous with a thought about Mozart, and so on. Now the Humean will need to know whether the *same* pain gets mentioned *twice over* in this list (in which case we shall be dealing with a single bundle or mind), or whether the two occurrences of the phrase "a pain in the back" refer to two distinct pains (in which case we shall be dealing with two distinct bundles or minds). But in fact there is no way for this issue to be decided. Not only do Humeans have no way of telling whether there are two pains or only one, they can surely have no conception of what might constitute the fact of the matter, one way or the other.

Hume's problem is that there doesn't seem to be anything, in the case of the mind, which can play the sort of role which space does in individuating meteorological events or pieces of wood. Distinct though exactly similar flashes of lightning can be distinguished by virtue of the distinct places in which they occur. But mental states don't literally occupy any space, for a weak dualist. So we can't say, "This pain is distinct from that exactly similar pain by virtue of occupying distinct places", since pains aren't supposed to have literal spatial positions – rather, they are *felt as emanating from* a place, and this can be the very same, as in the case of the Siamese twins.

What we should say here, of course, is that there are two pains if there are two people, and that there is only one pain if there is only one person. We should treat questions of identity and distinctness among pains as depending upon questions of identity and distinctness among people. Then since we should certainly say that the two Siamese twins are two distinct people, we shall say that we are dealing with two distinct (though exactly similar) pains, rather than with only one. The particularity of persons is thus prior to the particularity of experiences, rather than (as Hume would have it) the other way round.

The conclusion of this argument is that minds cannot be mere bundles of mental states, because we can have no conception of the particularity of mental states prior to, and independently of, a conception of the particularity of persons. The only way in which we can distinguish and identify particular mental states is by first distinguishing and identifying the people (the selves) who possess them.

Before leaving this topic, however, we should note that the dispute between Hume and Descartes which we have been discussing has been premised on an assumption of (at least) weak dualism. The question has been: given that mental states are non-physical states, are minds mere bundles of such states, or must there be some underlying self in which those states inhere? In arguing for the latter of these two options, we have given the victory in the debate decisively to Descartes. But the dispute between them can also be seen in another way, as being about the *architecture* or *mode of organization* of the mind. Descartes is defending a sort of *ego theory*, claiming that in addition to the mental states themselves, there is a further mental item (the self) which is aware of, directs, and oversees the rest. Hume is denying this. It may well turn out that on this issue, framed within the context of physicalism, Hume is correct, as we shall see in our discussion of functionalist and so-called "theory-theory" accounts of the mind in Chapter 7.

Conclusion

Over the course of this chapter we have managed to develop a powerful case in support of strong dualism. We were able to set out a seeming-proof of the existence of the soul, which was then capable of surviving a range of different challenges and attacks. Strong dualism was able to survive the objection from periodic unconsciousness, as well as the argument that causal relations between mind and body are impossible in principle. It has now survived a sustained challenge to the validity of the original argument we provided in its support. This was Hume's claim that the existence of a thinking thing (a substantial soul, as opposed to a mere collection of thoughts and experiences) cannot be known. Thus far, then, strong dualism appears quite well-supported. In the next chapter we will explore our conception of the soul still further, asking whether it is really a coherent one.

Questions for discussion

1. Try to imagine, in as much detail as you can, what disembodied existence might be like. How would you know, on the basis of your experience, that you were really disembodied?
2. How convincing do you find the argument for the existence of the soul? What, in your view, is its weakest point?
3. If souls are essentially-mental entities, then what might become of your soul during sleep and other periods of unconsciousness?
4. How plausible is it that the mind is just a "bundle" of different mental states (lacking any underlying *ego*, or thinking thing), in something like the way that a thunderstorm is just a bundle of meteorological states?
5. Can we, in principle, count the numbers of individual mental states existing in some context, in advance of knowing how many thinkers there are of such states?

Further reading

Descartes, R. (1637) *Discourse on the Method*, (Many translations available.)

Descartes, R. (1641) *Meditations on First Philosophy*, 1, 2 & 6. (Many translations available.)

Hume, D. (1888) "Of personal identity", *A Treatise of Human Nature*, book 1, part 4, section 6.

Malcolm, N. (1965) "Descartes' proof that his essence is thinking", *Philosophical Review*, vol. 74. Reprinted in W. Doney (ed.) (1967), *Descartes* London: Macmillan.

Malcolm, N. (1972) *Problems of Mind*, London: Allen and Unwin, Chapter 1.

Shoemaker, S. "On an argument for dualism", in Ginet, C. and Shoemaker, S. (eds.) (1983), *Knowledge and Mind*, Oxford: Oxford University Press. Reprinted in Shoemaker's (1984) *Identity, Cause and Mind*, Cambridge: Cambridge University Press.

Swinburne, R. "A dualistic theory" in Shoemaker, S. and Swinburne, R. (eds.) (1984) *Personal Identity*, Oxford: Blackwell.

3

⸺⧫⸺

Identity and the soul

Our task in this chapter is to investigate in more detail the dualist conception of the soul as an individually existing thing, whose existence is independent of the existence of the body. Since strong dualism maintains that bodies and souls are distinct existences, it does at least hold out the possibility of life after (bodily) death.

We shall now consider what answers a strong dualist might give to two related questions:

(A) Under what conditions would a particular disembodied soul after my death be *my* soul? (Under what conditions would it be *me*?)

(B) What would fundamentally distinguish different disembodied souls from one another? (What makes me distinct from you?)

After a section elucidating the concept of identity, question (A) will then form the topic of section 2, and question (B) will form the topic of section 3. Since our answer to question (B) will cause severe problems for dualism, in section 4 we will then return to re-evaluate the argument for strong dualism.

1 The concept of identity

Since both of the main questions to be addressed in this chapter involve the concepts of identity and distinctness, we shall begin by trying to elucidate the latter. (Note that our refutation of the bundle theory provided in Chapter 2:4 above has already relied upon them.) There are a number of points and distinctions to be introduced. Some of these may seem insignificant, but will later turn out to be of the highest importance. (Indeed, it will turn out in section 3

73

that one can construct a seeming-proof of the *non*-existence of the soul, turning on some of the theses defended in the present section.)

1.1 Qualitative versus numerical identity

Notice to begin with that there are two very different kinds of use of the words "same" and "identical". Thus the question, "Is this the same car as was involved in the robbery?" is easily seen to be ambiguous. Is it being asked whether the car in question is *similar to* (is of exactly the same kind as) the one which was involved in the robbery? Or is it being asked whether it is *the very same car*? I propose to use the terms "qualitative identity" (or "qualitative sameness") and "numerical identity" (or "numerical sameness") to mark this distinction.

Qualitative identity has to do with similarities between a number of different objects, or between different temporal stages in the life of the very same object. It is this notion which is involved in the statements, "You are exactly the same as when I saw you last", "I have just bought a new car identical to my old one", and in the question, "Are the twins identical?" Conversely, qualitative *non*-identity has to do with changes in the qualities of an object over time, or with the lack of similarity between different objects. For example: "She has not been the same since she got married", and, "The vase you bought me as a replacement is not identical to the one you broke".

Note that in order to be qualitatively identical, things don't have to be the same in every respect. They only have to share some restricted range of properties. Thus identical twins need only be similar in basic appearance and genetic potential; otherwise they can be as different as you please while still remaining identical. Also, identical cars need only be similar in make and appearance; they need not be owned by the same people, nor be in the same part of the country. In fact when the words "same" and "identical" are used in this way, what is really being talked about is qualitative similarity (indeed, often, qualitative similarity in some quite restricted respect).

Numerical identity, on the other hand, has to do with the number of individual objects involved in some context; and it is numerical identity which is involved in answers to questions of "How many?". If x and y are numerically identical, then there is just one object involved (i.e., x and y are "one and the same" object, they are "the very same"). And if x and y are *not* numerically identical, then there are *two* objects involved (i.e., x and y are distinct objects). It is this notion which is at issue when a jury are considering their verdict in a court of law: is the accused the very same person as the person who committed the crime, or are they, on the contrary, two different people? Note that the jury are not asked to judge whether the accused is *similar to* the criminal, nor whether he has changed since committing the crime. They are only asked to decide whether or not he *is* (is identical with) the criminal. This is a question of numerical, not qualitative, identity.

Clearly it is the notion of numerical identity which is involved in our two questions about the conditions for identity and distinctness among souls. Equally clearly, it is numerical identity of persons which concerns us if we are interested in the possibility of an afterlife. For of course I should not be greatly comforted to learn that after my death there will exist a person exactly like (i.e., qualitatively identical with) myself (e.g., a clone). Nor should I be greatly disconcerted to learn that after my death I shall continue to exist, but much changed (i.e., *not* qualitatively identical with my earlier self). All I really want to know is: shall I, myself, survive? So it is on the notion of numerical identity that we need to focus our attention.

1.2 Leibniz's Law

This is a logical law governing the notion of numerical identity. It may be expressed like this: if two objects are numerically identical (are one and the same), then anything true of the one must be true of the other also. Thus: if the accused is (is identical with) the criminal, then if the accused has a mustache, so too must the criminal have a mustache. Expressed less paradoxically it is this: if two ways of referring succeed in referring to one and the same entity, then sentences that differ only in that the one way of referring has been substituted for the other will always share the same truth-value. Thus: if "the accused" refers to the very same individual as does "the criminal", then if, "The accused has a mustache" is true, so too must be, "The criminal has a mustache".

Leibniz's Law may be represented in symbols thus: if $x = y$, then x has the property F if and only if y has the property F. The truth of this law is intuitively obvious. For if two objects are one and the same, then how could the "one" have properties which the "other" lacks? For if they really are one and the same, then there is no "one"

75

and "other" here, but only one thing, which may perhaps be being thought about or referred to in a number of different ways. (Hence the air of paradox in our initial statement of Leibniz's Law, when we used the phrase, "If two objects are identical".)

There might appear, on the face of it, to be some counter-examples to Leibniz's Law. Thus suppose that the police believe Mr Hyde to be the murderer, and suppose that Mr Hyde is in fact Dr Jekyll. It doesn't follow that the police believe Dr Jekyll to be the murderer, for they may not yet have discovered that Jekyll and Hyde are one and the same man. So isn't this a case in which we have: x = y, and x is F, but y is not F? Similarly, from the fact that Jocasta is the mother of Oedipus, and the fact that Oedipus wishes to marry Jocasta, it doesn't follow that he wishes to marry his mother. For he doesn't yet know that Jocasta *is* his mother.

In fact these examples don't genuinely conflict with Leibniz's Law, properly understood. For recall from earlier discussions that properties such as belief and desire are *intentional*: they always involve particular ways of representing the things which they are about. If we speak of the contexts created by such phrases as, "The police believe that ..." and, "Oedipus wishes to ..." as "intentional contexts", then the important thing to realize is that words within an intentional context don't have their normal reference. Instead, they refer to particular ways of representing, thinking or conceiving *of* those things.

Thus the name "Mr Hyde" within the context of the sentence, "The police believe that Mr Hyde is the murderer", doesn't refer to Mr Hyde himself, but rather to the way in which the police think about or represent Mr Hyde. For it isn't facts about Mr Hyde which make that sentence either true or false. (Indeed, as we saw in earlier, the sentence can be true even if no such person as Mr Hyde exists.) The only facts which are relevant are facts about the police. It can also be a fact about the police that, represented in one way (as "Mr Hyde"), they believe of Mr Hyde that he is the murderer, whereas represented in another (as "Dr Jekyll") they believe of him that he is not.

Leibniz's Law tells us that if two ways of referring in fact refer to one and the same thing, then sentences which differ only in that the one way of referring has been substituted for the other must share the same truth values, *so long as* those sentences are genuinely about the things to which those ways of referring normally refer (i.e., so long as the sentences do *not* put those ways of referring within an intentional context). Then since the sentences, "The police believe that Dr Jekyll is the murderer", and, "Oedipus wishes to marry Jocasta" are not genuinely about Dr Jekyll and Jocasta, respectively, the examples we gave above are not genuine counter-examples to Leibniz's Law.

It is important to keep the application of Leibniz's Law distinct from the notion of qualitative sameness, discussed in sub-section 1.1 above. For one thing, Leibniz's Law states that numerically identical things will share absolutely all of their properties; whereas qualitative identity generally has to do with some restricted range of properties, as we saw. For another thing, numerical identity is entirely compatible with considerable change of properties over time (i.e., with qualitative non-identity). So the fact that numerical identity is governed by Leibniz's Law (sameness of properties) does not mean that it implies qualitative identity.

Thus, the accused person may be (may be numerically identical with) the criminal, although he has become quite different (in the qualitative sense) in the time which has elapsed between the crime and the trial. This doesn't refute Leibniz's Law, since the proper understanding of that law requires us to make suitable transformations of the tenses of the verbs involved. Thus if the accused is (is identical with) the criminal, and the criminal had dark hair, then it is now true of the accused that he *did have* dark hair. If the accused is now white-haired, then it was true of the criminal at the time of the crime that he *would later be* white-haired. So despite the change (despite the qualitative non-identity) the two share the very same properties, namely: "having dark hair at the time of the crime" and, "having white hair at the time of the trial".

1.3 Transitivity, symmetry and reflexiveness

Other important features of numerical identity are that it is transitive, symmetric and reflexive.

A *transitive* relation is one which reaches across chains of individuals who are related by the relation. (For example: if John is taller than Mary, and Mary is taller than Joan, then John is taller than Joan.) Thus: if x = y, and y = z, then x = z. Again this is intuitively obvious. For if x and y are the very same thing, and y and z are the very same thing, then how could x *not* be the very same thing as z? (If Jekyll is Hyde, and Hyde is the tallest man in the room, then Jekyll must be the tallest in the room.)

77

A *symmetric* relation is one which, if an individual bears that relation to another, then the other bears the same relation to the first. (For example: if John is married to Mary, then Mary is married to John.) Thus: if x = y, then y = x. Plainly, if Jekyll is none other than Hyde, Hyde must be none other than Jekyll.

A *reflexive* relation is one which everything bears to itself (if it stands in that relation to anything at all). (For example: everyone is the same height as him or her self.) Thus: x = x. Again this feature of identity is obvious: everything is identical with itself.

These general features of identity, together with Leibniz's Law, will prove to be of some importance in our later discussions, both in this chapter and in Chapters 5 and 6.

1.4   Identity over time and individuality at a time

We can distinguish two different kinds of judgment of numerical identity. On the one hand there are judgments of identity *over* time, which take the form: object x at time t_1 is the very same as object y at time t_2. On the other hand there are judgments of identity *at* a time, which take the form: object x at time t is the very same as object y at time t. An example of the first form would be: "The person now in the cells is the person who yesterday committed the murder". An example of the second form would be: "The tallest living person is the oldest living person". I shall refer to judgments of the first form as "judgments of identity (over time)", and to judgments of the second form as "judgments of individuation (at a time)".

I shall argue that there must be more to judgments of numerical identity and individuation than is given in Leibniz's Law. In the case of a judgments of identity, one must also judge some relation to exist between the earlier and the later objects which *constitutes* them as one and the same object. In the case of a judgment of individuation, one must also judge that there is some property of the objects *in virtue of which* they are one and the same object. There must, indeed, be "criteria" of identity and individuation. So to say that x is numerically the same as y will be to say, in part, that Leibniz's Law applies to them. But it will also be to say that x and y satisfy either the criterion of identity or individuation for things of the kind to which they belong (depending upon whether what is in question is a judgment "over time" or "at a time").

I thus propose as a general thesis, that for every kind of object there must be such a thing as a criterion of identity for objects of that kind. The criterion will be a possible relation between earlier and later stages in the life of an object which would constitute them as one and the same thing. To illustrate: in the case of many types of physical object it is arguable that their criterion of identity is the relation of *spatio-temporal continuity*. That is: object x at t_1 is identical with object y at t_2 if and only if x has traveled in a continuous path through space to reach, at t_2, the place occupied by y. For example, suppose someone raises the question whether the human being now in the cells is the very same as the human being who committed yesterday's murder. What would we take as settling the issue? I suggest the following: suppose a private detective witnessed the murder and trailed the culprit continuously ever since, never once taking her eyes off him for a moment. She would then be in a position to answer our question with complete certainty.

It is important to distinguish between a *criterion* of identity and mere evidence of identity. For example, in our judgments of identity of human beings we often rely upon such things as sameness of appearance and sameness of fingerprints. But clearly these form no part of our conception of sameness of human being (of what "same human being" means), since we know that different people can look the same (identical twins), and since we acknowledge as a logical possibility that two different humans might have the same fingerprints. Equally, we know that one and the same person can come to look very different (plastic surgery), and can have their fingerprints removed or altered. We have merely discovered empirically that sameness of fingerprints is *reliable evidence* of sameness of human being. A *criterion* of identity, on the other hand, is logically implied by statements of identity between things of the appropriate kind.

I also propose as a general thesis, that for every kind of object there must be such a thing as a criterion of individuation for objects of that kind. This will be a possible property of those objects, such that sharing it would constitute them as one and the same object. To illustrate: in the case of physical objects it is arguable that their criterion of individuation is spatial position. That is: object x, at a given time, is identical with object y, at the same time, if and only if x and y both occupy the very same region of space at that time. For example, consider what would conclusively settle the question whether the tallest person in the world is identical with the oldest person in the world. I suggest the following: send off one group of researchers to rank all living people in terms of height, and another group to rank them in terms of age. Then our question will be answered affirmatively if and only if the person who comes top of the one list occupies the very same region of space as the one who comes top of the other.

Note that it is criteria of individuation which are involved in counting, enabling us to answer questions of "How many?". Thus, if I am set the task of saying how many chairs are in the room, I shall use disjoint space-occupancy as the criterion. Each filled and bounded region of chair-shape space counts for one, and none for more than one. All other properties of the chairs (their colors, weights, designs, and so on) can be ignored.

1.5   Why must there be criteria of individuation?

What argument is there for saying that there must exist criteria of individuation in connection with every kind of individual thing? (For the sake of brevity I confine myself to judgments *at* a time.) There are only two other possible alternatives. Either numerical identity simply *is* complete sameness of properties, where none of these properties has any privileged status. Or there is indeed more to the notion of identity than complete sameness of properties, but the "more" is nothing other than identity itself. I shall argue against these alternatives in turn. Although the issues are abstract, they are of the highest importance, both theoretical and practical. On this question may depend the possible existence of the soul, as we shall see in section 3.

Might numerical identity be nothing more than sameness of properties? An argument against this is that there is no way in which we could ever hope to check through every single property of two objects in order to see whether or not they coincide. For there will always be too many properties. It would seem that if we are ever to make judgments of individuation with any confidence, then we must pick upon some property to constitute the identity-at-a-time of each sort of thing.

It might be replied that this argument relates only to what is necessary for us to have knowledge of identity, not to what is actually necessary for any given kind of individual thing to exist as such. It may indeed be the case – so the reply goes – that we have found through experience that some properties of things (e.g., spatial position) are very good evidence that the remainder of the properties of the things will also coincide. But it is quite another thing to claim that these properties form part of the very notion of physical-object identity. It is yet another thing again to claim that there must be criteria of individuation in connection with every kind of individual thing.

My response is that a criterion of individuation isn't merely required for knowledge of identity (though it is indeed required for that), but also by our very conception of what it is for an individual thing to have a property at all. It seems to me unintelligible that the coincidence of two descriptions (e.g., "the desk in the corner" and "the only item of furniture in the room") might consist in the bare fact that the things they refer to happen to share all of the same properties. For until we possess a criterion of individuation we cannot even begin to *assign* properties.

For example, suppose that the desk is in fact red on one side and green on the other. Now are we dealing with two distinct objects here or only one? Are there two items of furniture, one of which is red and the other of which is green? Or is there only a single item of furniture, part of which is red and part of which is green? Lacking any conception of what distinguishes different items of furniture from one another (besides distinctness of properties) there is no way in which we can even begin to answer these questions. For here, of course, the idea of complete sameness of properties cannot help us. We know that there are distinct properties alright – namely red and green – but in the absence of a criterion for identifying and distinguishing items of furniture, we cannot even begin to decide whether they are properties of two different objects, or of different parts of the same object.

The general point to emerge is that we couldn't ascribe properties to things at all if our only conception of the identities of those things were given by complete coincidence of properties. Lacking any conception in advance of what distinguishes different things from one another, we should never know whether we were dealing with properties of distinct things, or of different parts of the same thing. Thus in the example above, what in fact determines that the colors are properties of the same object, is that the surfaces they apply to belong to an object which occupies a single discrete region of space, and which fulfills a given function (that of providing a flat surface for writing).

Similar considerations apply to the idea that there may be nothing to the identity and distinctness of things beyond this: their identity or distinctness. If we had no conception of what makes distinct items of furniture distinct, beyond the bare fact that they are indeed distinct, then we still couldn't even begin to ascribe properties to them. This is so unless, that is, we were supposed to have some special mental faculty which allowed us to know by direct intuition whether we were dealing with two distinct items of furniture or only one. But this would pose even more problems than it solved. How do we know that we have such a faculty of intuition? How do we know whether it operates correctly? How are the mere facts of identity and distinctness supposed to cause in us the appropriate intuitions? And so on.

Since the alternatives are both equally unacceptable, I conclude that there must exist a criterion if individuation (at a time) in connection with every kind of individual thing. A similar argument will establish that there must always exist a criterion of identity (over time). It is these criteria which provide us with our conceptions of what basically distinguishes different things from one another, and of what constitutes the continued existence of those things through time. In the absence of such criteria, the world would be wholly unintelligible to us: we should be unable even to begin ascribing properties to things.

1.6 Conclusion

The two questions with which we began this chapter may now be phrased more precisely.

(A)   What is the criterion of identity (over time) for souls?
(B)   What is the criterion of individuation (at a time) for souls?

In the sections which follow we will take up these questions in turn. But note an important general constraint upon the success of the enterprise: any criteria we propose must yield judgments broadly in line with our considered judgments of personal identity and individuation. For remember, the dualist's thesis is that souls *are* persons. So if the only available criteria were wildly at variance with our considered judgments about ourselves, then dualism would pass beyond all possibility of belief.

2   Soul identity over time

Our task in this section is to see whether or not we can construct an adequate criterion of identity (over time) for souls. Our main focus will be on developing an account of soul identity which can be defended as *coherent*. (In section 2.5 we will look briefly at the question whether the account is not only *possible* but *plausible*.) Many philosophers have claimed that this cannot be done, and that the very idea of a non-physical soul can be rejected as a result.

What we require is a statement of the conditions necessary and sufficient for the truth of judgments of the form: soul x at t_1 = soul y at t_2. We need a relation between the soul at the earlier time and the soul at the later time which can constitute them as one and the same soul. But this relation must yield judgments of soul-identity broadly in line with our considered judgments of personal identity. Obviously the relation in question can't be a physical one (such as, "is causally connected with the same human body"), since our account has to be such as to allow for the possibility of disembodied existence.

To start with we might try modeling our account as closely as possible upon that sketched earlier for physical-object identity, which took the form: physical object x at t_1 = physical object y at t_2 if and only if x is spatio-temporally continuous with y. The intuitive idea was of smooth motion between the place occupied by x at t_1 and the place occupied by y at t_2. Now motion consists of change in spatial position. So remembering that souls are supposed to be essentially thinking and experiencing entities, in the way that physical objects are essentially space-occupying entities, we might try the following:

> *Definition 1:* Soul x at t_1 = soul y at t_2 if and only if x and y are linked by a smoothly changing series of thoughts and experiences.

We could then construe this definition in such a way as to allow for periods of unconsciousness, by making the waking soul identical with the earlier soul whose experiences it resembles most closely.

Given the way in which our thoughts can jump from one thing to another, and given the radical discontinuities which can exist in our experiences, this account looks completely hopeless, however. Imagine falling asleep on an overnight train, your last thoughts before losing consciousness being of the repairs to the Statue of Liberty; then waking up the next morning in a completely different part of the country, thinking of the political situation in Guatemala. Obviously, someone else may wake up with states of consciousness which resemble those you had the night before more closely than do your own. For example: someone who traveled on a train in the opposite direction, who happens to wake up thinking of the Statue of Liberty. So if we adopted the criterion of soul-identity proposed above, then we should have to say that your soul had changed bodies in a case of this sort.

2.1 The memory criterion

What we need is a state of consciousness which can somehow bridge the discontinuities in thought and experience. The obvious candidate is *memory*. Thus although you awoke, in the example above, with an entirely new set of thoughts and experiences, you could of course recall, if you wished, much of what you had thought and experienced the previous day: where you were, what you did, what you saw. Then we might propose this:

> *Definition 2:* Soul x at t_1 = soul y at t_2 if and only if y can, at t_2, remember something thought or experienced by x at t_1.

An account of this kind was first put forward by the English philosopher John Locke. We shall now spend the remainder of this section developing and refining it.

Obviously the proposal isn't satisfactory as it stands, since identity is transitive, whereas memory is not. Thus someone might, as a child, steal apples from a neighbor's orchard, and then as a young woman recall that event while graduating with a degree in law. As an ageing judge she might still recall her graduation day, but have completely forgotten about the childhood theft. Then the situation could be represented diagrammatically, as in Figure 3.1.

But now if we apply the definition above we should have to say that the young woman is the same person (soul) as the child, and the old lady the same person as the young woman, but the old lady isn't the same person as the child. This would be absurd. Alternatively the old lady might still be able to recall the childhood theft, while having lost all memory of her day of graduation. (More recent memories tend to decay first, in fact.) Then the situation

84

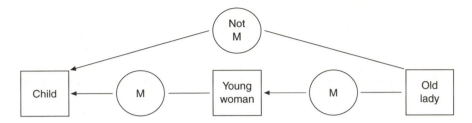

Figure 3.1 The forgotten theft.

would be as represented in Figure 3.2, and we should have to say that the old lady is the same person as the child, and the young woman is the same person as the child, but the old lady is not the same person as the young woman. This, too, would be absurd.

The solution to these difficulties is to extend the definition given above in such a way as to allow a series of overlapping memories to give identity of soul (and hence of person), as well as direct memories. We can do this by giving our account in two stages, first stating that direct memory gives identity, and then building on this to say that identity of soul carries across any series of souls linked together by direct memories. The neatest way to express this is as follows:

> *Definition 3:* Soul x at t_1 = soul y at t_2 if and only if *either* (a) y can remember things thought or experienced by x at t_1, *or* (b) y is, by repeated applications of clause (a), identical with someone who is, again by clause (a), identical with x at t_1.

This definition applied to the examples above would have the consequence which we intuitively want. Namely: that the child, the young woman and the old lady are all different stages in the life of the very same person.

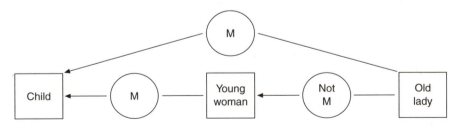

Figure 3.2 The forgotten graduation.

2.2   *The circularity objection*

A more awkward difficulty is that memory itself presupposes personal identity, and so cannot be used in an account of the criterion of soul-identity without vicious circularity.

Definitions and explanations are *viciously circular*, in general, if they take for granted a grasp of the very thing being defined or explained. Thus suppose you are explaining what a bachelor is to some non-English speakers. You say, naturally enough, that a bachelor is an unmarried man. But they reply that they don't understand the term "unmarried". If you respond that to be unmarried is to be either a bachelor or a spinster, then your explanations have become viciously circular. For they will be unable to understand your first definition until they understand your second. But they also cannot understand your second definition unless they already understand your first. (The second definition would have other faults as well: a two-year-old child can be unmarried, but is neither a bachelor nor a spinster.)

I shall argue that a definition of soul-identity in terms of memory must be like this. For I shall argue that, "Mary remembers experiencing event *e*" implies, "Mary really did experience *e*", which in turn implies, "Mary is the very same person as the person who experienced *e*". This of course brings us round to the very same relation – sameness of person, or soul – which we started out trying to define.

Notice, first of all, that memory is a species of knowledge. One of the distinctive features of knowledge, as opposed to belief, is that it implies truth. If I claim to know something, and what I claim to know isn't in fact the case, then I don't really know it but merely believe it. (In contrast: if I claim to believe something, and what I claim to believe isn't in fact the case, then this *doesn't* show that I don't really believe it.) In the same way, if I claim to remember something which didn't in fact take place, then I don't really remember it, but only *seem* to remember it. Thus: "Mary remembers *e*" implies, "*e* really did happen".

Secondly, notice that there are two very different kinds of memory. There is what might be called "impersonal memory", or "memory of fact", whose canonical form of expression is, "I remember *that* such-and-such". (For example "I remember that the Battle of Hastings was fought in AD 1066".) But there is also what might be called "personal memory", or "memory of experience", whose canonical means of expression is simply, "I remember such-and-such". (For example, "I remember the Battle of Hastings".) This second kind of memory is the sort which was involved in our most recent definition of soul-identity. Yet it always involves an implicit claim to have done or experienced, yourself, the thing in question. (You cannot remember the Battle of Hastings unless you yourself were really there.) So if this implicit claim is false, then you don't really remember the thing after all, but merely seem to remember it. Thus: "Mary remembers experiencing *e*" implies, "Mary is the very same person as the person who really did experience *e*".

It may be worth noting a further feature of personal memory, which will prove to be of some importance later, namely that it is a *causal* notion. You only really remember event *e*, if the experience of *e* is the cause of your current belief. Suppose that I have an experience which leaves no trace in my memory at the time. But later a neuro-surgeon implants in my brain a state exactly like a memory of that experience. Here I think we should say that I don't really remember it. Although everything seems to me as though I remember it, and although I did in fact have such an experience, what I have isn't really a memory, because it wasn't caused by the experience to which it relates.

Now consider the following example. Suppose I claim to remember falling out of a tree as a child and breaking my arm. I seem to recall my hand slipping on the branch, terror as the ground came up to meet me, then pain combined with astonishment at the strange angle of my arm in relation to my body. All this seems like yesterday. Yet it wasn't I who fell out of the tree but my sister. She afterwards described the experience to me so vividly that I had regular nightmares for some weeks, in which I dreamed that it was I who fell. Somehow over the years this became transformed into a seeming-memory of having fallen out of the tree myself. (As we shall see in Chapter 4:3, acquiring memories is a *constructive* process, and one which is easily interfered with.)

Clearly we should say in this case that I don't really remember falling out of the tree. For although my belief feels to me just like a memory (it comes to me, as it were, "from the inside"), and although what I believe is in fact a truth about someone (i.e., my sister), and although my belief is caused (via my sister's description) by the experience I claim to remember, it wasn't *I* who did and experienced those things. Since this is sufficient to disqualify it from being a genuine memory, personal memory of an experience must itself imply the identity of the rememberer with the person who underwent the original experience. In which case it is, as I claimed, viciously circular to define identity of soul in terms of personal memory. Or, put differently: memory relations can't be constitutive of personal identity, if memory is partially constituted by relations of personal identity in turn.

2.3   Avoiding circularity

The solution to the problem of circularity is to introduce a new concept of "quasi-memory", which is to be like personal memory in all respects except that it *doesn't* imply personal identity. Thus:

> *Quasi-memory:* someone quasi-remembers experiencing *e* if and only if: (a) they believe that an experience of type *E* took place, finding it natural to describe this experience "from the inside", (b) this belief is a true belief about someone (not necessarily him or herself), and (c) this belief is itself caused by an experience of type *E*.

By employing the notion of quasi-memory, soul identity may be non-circularly defined as follows:

> *Definition 4:* Soul x at t_1 = soul y at t_2 if and only if *either* (a) y can quasi-remember things thought or experienced by x at t_1, *or* (b) y is, by repeated applications of clause (a), identical with someone who is, again by clause (a), identical with x at t_1.

This avoids the charge of circularity, but now lets us in for a difficulty of another sort. The relation of quasi-memory can *branch*. But identity, because of its transitivity and symmetry, leaves no room for the possibility that two distinct persons might each be identical with a third. For instance, both I *and* my sister may quasi-remember falling out of the tree. Then applying the definition above, we should have to say that both I and my sister are, now, one and the same person, since each of us would be identical with the person who fell out of the tree – which is absurd.

We can apparently solve this difficulty by making our account a majoritarian one, since my sister will presumably have more quasi-memories about the tree-falling episode than I do myself. Thus:

Definition 5: Soul x at t_1 = soul y at t_2 is and only if *either* (a) y can, at t_2, quasi-remember more things thought or experienced by x at t_1 than can anyone else at t_2, *or* (b) y is, by repeated applications of clause (a), identical with someone who is, again by clause (a), identical with x at t_1.

Now it might seem that the occurrence of the phrase "than can anyone else" in clause (a) of this definition would render the whole account viciously circular. For who is "anyone else" except: someone who is not identical with y? In which case, doesn't the definition itself employ the very notion which it tries to define? But in fact the full phrase is: "than can anyone else at the time of y's quasi-memory". This makes all the difference. For it only introduces the notion of personal individuation *at* a time, whereas we were concerned to define the notion of personal identity *over* time. There would only be a vicious circularity here, if individuation at a time itself presupposes identity over time. As we shall see in the next section, it does not.

There is, in fact, a minor difficulty with definition 5. For although we might reasonably expect that my sister should quasi-remember more details of the tree-falling episode than I do myself, this won't necessarily be the case. (She may have forgotten all about it.) Yet it would obviously be absurd to conclude, in that event, that I am the person who fell out of the tree after all.

We can avoid this difficulty by insisting that in cases of conflict, clause (b) of the definition should take priority. For presumably on the day after the episode my sister could quasi-remember a great deal more about it than I could myself. (Indeed, at that time I quasi-remembered nothing, since I had only just been told about it, and the nightmares hadn't yet begun.) That person is, by clause (a), identical with someone (i.e., my sister on the day after that) who is, by clause (a), identical with someone who is ... identical with my sister now. We may thus let a series of overlapping majoritarian connections take precedence over any single direct majoritarian connection.

2.4 *Adding connections*

It is beginning to look as if the dualist can at least provide us with a *possible* criterion of soul-identity. Yet it is easy to become puzzled at the immense weight being placed on the concept of memory (or rather quasi-memory) within the account. For is memory really so very important? Is there any independent reason for thinking that memory has an important part to play in our concept of ourselves as individuals? Or has the account been constructed in terms of memory merely because it provides the dualist with a convenient means of bridging the discontinuities in consciousness?

By way of partial answer, notice that memory covers a great deal more than mere recollection of past events and experiences. Perhaps it really would be extraordinary to claim that such memories are so important to my existence as an individual that I should be counted as surviving just in case I retain them. But in fact, without memory I should merely find myself desiring certain things, and taking an interest in certain things, without being able to distinguish between my life-long interests and goals, and my passing fancies. Indeed, perhaps the most important part of knowing who I am, isn't memory of where I come from, what my name is, or what I have done and experienced in the past, but rather memory of who and what I really care about.

Not everything which intuitively belongs to our sense of our own identities can plausibly be brought under the umbrella of "memory", however. For it is one thing to remember what I *have* wanted, and quite another to continue to want those things. What makes my present existence into part of a relatively coherent integrated life, isn't simply memory of what I desired and intended in the past, but also that I still have many of those desires, intentions and ties of affection. (This point is easily missed, since we would normally understand the statement, "I remember what I want" in such as way as to imply that I still do want those things.) Indeed the whole business of forming plans and intentions for the future would be pointless if our desires were not, in general, relatively stable. No plans would ever get executed unless we still had the same desires once the time for planning was past, and the time for action had come. It may thus be more plausible to define soul-identity, not merely in terms of connections of memory, but also in terms of connections of desire.

Desires, like memories, may be distinguished into impersonal desires on the one hand (such as my desire that a particular party should win an election), and personal, or "self-referring", desires on the other (such as my desire that I should be rich). Self-referring desires, being for things to happen to my future self, presuppose the notion of personal identity over time, and so cannot be used to define it. But, as in the case of memory, we can introduce a concept of *quasi-desire* (and of quasi-intention) in terms of which we may define personal identity without vicious circularity. Thus:

> *Quasi-desire*: a quasi-desire for a piece of chocolate is (a) a desire that an eating of chocolate should take place, where (b) that event is naturally represented by me "from the inside".

Also like memory, desire is a causal notion. Just as something only counts as a genuine personal memory if it is caused by the experience which it purports to be a memory of, so something only counts as a genuine desire if it is apt to cause (via the causation of action) its own satisfaction. If I want (really want) to eat a piece of chocolate, then I am in a state which is apt to cause an eating of chocolate to take place. (Note that this implies that a particular personal desire d should only be counted as the very same as an earlier desire c, if d is the "causal descendant" of c. That is: if the existence of c is the direct cause of the later existence of d. For only if this is so can we say that by acting on the later desire d, the person is thereby satisfying desire c.)

Let us now introduce the concept of "psychological connectedness" between persons at earlier and later times. Let us say this:

> *Psychological connectedness*: a person x at t_1 and a person y at t_2 are psychologically connected with one another to the extent that: (a) person y can quasi-remember x's thoughts, experiences, quasi-desires and quasi-intentions, (b) x and y have the same impersonal desires and interests, and (c) x and y have the same personal quasi-desires and quasi-intentions; where (d) y's psychological states at t_2 are causal descendants of those of x at t_1.

We can then put this notion to work in a rather more plausible account of soul-identity, while preserving all the virtues of definition 5, as follows:

> *Definition 6:* Soul x at t_1 = soul y at t_2 if and only if *either* (a) y is, at t_2, more strongly psychologically connected with x at t_1 than is anyone else at t_2, or (b) y is, by repeated applications of clause (a), identical with someone who is, again by clause (a), identical with x at t_1. (Clause (b) to take precedence in cases of conflict.)

91

This account is surely coherent in itself. It also seems to match our considered common-sense judgments of personal identity pretty adequately, too. The next sub-section will briefly illustrate the latter point.

2.5 Are psychological connections what matter?

First, how plausible is it that the sort of psychological connected-ness which figures in definition 6 is genuinely *sufficient* for personal identity, and for my own continued existence? Second, how plausible is it that such connections are actually *necessary* for personal survival, so that I should fail to exist without them? I shall briefly present two examples. (We will consider many more examples of this general sort in much greater detail in Chapter 6.) The first example supports the idea that psychological connectedness is sufficient for personal identity, and the second supports the claim that it is necessary – just as definition 6 implies.

First example: Imagine that there is a magician who claims to be able to make people swap bodies. I am standing next to my sister when the magician pronounces the words, "Abracadabra Peter–Ann swap". Next moment, my visual experience of the world is from a slightly different point of view, I can feel that my body has softened in its outlines, and I can look across at my old body as if seeing it in a mirror. But I can still remember many of the things I once did with that body, and still have many of the same goals and desires. Meanwhile, the converse experience has happened to Ann: she is now seeing the world from my body. If a case of this sort were to occur, I think we should say that the two people Peter and Ann had swapped bodies, hence using the relation of psychological connect-edness as a *sufficient* condition for personal identity over time.

Second example: Now imagine that the magician claims to be able to wipe a soul clean of all psychological connections. He claims that if he were to say the words, "Abracadabra Peter blank", then I should permanently lose all psychological connections with my earlier self – all personal memories, desires, ties of affection and so on would be lost forever. It seems to me clear that if I believed in the magician's powers, I should fear his pronouncing those words in just the same way that I fear my own death or annihilation. In which case I would be treating the relation of psychological con-nectedness as a *necessary* condition of personal identity over time.

We will return to these issues at much greater length in Chapter

6. For the moment, the point is just that the account of soul identity represented in definition 6 seems capable of meeting the criterion of adequacy which we laid down at the conclusion of section 1 above – that of meshing successfully with our considered common-sense judgments of personal identity and distinctness.

2.6 *Intermittent existence revisited*

We have been developing an account of soul identity over time which appears to be both coherent and plausible. But what are its implications for the intermittent existence of souls though periods of complete unconsciousness, which was mooted in Chapter 2:2? On the face of it the present account fits quite well with that idea. What would link together an earlier and a later soul, through a period of unconsciousness in which no such soul exists, would be the relations of quasi-memory whose contents seem ideally fitted to reach across the intervening period of time.

The trouble, however, lies in the *causal* component which we wrote into the idea of a psychological connection. In order to count as the same quasi-memory or the same quasi-desire, we insisted that the later state would have to be a causal descendant of the earlier, existing *because* the earlier one did. But now the puzzle is how causal relations can exist across times during which there is nothing in existence – in particular, no soul – to serve as the vehicle of, or ground for, those relations. Can a state of a later soul be caused by a state in an earlier one if there is nothing in between to transmit the causal "force" from the one to the other? If not, then our definition 6 won't really have found room for the idea that the later soul can be the very same as the earlier, if there is an interval of unconsciousness during which no such soul exists.

We are now into difficult waters concerning the philosophy of causality. The question is, must all causation be *proximate* in time (and, for physical causality, space)? Or can there be *action at a distance* in time (and space)? Put differently, when a cause *c* at one time brings about an effect *e* at a later one, must there always be some intervening causal mechanism to bridge the temporal (and spatial) gap between *c* and *e*? Or can *c* be a *bare* cause of *e*, with nothing causally relevant to the production of *e* happening in the interval?

Many philosophers have the intuition that action at a distance (in time or space) is impossible. Many scientists, too, have had similar intuitions. Instead of resting content with the discovery that an earlier event *c* brings about a later event *e*, or with the discovery that an event in one place brings about an event in another, scientists characteristically assume that there must be an intervening mechanism of some sort, and set out to discover what it is. Regarded as a piece of scientific methodology, this has been extremely fruitful, leading to discovery after discovery. But this isn't enough to show that action at a distance is actually impossible. Indeed, this is now an idea which is being taken quite seriously within quantum mechanics.

As we suggested in Chapter 2:2, it might be that causal relations between distant events only really require (a) laws linking events of that kind, and (b) relations of counter-factual dependence between the particular events in question. In which case, provided there is a law of psychology that earlier memories cause later ones, in certain circumstances; and provided in the situation in hand the later quasi-memory would not have existed if the earlier one hadn't; then we can regard the causal component in the idea of quasi-memory as satisfied, and intermittent existence of souls will be possible after all.

Fortunately, however, we don't need to resolve this issue in order to establish that strong dualism remains defensible. For as we saw in Chapter 2:2, strong dualists have at least two other options for dealing with the problem of unconsciousness. Either they can deny, on the one hand, that complete unconsciousness ever really exists; or they can claim, on the other, that unconscious mental states as well as conscious ones can figure among the identity conditions for souls – and there is nothing in definition 6 above to rule this out.

3   Soul individuation at a time

There are no insuperable obstacles in the way of providing an adequate criterion of identity over time for souls. Our question now, is whether it is possible to back this up with an adequate criterion of individuation *at* a time. Recall that in section 1 above I argued that for every kind of object there must be something which determines whether two ways of referring to an object-at-a-time succeed in identifying one and the same object, or two distinct objects; this being the criterion of individuation for objects of that kind. Then if it can be shown that there cannot be an adequate criterion of individuation for souls, it will follow that souls cannot exist as distinct individual objects.

94

3.1 *General points*

It is important to note that criteria of individuation are logically more basic than criteria of identity. Before we can begin to keep track of an object over time, we must be able to identify it – to pick it out from other individual objects of the same kind – in the first place. No one could have a conception of what constitutes the continued existence of an entity over time, unless they also had a conception of what would distinguish it from other entities of the same sort at any particular time during its existence. Someone could, on the other hand, have a conception of what individuates an entity at any particular time, without yet having any conception of what would constitute the continued existence over time of any one such entity. So in this sense criteria of individuation are logically more fundamental.

In section 1 we suggested that it might be spatial position which provides the criterion of individuation for most kinds of physical object. Thus, what ultimately determines whether, "The car in the garage" refers to the same or a distinct entity from, "The only car in town painted in black and white stripes", is whether or not the cars in question occupy the same or distinct regions of space. It is therefore occupancy of disjointed regions of car-shaped space which one would use in counting the number of cars on a street. Now notice that spatial position can only be successful as a criterion of bodily individuation in virtue of the truth of the following three principles:

(i) Every physical object must always be in some place.
(ii) One physical object cannot be in two places – separated by a region of space in which no part of that object occurs – at once.
(iii) Two distinct physical objects cannot occupy the very same place at the very same time.

Principle (i) guarantees that you can always individuate an object by giving its spatial position. If it were possible for a physical object to exist without occupying any place, then it would have to be some other feature of it which distinguished it from other such objects. Principle (ii) guarantees that it isn't necessary to mention more than one place in order to establish the identity of an object. If it were false, then occupancy of two distinct places wouldn't be sufficient to establish that we were dealing with two distinct objects, and once again it would have to be some other feature of them which settled the issue. Principle (iii) guarantees that mention of a particular place is sufficient to distinguish one physical object from all others. If it were false, then it would have to be something other than occupancy of a particular place which determined whether we were dealing with just one object, or with more than one.

Note, too, how the above principles undergird our practice of *counting*. Recall what I do when I am counting the chairs in a room – I check off one numeral for each chair, taking care that I conduct an exhaustive search, that I don't miss any, and that I don't count any chair twice. It is principle (i) which guarantees that an exhaustive search of the space in question (the room) will turn up all of the chairs. Then, it is the claim that each chair must occupy a unique space – entailed by principles (ii) and (iii) – which guarantees that by correlating one and only one numeral with each discrete chair-shaped region of filled space, I am not counting more or less than I should.

If souls exist as distinct individual entities – as they must do if souls are selves, since selves are distinct individual things – then there has to be a criterion of individuation for them. There must be some range of properties, analogous to spatial positions for physical objects, which would enable us to pick out and refer to one individual soul rather than another. Or to put it another way: there must be something which fundamentally distinguishes souls from one another. There must thus exist some range of properties – call it "Φ" – such that the following three principles hold:

(a) Every soul must always satisfy some property from the Φ-range.
(b) One soul cannot satisfy two different properties from the Φ-range at the same time.
(c) Two distinct souls cannot both satisfy the same property from the Φ-range at the same time.

Unless these three principles hold good, then we cannot be guaranteed to individuate any particular soul by saying, "It is the one which is F" (where F is some property from the Φ-range). In which case it would have to be some other property of souls which makes the difference.

What sort of property might an item from the Φ-range be like? Plausible candidates would be complete modality-specific properties, such as might be given by a complete and fully-detailed

96

description of someone's visual field or auditory field at any one time. For this certainly makes it plausible that principle (b) should hold good: while one person can experience both red and green at once (i.e., in different regions of their visual field), one person surely can't undergo two distinct completely-described sets of visual experiences at one and the same time. Ditto for complete descriptions of someone's auditory experience, and so on.

3.2 The search for criteria of soul individuation

It is obvious that connectedness with a particular body can't provide the criterion of soul-individuation, because of principle (a) above. If it is supposed to be logically possible that souls should exist unconnected with any body, as the dualist believes, then what fundamentally distinguishes souls from one another cannot be their association with different bodies. Connectedness with a particular body can at best be evidence of soul-individuation, rather than a criterion of it. In fact we need a criterion which could serve to distinguish disembodied souls from one another, were it to turn out that disembodied existence does indeed occur.

Nor can we give our account in terms of connectedness with a particular body, while allowing for the possibility of disembodied existence, by providing for appeals to past facts about the souls in question, namely which bodies they were connected with in this life. Thus we cannot say this:

> *Definition 1:* soul x at t_1 = soul y, also at t_1, if and only if *either* (a) x and y are now connected with the same body, *or* (b) x and y were once connected with the same body at some time prior to t_1.

For the possession of a past (or future) property involves the identity of the object over time, and hence presupposes both criteria of identity and individuation for objects of that kind. In which case the above account of soul-individuation would be viciously circular. Thus, "Soul x at t_2 was connected with body B at t_1" says the same as, "Soul x at t_2 is the very same soul as the soul which is, at t_1, connected with body B". This then presupposes that we already have a conception of what might enable us to identify both the earlier and the later soul.

The above argument generalizes, to show that the criterion of individuation for an object of any given sort cannot possibly involve either past or future properties without vicious circularity. Then if the criterion of soul-individuation cannot be bodily, and if it cannot involve either past or future properties, we must confine ourselves to present-tensed properties whose application does not in any way presuppose a connection with a particular body. We are, in effect, thrown back onto mentalistic terms such as "thought", "quasi-memory", "belief" and "experience". Then the question is whether it is possible to construct an adequate criterion of soul-individuation out of such terms. Consider the following proposal:

Definition 2: soul x at t_1 = soul y, also at t_1, if and only if x and y are thinking exactly similar thoughts at t_1.

This is obviously hopeless. There is no way in which it can satisfy principle (c) while at the same time remaining in line with our judgments of distinctness among persons. It is clearly possible for two distinct human beings to think exactly similar thoughts at exactly the same time. Indeed, this seems to happen quite frequently. So applying the proposed criterion of individuation for souls, we should have to say that any two such human beings momentarily possess the same soul, thus becoming the very same person. (Note, moreover, that we cannot get around this difficulty by appealing to the fact that the thoughts in question may occur as part of two different trains of thought. For this would be to import past and future properties into the criterion of individuation.) Essentially the same difficulty infects the following proposal:

Definition 3: soul x at t_1 = soul y, also at t_1, if and only if both x and y can, at t_1, quasi-remember exactly the same events and experiences.

For again this either runs foul of principle (c) or yields absurd individuations. Two different human beings suffering from total amnesia would both have exactly the same quasi-memories (i.e., in both cases none at all). So we should either have to say that they would possess the same soul, and thus be the very same person; or it would have to be something other than quasi-memories which serves to differentiate them from one another. It might seem that the following proposal can fare better:

Definition 4: soul x at t_1 = soul y, also at t_1, if and only if x and y are both undergoing, at t_1, exactly similar experiences.

For given that human beings always have different visual and auditory perspectives on the world, it might seem impossible that two of them could ever have exactly the same experiences at the same time. But imagine two humans fitted-up with viewing-goggles and headphones, and otherwise anaesthetized, to whom we simultaneously play exactly the same clip of film with the same sound-track. Then surely these two individuals would undergo exactly the same experiences? For we should have cancelled out all differences in perspective.

A dualist might reply that this example only shows that it is possible for two different human beings to receive exactly the same visual and auditory stimuli, not that the resulting experiences will be the same. Indeed this is correct: in general they would not be the same. For since the two subjects may have different memories, and different desires and interests, the stimuli will not have the same significance for them both. They may notice different things, concentrating their attention on different aspects of the experience. Or they may be distracted from different aspects of it by the thoughts which are occurring to them at the time. But all of this is only "may" (or at most "will"), not "must". Suppose that the two subjects are both suffering from total amnesia, that both happen to have the same desires and interests, and that the same thoughts occur to them as the experience begins. It may then be perfectly possible that they should undergo exactly the same experiences. We would then be committed to the absurd belief that they are in fact one and the same person (soul).

It might be objected on behalf of the dualist that these examples are purely imaginary, and are extremely unlikely to occur. But this would be to miss the point. For on any proposed account of the criterion for identifying souls – whether given in terms of some restricted range of mental states (such as thought or memory), or whether given in terms of the complete set of such states – it will follow that it is logically impossible for two distinct souls to share exactly the same states at the same time. Yet it is, on the contrary, surely conceivable that two distinct people might possess qualitatively identical (exactly similar) states of consciousness at exactly the same time.

3.3 A proof of the falsity of strong dualism?

Our argument against strong dualism which we have been developing over the course of sections 1 and 3 may now be summarized as follows:

(1)   The dualist believes that selves (persons) are non-physical souls.

(2)   Selves are distinct individual entities.

(C1) So the dualist must believe that souls are distinct individual entities.

(3)   There must be a criterion of individuation in connection with every kind of individual thing.

(C2) So (from (C1) and (3)), if dualism is true, then there must be a criterion of individuation for souls.

(4)   Any conceivable criterion of soul-individuation will entail that it is logically impossible for two distinct souls to possess qualitatively identical mental states, either in general, or for some restricted range of such states.

(5)   It is, on the other hand, logically possible for two distinct people to possess qualitatively identical mental states, either in general, or for some restricted range of such states.

(C3) So (from (C2), (4) and (5)), either no such things as souls exist, or souls aren't selves.

(C4) So either way, strong dualism is false.

This argument gives every appearance of being a proof. The argument as a whole seems valid, and each of the premises (1)-(5) seems either indubitable in itself, or to have been adequately supported by arguments given previously.

3.4   Can the strong dualist reply?

It may be objected against the above argument, that from the fact that we have failed in our attempts to frame an adequate conception of souls as individual entities, it doesn't follow that no such things can exist. For after all, there are surely all sort of things in the world for which we have, as yet, formed no adequate conception. But this objection mistakes the nature of the argument, on two counts. First, the argument doesn't merely deal with our concepts and capacities, but with what is possible in the world. The claim wasn't merely that in order for us to have a conception of souls as individual things, we must be capable of distinguishing them from one another. It was rather that in order for souls to exist as individual things, there must be some properties (whether we know of them or not) which serve to render them distinct from one another. Secondly, the argument wasn't merely that we haven't yet found an adequate criterion of individuation for souls, but that there cannot be such a criterion. For it would have to be either bodily or mental, and as we have seen, neither can serve.

A dualist might try adapting the reply we made on behalf of the bundle theorist in Chapter 2:4, responding to the problem of what brings unity to the bundle (i.e., to the problem of what makes all of my various different mental states belong to one unitary mind). We said, there, that one might appeal to an underlying *capacity* for higher-order awareness of the co-occurrence of different conscious states. Why then can't the dualist say the same thing now? Why can't the dualist say that what makes it the case that two people undergoing exactly similar experiences are two souls rather than one, is that in neither of them is there any capacity for introspective awareness of the experiences of the other?

The difference, however, is that at that stage in our discussion of the bundle theory we were allowing ourselves to take for granted the individuality of particular mental states (e.g., *this* pain rather than *that* exactly similar one) as being prior to the individuality of minds. For the bundle theory claims precisely that individual minds are constructed out of individual mental states. (Indeed, this proved to be its downfall, as we saw later in Chapter 2:4.) In the present context, however, it will only be the case that there are two exactly similar sets of experiences in question, if it can first be established that we are dealing with two distinct people (souls). So we can only allow ourselves a *general* description of the properties in terms of which we are hoping to individuate souls. From this perspective it is plain that two distinct people might not only have exactly similar experiences, but that they might also have exactly similar introspective capacities – so we should still lack any property to individuate them as non-physical souls.

The last refuge of the dualist is to claim that there might be properties of souls which serve to individuate them which are neither bodily nor mental, of a sort of which we as yet have no knowledge. But if we have no idea of the properties which individuate them, then we have no conception of souls as individual things. Then to believe that I am a soul, or to hope that I might survive physical death as a disembodied soul, would be a bit like "believing" that there is a snark on the other side of the island, and "hoping" to capture it. (See Lewis Carroll's poem, "The Hunting of the Snark", which closes by revealing that the snark is a boojum. The point of the poem is that you cannot look for, nor hope to find, something which you have no conception of.) I should literally have no idea what I believe, nor what to hope for. I should be left merely with the words, "I am a soul, and the soul may survive the body", without having any idea what they might mean. You cannot believe what you cannot think. The effect of the last refuge suggested above is that we cannot think of souls as individual entities.

Perhaps this point is expressed a little too strongly here. For (in contrast with the snark) we do have at least *some* conception of what souls are supposed to be – we know that they are supposed to be non-physical, for example, and that they are supposed to possess mental properties of various kinds. So I can surely hope that I am some kind of non-physical thing which possesses mental states, and which might survive the destruction of my body, even if I can't say what *kind* of thing I hope that I am (i.e., even if I don't have a criterion of identification for things of that kind).

A fairer way to express the conclusion of the argument would be this. As a matter of fact we make confident judgments of identity and distinctness among persons (selves). But if strong dualism were right, then we would lack any basis for such judgments, since we should lack any conception of what fundamentally distinguishes different souls from one another. So we cannot believe in strong dualism without giving up the claim that our practices for individuating people are warranted. Put differently: there is no way for strong dualists to satisfy the requirement which we laid down at the outset, namely that their account of the criteria of identity and identification for souls should line up with our considered judgments of identity and distinctness of persons.

4   The argument for dualism reconsidered

We are faced with a paradox. In Chapter 2:1 we constructed an argument for the truth of dualism which gave every appearance of being a proof. Yet now in section 3 of this chapter we have constructed an argument for the falsity of strong dualism which appears almost equally convincing. The correct conclusion to draw from this (since dualism cannot be both true and false) is that something, somewhere, must have gone wrong with one or other of those arguments. Our immediate problem is to find out what.

4.1   *Imagining versus conceiving*

One possible weakness in the argument for dualism might seem to lie in its first premise, which states that it is conceivable that I might have disembodied thoughts and experiences. We argued for this on the basis of my being able to imagine a sequence of experiences which do not in any way involve the experience of having a body. Now so far this is correct: it is indeed possible to imagine having such experiences. But it doesn't follow from this that it is really conceivable that I should have experiences which are not in fact the experiences of a physical thing. For I might have a sequence of experiences which don't involve the experience of having a body although I am, not disembodied, but merely hallucinating. Although I have experiences of moving through walls, of perceiving my own body from a perspective outside it and so on, it may be that I am all the time lying motionless in a hospital bed. From the fact that I can imagine a sequence of experiences which would, from my point of view, be indistinguishable from those of a disembodied being, it doesn't follow that disembodied experience is really logically possible.

Some have thought that there is a general moral to be drawn here about the limited usefulness of imagination in helping us establish what is logically possible or genuinely conceivable. To imagine something is to represent to oneself the appearance of that thing: to have a visual mental image is to represent to oneself how something would look, to have an auditory mental image is to represent to oneself how something would sound, and so on. So anything which goes beyond appearances – which isn't simply a matter of the look of the thing, or the sound of the thing – doesn't strictly speaking belong to the content of the image itself. Rather, it will have been added in thought. There is no telling from the image alone whether its conjunction with that thought mightn't yield a contradiction.

Thus if I imagine a pig flying, what I really do is represent to myself how it would look to me if a pig flew: I imagine a sequence of experiences which I should naturally describe as being "of a pig flying". But this doesn't by itself show that it is logically possible for a pig to fly (though I have no doubt that such a thing *is* possible). The most that it shows is that it is possible to hallucinate a pig flying. For from the fact that those imagined experiences are logically possible, it doesn't follow that the thing itself is similarly possible.

Consider a somewhat more plausible comparison: I can imagine a sequence of experiences which would, from my own point of view, be indistinguishable from having traveled back into the twelfth century, and which I should naturally describe in those

103

terms. I can imagine stepping into a large box, and stepping out again a moment later to have experiences of a world in which people use oxen to draw wooden wagons and carts and so on. But it doesn't follow from this that time-travel is logically possible. For the thought, "And I should then be in the twelfth century" goes beyond anything which I have certainly imagined. All that I can be certain of having imagined, is a particular sequence of experiences. But these might be hallucinatory, or they might be experiences of a world which has miraculously changed in a moment into an exact replica of the world of the twelfth century. So from the fact that those experiences are logically possible, it doesn't follow that time-travel itself is logically possible.

Indeed, there are familiar paradoxes of time-travel which suggest that it mightn't be logically possible to travel in time. For if time-travel were really possible, it would be possible for the time-traveler to kill one of his own ancestors, thus bringing it about that he himself never existed. I can certainly *imagine* killing my own ancestor. For example, while looking at a photo of my father as a young boy, I can imagine stepping up while the photo was being taken and killing that very individual. But it seems plain that the thought, "I kill my own ancestor at a time prior to the possibility of my conception" contains a covert contradiction: for if I perform the act in question, then I never even exist.

Similarly then: when I try to imagine disembodied thought and experience all that I can be certain of doing is imagining a sequence of experiences which don't involve the experience of having a body. Then to this image I add the thought, "And as a matter of fact these are not the experiences of any physical thing". But this thought is not strictly speaking part of the content of my image itself. Therefore, it may be that its conjunction with what I imagine yields a contradiction. Certainly such *experiences* have been shown to be logically possible by my act of imagination. But it is quite another matter to claim that they could possibly be the experiences of a non-physical thing.

Although we may have found an error in the argument for dualism, it certainly isn't an obvious one. It has required no little labor to expose it, since we have had to draw a subtle distinction between *imagining* (which is claimed to be confined to appearances) and *conceiving* (which can go beyond them). So it remains explicable that many intelligent people should have become convinced of the truth of dualism.

4.2 Conceiving the impossible

I have been worrying away at whether the mere *imaginability* of disembodied experiences is sufficient to show that such experience is genuinely *conceivable*. However, this may not be the best way to respond to the argument for strong dualism. For even granting (as seems plausible to many people) that disembodied thought and experience are conceptually possible, we can still reject the first premise of the argument. We can allow that there is nothing incoherent in the thought of my disembodied experience, and that the statement, "I could have conscious states which weren't the states of any physical body" is not in any way self-contradictory. But still it doesn't follow from this that I am not a necessarily physical thing.

It may be that I *am* a physical thing – perhaps a particular brain – and hence that I am necessarily physical, despite the fact that I can conceive of myself being non-physical. The crucial point is this: *not all necessities are conceptual ones*. Some necessities obtain, not merely in virtue of relations between the elements of our thoughts (concepts), but in virtue of facts about the world. As it is sometimes said, some necessities are *metaphysical* rather than conceptual.

In order to see that this is so, consider once again the fictional example of Dr Jekyll and Mr Hyde. Suppose that you are a police officer investigating a series of murders, which you now know to have been committed by Mr Hyde. You know what Mr Hyde looks like, having received a number of accurate descriptions from witnesses, and perhaps having seen him, yourself, at the scene of one of his crimes. You also know quite a lot of facts about his movements and so on, but have not yet been able to capture him. Now suppose also that you happen to know Dr Jekyll quite well. Perhaps he has been your family doctor for many years, and you consult him regularly about the treatment of some illness of yours. Of course you know what he looks like (he looks somewhat different from Mr Hyde), you know where he lives and works, and you remember many conversations which you have had together in the past. You believe Dr Jekyll to be a fine upstanding citizen, to whom you gladly entrust the lives of yourself and your children.

Naturally it never occurs to you that Dr Jekyll and Mr Hyde are one and the same man. From your perspective – thinking of them in the way that you do – it is at least conceptually possible that they are different people (indeed, you may be quite sure in your own mind that they *are* different). You can, for example, easily conceive of circumstances in which Dr Jekyll would still have existed although Mr Hyde never does so – for example, a possible world in which Dr Jekyll is born as normal, but where Hyde's parents never happen to meet. You can also easily conceive of circumstances in which Dr Jekyll continues to live while Mr Hyde ceases to exist. For example, you can conceive of yourself shooting Mr Hyde dead at the scene of one of his murders, and then calling out Dr Jekyll to sign a death-certificate for the body. So, given the manner in which you conceive of them, it is true that Dr Jekyll is not (conceptually) necessarily Mr Hyde. On the contrary, Dr Jekyll is (conceptually) *possibly not* Mr Hyde.

Yet, for all that this is so, Dr Jekyll and Mr Hyde are in fact one and the same man. Given that they *are* the same man, they are *necessarily* the same man. There is no possible world in which Dr Jekyll is born but Mr Hyde is not. For since they are one and the same human being, they have the very same parents; so if Mr Hyde's parents had never met, then nor would Dr Jekyll's. Nor is there any possible world in which Dr Jekyll continues to exist while Mr Hyde ceases to do so. In fact, if you were to shoot Mr Hyde you would – necessarily – have shot Dr Jekyll also. You cannot shoot the one without shooting the other, for there is really no "one" and "other" here, but only one man whom you have come to conceive of in two different ways. Although you might *try* to call out Dr Jekyll to inspect Mr Hyde's dead body, you would necessarily fail, since they have one and the same body. So although you can *conceive of* Dr Jekyll and Mr Hyde as being two distinct people, since they are in fact one and the same man, they are so necessarily.

The moral of the story is that not all necessities and possibilities are conceptual ones. Something can be conceptually possible (conceivable) while being metaphysically *im*possible; and something can be metaphysically necessary which is not conceptually so. Indeed, precisely this sort of situation will arise whenever we conceive of what is in fact one and the same event or thing in a number of distinct ways.

Note, however, that we are still dealing here with what are genuinely cases of *logical* necessity and possibility. The necessity of Dr Jekyll being Mr Hyde is quite unlike the mere physical necessity that an object released near the surface of the Earth will fall. For there are possible worlds in which such an object does *not* fall, for example worlds in which there is anti-gravity instead of gravity. But there is no possible world in which Dr Jekyll – that very man who is your doctor – exists, whereas Mr Hyde – that very man who is in fact a murderer – does not. Nor is the impossibility of Mr Hyde dying while Dr Jekyll continues alive at all like the mere physical impossibility of someone (on Earth, unaided) jumping 100 meters into the air. For there are possible worlds in which someone does jump that high; but there can be no possible world in which Hyde dies but Jekyll doesn't, since they are one and the same man.

What follows from all this, is that even if we allow that I can conceive of myself surviving the destruction of my body and brain, it may be that – since I *am* that brain – it is metaphysically impossible that I should exist without it. Since I don't conceive of myself in physical terms (but rather in terms of the way in which my thoughts and experiences *feel* to me, subjectively) I may be able to conceive of myself continuing to exist in the absence of anything physical. But if I am, in fact, a physical thing, then such existence won't really be a logical possibility. For then there won't be *two* things in existence, one of which might continue intact while the other is destroyed, but only one.

I conclude, then, that the argument for the existence of the soul can be blocked at the outset. Although I may be conceivably-distinct from anything physical, this cannot show that I am (metaphysically) possibly not physical. It may be that I am in fact a physical thing, and that, by virtue of being so, my physicality is a necessary attribute of me. We have, at least, no conclusive argument to the contrary.

4.3 Validity and other minds

I have been arguing for a break in the link between *conceivability* and *possibility*. There may be things that one can conceive of which aren't really logically possible, like the death of Hyde without the death of Jekyll. But this then means that there is a sort of *validity*, too, which doesn't reduce to conceivability. There may well be arguments where one can conceive of circumstances in which the premises would be true while the conclusion is false which are nevertheless – as one might say – *metaphysically valid*. Despite what one can conceive, there might actually be no possible world in which the premises are true and the conclusion is false; it might really be logically impossible for the premises to be true while the conclusion is false. (A simple example would be: "Hyde is dead; so Jekyll is dead".) Let us briefly consider how this leaves us in relation to the problem of other minds, as originally laid out in Chapter 1.

One strand in the argument giving rise to the problem of other minds was the claim that there can be no deductively valid arguments from descriptions of physical circumstances and behavior to descriptions of other people's mental states. This was because it will always be possible to conceive the premises of such an argument to be true, while conceiving the conclusion to be false. (Remember the possibility of pretense, and the conceivability of zombies.) But now it seems that such arguments might, after all, be metaphysically valid ones. (Maybe zombies, although conceivable, aren't metaphysically possible.) So does this mean that the problem of other minds can now be solved? Unfortunately not.

The original point of the contrast between *deductive* and *inductive* arguments in Chapter 1 was an epistemic one (i.e., pertaining to sources of knowledge), not metaphysical. It was a contrast between what one could know *just by thinking* on the basis of available facts about other people, on the one hand, and what one could know on the basis of *reasonable scientific inferences* of various sorts, on the other. Granted, it now turns out that there are some (metaphysically) valid arguments whose validity can't be established by thought alone. But that then just pushes them into the other available (broadly scientific) category, and we still face the problem of how we can be justified in believing the conclusion given the premises.

Let me make essentially the same point in more concrete fashion. Suppose that as a matter of fact pain is (is strictly identical to) brain-state X. Then arguments of the form, "Person A is in brain-state X; so person A is in pain" will be metaphysically valid ones: it will be logically impossible for the premise to be true while the conclusion is false. (In the same way, if Mr Hyde is really Dr Jekyll, then the argument, "Hyde is dead; so Jekyll is dead" is metaphysically valid). But this doesn't help us with the problem of other minds by itself. It just places all the onus on to knowing that pain is actually brain-state X. Since this isn't something we can know just by thinking about it, it would have to be known on broadly inductive grounds. That then pushes us onto the other horn of our dilemma in Chapter 1. For without relying on claims about other people's mental states, how could I ever discover that pain (not just in me, but in general) is identical to brain-state X?

Conclusion

At last we have found an error in the argument for strong dualism: its first premise is insufficiently supported. But I can't see any errors in the argument of section 3 above, the conclusion of which is that disembodied existence *isn't* logically possible (or at least, whose conclusion is at least that disembodied existence can't be made to cohere with our actual practices in counting and individuating people). So we can apparently conclude that dualism is false. Yet we are still left with the arguments of Chapter 2:4 against the bundle theory of the mind, the conclusion of which is that mental states must be the states of some individually existing thing. It therefore follows that mental states must be the states of some physical thing: either the living human organism, or some part thereof (e.g., the brain).

We seemingly have no option but to say that the person or self – the subject of thoughts and experiences – is a physical thing. This is a version of physicalism. But it is, as yet, only weak physicalism. For it doesn't follow from anything which has so far been shown that mental states are themselves physical states. So although we have, in this chapter, provided good reason for rejecting strong dualism, weak dualism remains a possibility: it remains possible that mental states are non-physical states of a physical thing. We will return to examine weak dualism in Chapter 5. In Chapter 4 we shall remain focused on strong dualism, considering the empirical evidence which is alleged to support the existence of the soul.

Questions for discussion

1. Could there be nothing more to the identity of "two" individuals than the fact of their identity? Or must there be criteria of identity and individuation?
2. What is the *circularity objection* to the memory theory of personal identity? Is the introduction of a concept of "quasi-memory" an adequate response?
3. If a person today is to be the very same individual as a person last year, is it logically *sufficient* that they should be linked together by a continuous chain of psychological connections?
4. If a person today is to be the very same individual as a person last year, is it logically *necessary* that they should be linked together by a continuous chain of psychological connections?

5. Could there be two distinct people possessing exactly similar mental states at the same moment in time?
6. Is everything imaginable also conceivable? And is everything which is conceivable also logically possible?

Further reading

Butler, J. (1736) "Of personal identity", *The Analogy of Religion*, appendix 1. Reprinted in Flew, A. (ed.) (1964) *Body, Mind and Death*, London: Macmillan and in Perry, J. (ed.) (1975), *Personal Identity*, Berkeley: University of California Press.

Locke, J. (1690) "Of identity and diversity", *Essay Concerning Human Understanding*, vol. 1, book 2. Reprinted in Flew, A. (ed.) (1964) *Body, Mind and Death*, London: Macmillan and in Perry, J. (ed.) (1975), *Personal Identity*, Berkeley: University of California Press.

Mackie, J. (1976) *Problems from Locke*, Oxford: Oxford University Press, Chapter 6.

Perry, J. "Personal identity, memory and the problem of circularity", in Flew, A. (ed.) (1964) *Body, Mind and Death*, London: Macmillan and in Perry, J. (ed.) (1975) *Personal Identity*, Berkeley: University of California Press.

Shoemaker, S. (1970) "Persons and their pasts", *American Philosophical Quarterly*, vol. 7. Reprinted in Shoemaker, S. (1984) *Identity, Cause and Mind*, Cambridge: Cambridge University Press.

Swinburne, R. (1984) "A dualistic theory", in Shoemaker, S. and Swinburne, R. (eds.) *Personal Identity*, Oxford: Blackwell.

4

⇒⋗⋖⇐

Rationalism, Empiricism, and the soul

This chapter begins by presenting a challenge to the way in which we have proceeded so far in this book. This is the Empiricist attack on all attempts to obtain substantive knowledge (such as knowledge of the existence or non-existence of the soul) through thought alone. With that challenge tentatively endorsed, we will then discuss and evaluate the empirical evidence for the existence of the soul, such as that provided by near-death and out-of-body experiences, and remembrance of past lives.

1 Rationalism *versus* Empiricism

In Chapter 3:4 we criticized the attempted proof of the existence of the soul which had been developed in Chapter 2:1. We maintained that one cannot soundly argue from claims of conceptual possibility to claims of metaphysical possibility. There is a related, though more radical, reply to the argument for strong dualism. This doesn't consist in an objection to any particular premise or step in the argument, but is rather a rejection of the whole attempt to prove the existence of the soul by reasoning alone. But the meaning of such a response, and the motivation behind it, will require some stage-setting in order to become clear.

1.1 *Historical background*

We have here come upon one of the major disputes in the history of philosophy: between Rationalists, on the one hand, and Empiricists on the other. (The two best-known Rationalists are the French philosopher René Descartes and the German philosopher Gottfried Leibniz. The two best-known Empiricists are the English

111

philosopher John Locke and the Scottish philosopher David Hume. See the list of further reading at the end of this chapter.)

Rationalist philosophers believe that it is possible to obtain substantial knowledge a priori (i.e., by reasoning alone, without consulting experience). By *substantial* knowledge is meant knowledge of a reality independent of our beliefs, or knowledge which doesn't simply deal with relations between our own concepts and ideas.

Rationalists believe that we can, just by thinking about it (without having to consult our experience or conduct experiments), discover such substantial truths as: that there is a God; that we have immortal souls; that we have free will; that every physical event has a cause; and so on. Most Rationalists have also included within their catalogue of the substantial truths of reason, the truths of mathematics and logic. For they have believed that such truths relate to an objective reality which is independent of our minds. Rationalist philosophers also maintain that a significant proportion of our substantive knowledge is innate or in-born. (I shall return to this point in the following sub-section.) Historically, Rationalists have believed *either* that our knowledge of substantive a priori truths has been implanted directly in our minds by God, *or* that God designed our minds in such a way as to contain a faculty of reason with the right sort of structure needed to generate the truths in question (or both).

Related to their beliefs about mathematics and logic, most Rationalists have also been *platonists* (named after the ancient Greek philosopher, Plato). They have believed that our reason gives us access to a realm of abstract (non-physical and changeless) objects, peopled by such things as numbers and geometrical figures (the number 17 and the perfect square) and Universals (justice, beauty and greenness). Thus they have held that when we arrive, by a process of thought alone, at a proof of some proposition of mathematics (such as, $17 + 16 = 33$), we have acquired knowledge of a genuinely objective fact which is independent of our minds. They believe that the number 17 existed long before there were ever any human beings, and would have existed even if there never had been any human beings; at which times and in which circumstances the same things were or would have been true of it. They hold that no matter what else might have been the case, the number 17 would still have had the property that when added to 16 it is 33.

How, though, are we supposed to achieve access to these facts concerning mind-independent abstract objects such as numbers and Universals? Rationalists have generally postulated a special mental faculty of *intellectual intuition*, at this point. For in the simplest cases, they have said, we can just *see*, merely by thinking, that 2 + 2 = 4 (for example). When we consider simple propositions of this sort, we have powerful intuitions, or inclinations, concerning their truth or falsehood. Rationalists then postulate that, just as we have special organs (i.e., eyes, ears, and so on) for detecting properties of the physical world, so too we have a special *intellectual* organ – quite literally a kind of "mind's eye" – for detecting properties of things in the abstract world.

Empiricist philosophers maintain, on the contrary, that all substantial knowledge must be grounded in experience. They have denied the existence of a priori knowledge, and historically they have rejected innate knowledge as well. They hold that knowledge which relates to things outside of us requires observation and experiment, and not just mere thought. Many Empiricists will agree that there are *some* things which we can know just by thinking about it. But they hold that such truths relate to nothing beyond the connections which obtain between our concepts themselves. Hence many Empiricists, while allowing that a truth such as, 17 + 16 = 33 is discoverable by reason alone, will deny that it relates to any reality which is independent of our minds. Rather, such a truth is a *conceptual* one, holding in virtue of the relations which obtain between our concepts (ideas) of 17, 16 and 33. So they maintain that the disciplines of mathematics and logic are purely conceptual in nature, dealing only with relations between concepts within our minds.

Other Empiricists are happy to allow that we have knowledge of an abstract realm of numbers and sets, but they deny that our knowledge of that realm is a priori. (The various possibilities are laid out in Figure 4.1.) Rather, they think that we only have reason to believe in the truths of mathematics because mathematics forms part of our well-grounded scientific theories. So the ultimate test of mathematical knowledge is experience, not thought alone, on this view. Yet other groups of Empiricists deny that mathematical statements are strictly *true*. They agree that such statements carry a commitment to the existence of abstract objects, but they deny that any such mind-independent objects really exist. However, they continue to explain how mathematics can be *useful*, enabling us to make sound inferences in using and evaluating scientific theories. But *all* Empiricists are united in denying that mathematics and logic give us a priori access, by a process of reason alone, to any supramental reality.

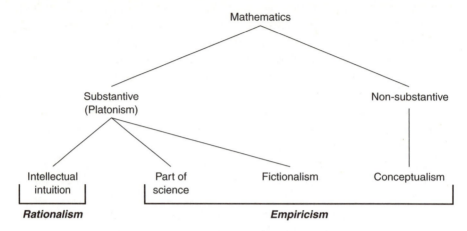

Figure 4.1 The nature of mathematics.

Now, notice that the argument for the existence of the soul presented in Chapter 2:1 was very much a Rationalist one. We were supposed to be able to arrive at the truth of each of the premises merely by thinking about what it is that it says, as well as to recognize the validity of the argument as a whole. We would therefore expect an Empiricist philosopher to object to such an argument on principle. The most that an Empiricist will concede is that the argument may be successful in bringing out something of how we *conceive of* ourselves. So if the conclusion of the argument were not that we *are not* physical things, but rather that we don't conceive of ourselves as physical things (or even that we *cannot but* conceive of ourselves as *non*-physical), then an Empiricist will presumably have no objection. Empiricists will thus allow that we may show, purely through the use of reason, that we don't conceive of ourselves in physical terms. This would be a truth about us and our concepts. But it is quite another matter to conclude that we are not in fact physical things. For how are we to know that our conception of ourselves is an adequate one?

Similarly, the argument *against* the existence of the soul presented in Chapter 3:3 was also a Rationalist one (at least in its initial formulation – in the end we claimed only that belief in the soul was inconsistent with our actual practices for individuating people). For it attempted to *disprove* the existence of the soul by reason alone. We should therefore expect an Empiricist to object to it too. Empiricists may allow that the Rationalist argument against the existence of the soul can establish that we cannot form an adequate *conception* of ourselves as non-physical things. But they will insist that it doesn't follow from this that we *aren't* non-physical in reality – it doesn't follow that we are physical beings. For how are we to know that it is possible for us to form an adequate conception of every fact about ourselves? Maybe we are in fact non-physical even though we cannot form an adequate conception of ourselves as such.

Anyone who has, for whatever reason, already become convinced of the Empiricist approach to knowledge, will thus be unmoved by the arguments so far considered in support of (and some of those against) strong dualism. Their objections will be entirely independent of their ability to spot a specific error in the arguments themselves, of the kind we claimed to exist in Chapter 3:4 above. But what, then, is the motivation for being an Empiricist? The Empiricist objection, on principle, to any attempted proof of the existence or non-existence of the soul will only be as strong as the reasons for accepting Empiricism in the first place. However, before we begin to tackle this question (in section 2 below), rather more needs to be said in elucidation of the Empiricist project.

1.2   *Other aspects of Empiricist–Rationalist debate*

The main historical focus for debates between Empiricists and Rationalists is the one we have been discussing, concerning the legitimacy of a priori reasoning (or thought alone) as a source of knowledge of substantial (mind-independent) matters of fact. This has not, by any means, been the only strand in the debate, however. The two sides have tended to disagree on other matters as well. These are summarized in Figure 4.2.

Both sides agree that experience can be a source of knowledge, of course. As we have seen, Rationalists accept, but Empiricists deny, that pure reason can be a source of substantive knowledge. But in addition, Rationalists have tended to think that we probably possess a great many innate (in-born) beliefs, while Empiricists have denied it. Most Rationalists have thought, for example, that beliefs concerning the basic principles of morality are innate – not arrived at through a process of reasoning and a priori proof, as in the case of mathematics, but believed by all normal people without the need for tutoring, nevertheless. They have maintained that these (and other) beliefs were planted in our minds by God. All we need to do

Sources of knowledge				
Experience	Pure reason	Innate beliefs	Innate concepts	Innate mental structures
Empiricists ✓	✗	✗	✗	*minimal*
Rationalists ✓	✓	✓	✓	*abundant*
			Elements of mind	

Figure 4.2 Empiricism *versus* Rationalism.

in order to discover that we have them is introspect carefully, free of distractions and interfering emotions.

Not only have Rationalists believed that many beliefs are innate, they have also thought that a great many of our concepts, too, are innate. Empiricists have insisted, in contrast, that all concepts have to be acquired from experience, through some sort of process of *abstraction*. Rationalists have thus thought that our minds contribute a good deal to the overall shape of our experience of the world – we bring to our experience from the outset a basic framework of categories and concepts in terms of which those experiences become organized, rather than (as Empiricists think) deriving those concepts from the nature of our experience itself. Empiricists have maintained, in contrast, that our initial experience of the world is a "booming buzzing confusion", and that it is only by gradually noticing similarities and recurring patterns within it that we start to acquire the concepts which enable us to organize and make sense of it.

Finally, Empiricists have generally been highly minimalist about the basic sorts of mental structures and processes which they are prepared to allow. All mental activity is to be reduced to a number of simple processes of *copying* (of ideas from previous experiences) and *storage* (in memory), as well as *comparison* and *association*, for example. Of course, everyone has to allow that *something* in the mind is innate. Although much may be learned, the basic principles

of learning can't themselves be learned. But Empiricists have historically been concerned to minimize as far as possible the number of
innate principles and processes which they have to countenance.
Rationalists, in contrast, have for the most part believed in an abundant suite of richly structured innate processes, perhaps different for
different domains of the mind (e.g., for dealing with language, or
with vision).

It is important to note that these different strands in the
Empiricist–Rationalist debate are logically independent of one
another. Thus the existence of substantial a priori knowledge (a set of
truths discoverable by a process of reasoning alone) doesn't entail the
existence of any innate beliefs, nor vice versa. Nor are either entailed
by the existence of innate concepts or abundant innate mental structures. It could perhaps be argued that innate beliefs entail innate concepts, at least, on the grounds that if beliefs are in-born, then surely
the concepts out of which those beliefs are composed have to be in-
born too. But even this is fallacious. For it might be that all concepts
first have to be learned through abstraction, but thereafter a bunch of
beliefs involving those concepts make their appearance spontaneously, without learning. (The crucial point here is that innate items
don't have to be present at birth; they just have to emerge through
normal maturation without learning – think of beards in men or
breasts in women, for example.)

The shape of the historical debate therefore presents us with
something of a puzzle. Why did the participants in that debate line
up as they did? One just has to glance at Figure 4.2 to see that there
are many possible combinations of views which seem to have gone
undefended. Why didn't anyone reject the use of pure reason but
accept the existence of innate beliefs and/or concepts, for example?
Since the different strands of the debate are logically independent,
we need some account which explains why the early participants in
these debates nevertheless saw them all as belonging together. In
particular, what unifies the different strands in Empiricists' rejection
of pure reason, innate beliefs, innate concepts, and rich innate
mental structure?

1.3   The core of Empiricism

We are now into difficult and controversial waters. But my own
view is that the basis of the Empiricist attitude turns out to consist
in this: *we should only allow that someone knows something when*

we can provide at least the beginnings of a plausible scientific account of how *they know that thing.* Thus the basis of the Empiricist objection to platonism, for example, is that it is impossible to explain, in terms acceptable to science, how an abstract (non-physical, changeless and eternally existing) object could have an effect upon the human mind, leading us to have true beliefs about its properties. There is, on the other hand, no Empiricist objection to knowledge which is based upon experience, since we have at least *some* idea of how our perceptual faculties might operate.

I propose that the core of Empiricism should be seen as lying in the idea that epistemology – or "theory of knowledge" – is constrained by science (and by psychology in particular). The most basic Empiricist commitment is to the thesis that claims to knowledge should only be granted on condition that they can be rendered consistent with our best theory of the powers of the human mind, and of the mind's natural modes of access to reality. No knowledge-claims are to be allowed, except where we can provide at least the beginnings of a naturalistic account of the processes through which that knowledge is acquired. (A *natural* process is one which falls under causal laws. It is one which can in principle be subsumed within the laws of nature, whether those laws are known by us or not, and whatever form they might ultimately take – it is not presupposed at the outset that all natural processes are physical, for example.) But this is not to say that epistemology then becomes *absorbed into* natural science. Rather, it is to place an additional normative constraint on epistemology – namely, that we should be able to see how our claims to knowledge might be fitted into the framework of a natural science.

This account makes it obvious why Empiricists should reject the idea of substantive a priori knowledge – it is because we have no idea how to explain, in natural terms, how our reasoning faculty might have acquired such powers. Moreover, the basic reason why early Empiricists denied the existence of innate beliefs and concepts, on this account, was because the only theory available to them at the time, of the process through which an item might come to be innate, was a *non-natural* one, namely, direct intervention by God. (Of course, at the time when Locke and Hume were writing, Charles Darwin's theory of evolution through natural selection had not yet been proposed and developed.) Although the early Empiricists would have granted that intervention by God was conceptually possible, it conflicted with their overall attempt to fit our idea of ourselves and our knowledge into a broadly scientific framework.

(As for the reason why the Empiricists rejected abundant innately structured mental processes, this should be seen as arising from their attempts to develop a science of psychology. Since their goal was to constrain knowledge-claims by our best theory of the mind's powers, they correctly saw that they needed to develop some account of those powers: in effect, they needed a psychology. Following what they took to be accepted scientific practice at the time, they sought to minimize both the kinds of entities and the number of basic processes postulated by their theory. In effect, they were guided by considerations of *simplicity* or *parsimony*.)

But if this were really the reason why the early Empiricists rejected innate beliefs and concepts, then why didn't they say so explicitly? It may be that what I am calling their core commitment, formed such a fundamental part of their outlook as to be almost invisible, even to themselves. Alternatively, their real argument may not have been easily expressible in public, for political reasons. Most early Empiricists were also theists, and even those who were not had to respect the immense political power of the Church. (Witness the persecution of Galileo for suggesting – contrary to Church teaching – that the Earth isn't at the center of the universe. Witness also the lengths to which Hume had to go in disguising his own agnosticism in *The Dialogues Concerning Natural Religion*, which he held back from publication until after his own death.) An attack upon innateness on the grounds that it required us to believe in God's intervention in the human mind might have seemed like a direct attack upon theism. For if God exists, why shouldn't he intervene in the natural world if he chooses to do so? There is really no *argument* for insisting that natural events admit of naturalistic explanations, except the success of science in the long run. I suggest that instead of facing this issue head-on, and openly declaring their commitment to the explanatory adequacy of science, the early Empiricists may have chosen, either to argue against innateness on quite other grounds, or to assume its falsity and render the hypothesis of Divine intervention unnecessary, by providing an alternative account of the genesis of human knowledge through experience.

1.4 *Advantages of the account*

The main advantage of this proposed account of the core of Empiricism is that it enables us to unify the early Empiricist objections to innateness, on the one hand, and to substantive knowledge by reason alone (particularly platonism), on the other. In both cases knowledge-claims were rejected because there was available no naturalistic account of the belief-acquisition processes involved. In the case of innateness, the hypotheses that either knowledge, concepts, or information-bearing mental structures are innate, were rejected because they seemed to require non-natural intervention in the human mind by a veracious God. In the case of substantive knowledge by pure reason, the objection was that there could be no naturalistic explanation of how reason could have acquired the power to generate knowledge of anything outside of itself. It would apparently have required God's intervention to ensure that the structure of our reason accurately mapped the structure of the appropriate mind-independent realm.

Consider the platonist hypothesis of a special faculty of intellectual intuition, for example. This holds that we have a special mental organ – a kind of "mind's eye" – which enables us to *see* or *intuit* facts about the abstract mind-independent realm of numbers and universals. This was rejected because we cannot even begin to give an account of the psychological structure of such a faculty, nor of how there could be causal contact between necessarily-existing abstract entities and the human mind. Yet the only other alternative open to a platonist, namely the suggestion that our beliefs about the abstract realm are innate, brings us back to a non-natural model of belief-acquisition once again. God's intervention would apparently have been needed to ensure that our innate beliefs were true of the abstract realm.

The present proposal also coheres well with the fact that the early Empiricists immersed themselves in enquiries which were quite explicitly psychological. It is because they thought that the theory of knowledge had to be fitted into a broadly scientific outlook, and rendered consistent with our best scientific theories, that they regarded epistemological and psychological questions as belonging essentially together. Many later commentators, in contrast, have regarded the close conjunction of psychological with epistemological enquiry as being seriously confused. They have said that it is one thing to ask how the mind actually works, and how beliefs are actually formed, and quite another to ask what we can know, and how. The one is a factual, the other should be a normative–evaluative, enquiry. On my reading of Empiricism, however, these questions are intimately related to one another. For if epistemology is constrained by science in general, and by psychology in particular, then you cannot begin to settle the question what we can know without at least sketching the outline of the various faculties and psychological processes which are involved in the acquisition of our beliefs.

The present account also fits neatly with the ways in which both Locke and Hume explain the motivation of their work. In the Epistle to the Reader of Locke's *Essay Concerning Human Understanding* he tells us how, in the course of discussions with friends on an unspecified topic, they came to feel that if they were to make progress with it they should first examine their own mental powers. The task which Locke then set himself, was to see what subjects the human understanding was or was not fitted to deal with. In the Introduction he then writes in similar spirit, thus:

> This was that which gave the first rise to this *Essay* concerning the *understanding*. For I thought that the first step towards satisfying several inquiries the mind of man was very apt to run into was to take a survey of our own understandings, examine our own powers, and see to what things they were adapted.

The project, as I see it, was to attempt to settle disputes concerning the extent of human knowledge by first providing an outline of the faculties of the human mind, and of the mind's natural modes of access to the world, and then to regard knowledge-claims as constrained to be consistent with that account. This is precisely what I am maintaining to be the core Empiricist commitment.

Similarly Hume, in describing the main aim of his work in the Introduction to the *Treatise of Human Nature*, argues that there is a sense in which the science of human nature lies at the foundation of all the sciences, and that we may hope to make progress with the latter by studying the former first. Now he can hardly have meant (can he?) that we should expect particular discoveries in physics or chemistry to be consequent on advances in psychology. Rather, he is more plausibly read as saying that claims to knowledge, in general, have to be rendered consistent with the powers of mind ascribed to us by our best psychological theories; which is again the core Empiricist commitment. Even more explicitly, Hume writes as follows in the opening section of the *Enquiry Concerning Human Understanding*:

> The only method of freeing learning, at once, from these abstruse questions [of metaphysics], is to enquire seriously into

the nature of human understanding, and show, from an exact analysis of its powers and capacity, that it is by no means fitted for such remote and abstruse subjects.

Here again the project is the core Empiricist one, to constrain knowledge-claims by our best theories of the mind's natural modes of access to reality.

1.5 Contemporary Empiricism and the soul

If the above characterization of the core of Empiricism is correct, then it follows that contemporary Empiricists should have no objections to evolutionary versions of nativism. For unlike Divine intervention, the selection of innate characteristics through evolution is certainly a natural process. Indeed, it is one of which we not only have the outline of an account, but a well-developed scientific theory. Empiricists in the twentieth and twenty-first centuries will therefore have no principled reason for denying the existence of innate knowledge. Since we can indeed provide an account of the process through which a belief might come to be innate, the Empiricist constraint on nativist knowledge-claims no longer has any application.

If the present account of the core of Empiricism is correct, then the basis of the Empiricist objection to attempts to prove (or disprove) the existence of the soul, is *that it is impossible to explain how reason can have acquired such powers.* How is it that our faculty of reason has come to have within itself some structure which accurately reflects the existence (or non-existence) of a soul? In earlier ages a Rationalist might have replied that God had placed that information within the structure of our reason. But this is plainly not a scientific explanation, and so will not be acceptable to an Empiricist, if I have correctly characterized their position.

In our own era, the Rationalist answer to this challenge will presumably be in terms of evolutionary theory, since this is, we believe, how all other innate features of human beings have been arrived at. But then it is very hard to see how such an explanation might go. For in order to be selected in evolution, a feature has to confer on individuals who possess it some advantage in survival or reproduction – people who happen to possess that feature through random gene mutation, have to be more likely to survive and reproduce, hence passing on their genes to their children. But what advantage in survival would it confer, to have a faculty of reason which can construct a reliable proof of the existence of the soul? It is very hard to see any, or at least any which would require such a faculty of reason to be *reliable*, and so capable of generating *knowledge*. (Perhaps believing in the soul might make people happier, and this might make them more likely to attract a mate. But this will work *whether or not* the soul really exists.) In which case the Empiricist objection will remain in force.

It will be too big a task for us to attempt, here, to tackle the Empiricist–Rationalist dispute in detail and in full. For this is an issue which is still very much alive today, ramifying into many different areas of philosophy – into the philosophy of mathematics, the philosophy of science, and the theory of knowledge. It may be enough that we have been able to articulate a worry which many readers will have felt, concerning the very idea of attempting to prove the existence of the soul by reason alone. But we *will* need to reflect on what it is that lies at the basis of this worry. What is the motive for denying that we can arrive at substantial facts about the world or about ourselves by reason alone?

2 Should we be Empiricists?

My own view is that the main motive for being an Empiricist consists in an underlying commitment to the explanatory adequacy of science. As an Empiricist, I think that the reason why we shouldn't be prepared to accept claims to knowledge where we cannot foresee any scientific account of the process through which that knowledge is acquired, is that otherwise our possession of such knowledge would, to the best of our belief, forever have to remain inexplicable. Put otherwise (and very roughly) the commitment is: don't believe in miracles unless you absolutely have to.

2.1 An example: prescience

Can it really be reasonable to deny that we have knowledge of some subject-matter, merely because our present scientific beliefs provide us with no materials with which to frame a remotely plausible account of how we might have acquired that knowledge? Let us consider an example in some detail, as a test-case. Suppose that some person, or group of people, claims to be *prescient*. That is to say, they claim to have intuitive (non-inferential) knowledge of the future. Of course many people have actually made such claims, and many of these people were, no doubt, either crazy or fraudulent. But let us try to imagine an example in which it seems indisputable that the predictions very often turn out right. So these people apparently have true beliefs about the future which are not arrived at by inference from current tendencies. The question then, is whether we can give some account of the process by which those beliefs are acquired; and if not, whether we are justified in denying that these people may be said to have knowledge of the future.

I can think of at least three hypotheses which an Empiricist might propose, in order to explain away all those cases of the apparent phenomenon of prescience which have actually occurred. First, it might be suggested that the people in question are predicting the future on the basis of a *non-conscious inference* from their knowledge of current tendencies, in which case there would be nothing especially mysterious about their powers. But this may turn out not to be the case. For it is imaginable that they can predict future events which could not possibly have been deduced from current tendencies, such as the accidental death of a particular person in a car crash in two years' time, perhaps also predicting the date and place of the event.

Secondly, there is the possibility of fraud. It may be suggested that those who claim prescience are covertly bringing about, themselves, the events which they predict; or they may merely be *pretending* to have predicted the events prior to their occurrence. But again this might conceivably be ruled out, either because the events in question are wholly unprecedented and beyond the causal powers of any individual or group of individuals (such as the appearance of a new comet in the sky on a particular date), or because we can verify that the predictions have been made well in advance of the predicted event.

It might finally be suggested that the predictions are framed with sufficient vagueness to give merely the *illusion* of accuracy. This idea is already familiar from astrology, which purports to predict features of people's character and life-history from the distribution of the planets at the time of their birth. For provided that the predictions are sufficiently vague and general, and concern topics which people want very much to hear about (and which occur fairly commonly), then there is a high chance that those predictions will come to be regarded as having been fulfilled. An Empiricist could suggest that something similar may also be taking place in our imagined case of prescience. But again it may turn out not to be so. For the predictions in question may be quite precise, concerning

124

matters which are perhaps unusual, and of no particular human interest. It would then be hard to see how our impression of success could be illusory.

If a situation of this sort were actually to occur, it would be a serious embarrassment to Empiricists, given my characterization of their position. For we have not the faintest idea how there can be a reliable process for acquiring true beliefs about the future, except by inference from current tendencies. For how could a future event exert any kind of influence on the human mind? How could the mere fact that an event *will* take place at a particular time in the future, give rise to any process bringing someone to believe that it will? The idea seems barely intelligible. Yet in the example above, we would have powerful reasons for thinking that these people have knowledge of the future, based upon their past success. So in such a case, we could know that they have knowledge, having every reason to think that their beliefs about the future are in fact produced through a process which is reliable, although we cannot even begin to give an account of the nature of that process.

In fact, however, we can insist that the example is merely imaginary, and that a genuine case of prescience will never really occur. For Empiricists should not (of course) be claiming to know *on the basis of thought alone* that all knowledge must arise through natural processes of which we can in principle provide an account! Rather, their attitude should be seen as resulting from a more general commitment to the ultimate (or at least in-principle) scientific explicability of all natural phenomena, including the phenomenon of belief-acquisition. This commitment may be supposed to receive its justification from past scientific success. Empiricists should therefore respond to our example by saying that they are prepared to bet that a genuine case of prescience will never in fact occur – precisely because we cannot begin to see how there could be any natural process underlying the acquisition of our beliefs in such a case.

2.2   The adequacy of science

Looked at in the way I am suggesting, then, Empiricist constraints on knowledge-claims may be seen to stem from a more general belief in the ultimate adequacy of science. The sequence of thought would be this: if we were to possess knowledge on the matter in question (the future, say), then our beliefs would have to be caused by a reliable process; but if our current science is such that we cannot even begin to frame a hypothesis as to what that process might be, then this in itself provides us with good reason for doubting its existence.

An analogy may help here. Suppose someone suggests that zebras in the wild put on overcoats at night to keep warm. Are we not prepared to bet, in the light of our current knowledge, that this will never turn out to be true? Indeed, if someone were to present evidence of its truth, should we not do our best to dismiss or explain that evidence away? For if it *were* true, it would apparently be wholly inexplicable. Are we to imagine that zebras have their own secret technology which enables them to weave cloth? Or are we to imagine that they have an elaborate and so far undiscovered system for stealing overcoats from human beings? These ideas pass beyond the possibility of belief, given what we already know about zebras and their habitat. Similarly, I suggest, with our imagined case of prescience: given what we already know about the world, we may be sure that it will never happen.

This is not to say that the Empiricist constraint on knowledge-claims is an infallible one. Plainly it cannot be, since it led the early Empiricists to deny the existence of innate beliefs and concepts – incorrectly, as it turns out (as we shall see briefly in Chapter 7). It may nevertheless be a reasonable one. If we share the Empiricist belief in the ultimate explanatory adequacy of science (or at least their belief that all processes in nature are natural ones, happening in accordance with causal law), then we shall deny that there are any natural phenomena for which there is no natural explanation. We therefore have reason to deny that some suggested phenomenon will ever in fact occur, if to the best of our belief there can be no natural explanation of it. Into this category, in my view, fall not only claims of prescience, but also astrology, magic and various alleged psychic phenomena.

(Two points are worth noting, here. The first is that the sorts of cases which Empiricists should reject on principle form a *spectrum*, since there are differing *degrees* of in-principle-inexplicability. The case of prescience is especially strong, since our scientific world-view leaves no room for backwards causation of beliefs by remote future events. The case for rejecting astrology, in contrast, is less deep. It is merely that it is very difficult to see what influence the position of the planets at birth (and why at birth?) should have on the developing human brain. If the influence were gravitational, for instance, then one would expect more influence from being born next to a mountain or large building. The second point to note is that Empiricists should be led to reject, not just knowledge-claims where we can't provide a naturalistic account of the genesis of that knowledge, but more generally *all* phenomena where it looks like we can see in advance that they can't be absorbed into a scientific world-view. See the cases for discussion presented in Figure 4.3.)

We are now in a position to articulate the underlying motivation behind the core of Empiricism. It consists, first, in a commitment to the explanatory adequacy of science; and secondly, in the search for an explanatory coherence within the overall system of our beliefs. These commitments lead Empiricists to reject all phenomena, and all claims to knowledge, where our background beliefs give us good reason to think that there cannot be a natural explanation of the processes involved. In consequence, Empiricists will be led to *explain away* the apparent phenomena in question (e.g., appealing to fraud, or reinterpreting apparently substantive claims as merely conceptual ones, or whatever). (See Figure 4.4 for a diagrammatic summary of the sequence of thought here.) Such commitments are, now, eminently reasonable. It is obvious that we should try to weld our beliefs into a coherent system if we can. And the early Empiricists' methodological commitment to the explanatory adequacy of science has been amply vindicated by subsequent scientific progress.

That *we* are justified in believing in the explanatory adequacy of science, however – given the huge success of science – does not mean that the same can be said of the early Empiricists. On the

Cases for discussion	
Psycho-kinesis (spoon-bending) Levitation (lifting the body through meditation) Magic (causing events by casting spells) Miracles (events directly caused by God)	Events with no natural explanation?
Prescience (foreknowledge) Astrology Psychic knowledge (mind-reading) Knowledge of platonic/abstact objects Knowledge of soul by thought alone	Knowledge with no natural explanation?

Figure 4.3 Cases for discussion.

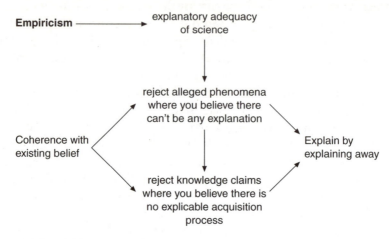

Figure 4.4 Empiricism's commitments.

contrary. While their commitment to science wasn't just a matter of blind faith, since notable advances in knowledge had already been achieved, it wasn't fully justified either. (So here may be a further reason why the early Empiricists didn't make clear the true nature of their opposition to innateness. For had they done so, they would have had to admit that their position was almost as reliant upon faith as that of their Rationalist theistic opponents.)

Our contemporary position, however, is surely quite different. Again and again in the last three centuries philosophers and others opposed to the explanatory adequacy of science have declared that there are specific limits on scientific understanding. Many once alleged, for example, that the origins of life must forever remain a mystery. But in each such case subsequent scientific discoveries have shown the doubters to be wrong. Either the puzzle in question was solved, or at least enough progress was made with respect to it for us to be assured that the process or phenomenon in question is genuinely natural, and for us to get some inkling of how it might eventually be fully understood. (This is the position we are currently in with respect to the so-called "problem of consciousness", I believe, as we shall see briefly in Chapter 8.) Given this track-record of success, it is surely reasonable to adopt, as a working assumption, that all real processes in nature are natural ones, happening in accordance with natural laws.

3   The empirical evidence for the soul

If Empiricists deny that we may know of the existence (or non-existence) of the soul by thought alone, then we might expect them to be more sympathetic to arguments which are based upon empirical evidence. A variety of such arguments for strong dualism have been suggested, of which there are three main ones: out of body and near death experiences; remembrance of past lives; and messages from the dead received via a medium or "psychic". Let us briefly outline each of these sources of evidence in turn, before we turn to discussion.

There have been many cases in which patients have been declared briefly dead, often following a heart-attack, or while under an anesthetic during the course of an operation. Their heart stops, and they cease breathing. When they are later revived, in a significant number of instances the patients report having had experiences of leaving their body at the time. They often claim to have looked down on their own body, and the efforts of the doctors trying to revive it, from a perspective elsewhere in the room. It is said that in some of these cases patients were able to report details which they couldn't have known in any other way. In other cases patients have the experience of traveling down a tunnel towards a bright light, while feeling an indescribable sense of peace and contentment. This is then evidence, it might be said, of the existence of the soul, and its independence of the body. Since their bodies were unconscious – indeed dead – while they themselves remained both conscious and able to adopt a perspective distinct from their bodies, surely people themselves must be entities which are distinct from their bodies.

A second source of evidence is provided by cases in which, it is alleged, people under deep hypnosis may be induced to recall details from the lives of people who have long been dead; or by cases in which young children claim to be reincarnations of people who have recently died. These beliefs come to the person under hypnosis, or to the child, in the manner of personal memory – the events in question being represented "from the inside", as if they had been personally experienced. More importantly, historical research sometimes reveals that the "remembered" events really did take place. Indeed, in some cases it is claimed that the person reporting the events would have had no opportunity during their life-time to have learned of the events they apparently recall, for example by reading history books or talking to relatives. This is then strong evidence, it

129

might be said, not only of the existence of the soul, but of the transmigration, or reincarnation, of souls from one body to another.

The final source of evidence to be considered concerns messages received from the spirit-world via a medium. Many people claim to have conversed with dead friends and relatives through the offices of a medium. Not only, they say, are the nature of these conversations consistent with what they know of the character and beliefs of the dead person, but the messages often concern trivial or intimate details which no one but the dead person could have known. The only way to explain such facts, it may be urged, is on the supposition that people have souls which may survive the destruction of their bodies, but which remain able to interact with the physical world via the minds of certain privileged individuals (psychics, or mediums).

I shall now spend a little while discussing the strength and reliability of the evidence for each of these three kinds of phenomena in turn. Then in section 4 we will turn to consider the question whether or not the *best* explanation of these sorts of phenomena – assuming them to be genuine – would be the existence of a non-physical soul. I shall be drawing on the work of the English psychologist Susan Blackmore, among others.

3.1 The quality of the evidence (1): near-death experiences

How powerful is this source of evidence? Not very, it might be claimed – on the grounds that it is by no means easy to rule out the possibility of fraud. For how are we to know that those people who report near-death experiences aren't fabricating their claims, consistent with what they know to have taken place in the operating theatre? It might be replied that this isn't a very plausible suggestion. For what possible motive could such people have? (Here there is a contrast with the cases of hypnotists and mediums, who often stand to gain very substantial financial rewards from their activities. I shall return to this point in the sub-sections following.) But this response might under-rate the intrinsic allure, for many people, of having something interesting to say. There is a very powerful attraction in being able to report something – whether it be a UFO landing or a near-death experience – which makes one stand out from the crowd and/or gets one's name into the papers.

There are a number of significant differences between UFO sightings and near-death experiences, however. One is that UFO sightings only began in the twentieth century in western cultures in which science-fiction literatures and films were increasingly common. Another is that such reports vary widely in content with time and place, with all sorts of different alien creatures and types of spacecraft being described. And thirdly, UFO sightings tend to occur in local "epidemics", following publicity given to an initial sighting. In contrast, historical and cross-cultural research shows that near-death experiences have occurred throughout human history and across all human cultures, with a "core" of consistent features recurring throughout (e.g., a tunnel of light, experience of one's own body from a perspective outside it, feelings of peace and contentment). Moreover, many of those who report near-death experiences are not publicity seekers, but only tell of their experience when directly questioned by investigators some time after the event.

In fact the *existence* of near-death and out-of-body experiences is now beyond question, following a number of decades of intensive study and research. Their existence receives corroboration from the fact that each of the components in such experiences can be induced in other circumstances – for example, by certain drugs and by certain forms of meditation. What remains much more controversial is whether out-of-body experiences are a genuine form of extra-sensory perception of the world, rather than a kind of hallucination or dream, or rather than involving perception via the ordinary senses. While there have been reported cases of people who experienced things during an out-of-body experience which they could neither have perceived by ordinary means, nor known about antecedently and woven into their "dream", none of these cases has so far received objective corroboration.

Admittedly, some near-death experiences have involved inaccessible details later corroborated by friends and relatives. Thus, for example, someone involved in a near-death experience may be able to tell us what color shoes the surgeon was wearing at the time, which is not something that they would have been able to see, even had they been conscious. Relatives may also confirm having seen the surgeon in shoes of that color on that day. But the facts of human psychology should make us wary of such cases in the absence of independent verification. For there is a natural tendency among loved-ones to seek agreement (especially in circumstances such as these!); and there is a tendency, too, to recall only positive items (i.e., features of the initial report which were agreed upon)

131

and to suppress the negative (i.e., features of the initial report which didn't secure agreement among listeners).

Nevertheless, those who have undergone near-death experiences can often describe in remarkable detail what took place in the operating theatre following their "death", such as the application of defibrillators to the chest, or an injection being given to the groin – all described as having been observed from a point on the ceiling, say. We will return in section 4 to consider whether or not such phenomena are best explained by the hypothesis of a non-physical soul which can leave the physical body at death.

3.2 *The quality of the evidence (2): past lives*

Here we need to handle the two different sorts of case separately – namely, memory recovery in adults through hypnosis and young children's spontaneous memories of a previous life – since they raise rather different issues. The former data are inherently suspect, because of the phenomenon of hypnotic *suggestion*. When hypnotized, subjects can be induced to do and believe all sorts of crazy things, as is well known. There is the possibility, then, that hypnotists may actually be guiding their subjects towards a set of memories *as of* a previous life, whether consciously or unconsciously, by means of subtle cues of one sort or another in their behavior and manner of questioning. (This will seem especially plausible in the light of the way that young children's suggestibility can be used to construct wholly fictitious "memories", as we shall see.) I therefore propose to set this sort of case to one side, as unreliable.

It might be objected that the data cannot be dismissed so easily. For what of the fact that subjects sometimes recover facts about a past life which they couldn't have known prior to the episode of hypnotic regression? The trouble, however, is that such cases are extremely hard to validate. For it is impossible to know what sources of information may have been available to the subject previously. Much more seriously, it is impossible to rule out fraud of one sort or another by the hypnotist (whether intentional or unintentional). For after all, such people stand to make considerable sums of money and/or become famous if they can convince other people that they can be assisted to recall a past life, at the same time demonstrating to them the reality of reincarnation. It would be little wonder if they should go to considerable lengths of one sort or another to secure the success (or rather, perceived success) of the enterprise. (I shall return to consider issues raised by the possibility of fraud at slightly greater length in the following sub-section.)

Let us turn, now, to consider cases of infant "reincarnation", where hypnosis is not involved. There have been a number of cases of young children who claim to remember events from a past life, many of which have been documented by the American psychologist Ian Stevenson. Sometimes the claims relate to the life of a dead relative, sometimes of someone more distant. It is claimed that the details of such "memories" can prove remarkably accurate. Such childhood reports tend to be much more common in cultures where there is a general belief in reincarnation in the surrounding population, however, which should make us somewhat suspicious. Moreover, there has never yet been a case where the genesis and development of such memory reports has been observed and/or recorded "on line" by independent observers. Given what is now known about memory-formation in general, and about young children's susceptibility to suggestion in particular, this is enough to devalue the whole genre of alleged evidence. Let me elaborate.

It is now well-established that memory is a *constructive* process. Forming a memory of an event is not at all like taking and storing a photograph. Rather it is much more like one person jotting down some notes at the time of an event, and then another person drawing that event from the notes alone. The end product will be a "complete" picture, but many of the details will have been provided by the subject, who makes inferences and imports assumptions into the construction process. ("It *must* have been like that!") Moreover, the process of construction takes place over time, with the "memory" being elaborated upon each time it is revisited or retold. (This is not to say that the construction process is necessarily unreliable, of course – if our background assumptions are true, then many of the constructed elements will actually be correct.) What is also the case is that facts provided by other people will be added to the construction process – for the most part "seamlessly", in such a way that the subject will be unable to tell from the finished product which parts were original, which parts he added, and which parts came from other people. On the contrary, the phenomenology of memory is such that the whole construction will *seem* like a faithful record of the original events.

Whenever a memory has been formed by frequent telling and retelling of an event to other people (which is the stage at which an investigator will first arrive at the scene in an infant "reincarnation" case), there is good reason to be suspicious, therefore. For many elements of the "memory" might in fact have been provided by others (who will at the same time have been constructing their own memories of the infant's life, of course, and in ignorance of the constructive nature of memory). Add to this the fact that memory formation in infancy is *highly* susceptible to suggestion, and we can see that no such reports can be treated as hard evidence until a great deal more "on line" research is done in such cases.

The question of the reliability of childhood memories came to the fore especially in the 1990s, when allegations of sexual abuse of children started to be widely investigated. For the children involved would be required to testify to a court, and the question was raised whether their testimony could be trusted. What emerged is that in almost all cases the children *intended* to be truthful – indeed, were reporting the facts as they now saw them. But it was *very* easy for wholly false memories to be created in young children by asking them leading questions – or indeed, by asking them repeated questions over a period of time, even if the questions themselves were not "leading".

In one experiment conducted by the American psychologist Stephen Ceci, for example, children went to visit a doctor (with parental consent). The doctor conducted a routine examination, listening to the child's chest and so on. Then afterwards the child was interviewed by an experimenter, and asked to describe what happened during the visit. When the child had finished their description (initially quite innocent, of course), the experimenter simply asked, "And is that *all* that happened?" The same sequence was repeated in interviews on subsequent days, with the same follow-up question. By the end of remarkably few interviews, many of the children were reporting acts of unthinkable abuse by the doctor who conducted the original examination – and not just reporting, but believing. A whole elaborate false memory of sexual abuse had been constructed by the simple expedient of expecting the child to have something more to say.

Given these facts, it should be obvious that no weight can be placed on childhood memories of past lives unless and until investigators have full access to the child from the moment of first report. By the time the child is actually seen by investigators in real cases, the child will of course have been questioned many times by relatives and interested neighbors, giving plenty of opportunity for elaboration, and for incorporation of accurate details intentionally or unintentionally provided by those questioners.

3.3   The quality of the evidence (3): messages from the dead

Turning now to consider cases of messages from the dead provided through a medium, the obvious possibility to consider is fraud. For such messages are supplied by someone (the medium or psychic) who makes a living out of doing just that. So: no messages, no money. It might be objected that in many such cases (and also in many cases of memory-recovery through hypnosis), it will be difficult to see *how* a fraud might have been perpetrated. For it will often be hard to see how the person in question could have had any normal (non-spiritual) access to the facts which they report. Thus, a hypnotized subject may report details from a past life which simply do not figure in any historical document to which they could apparently have had access. Also, a medium may transmit intimate details which, so far as can be seen, could only have been known to the dead loved one.

However, these points are not particularly impressive. For we know that magicians and illusionists, similarly, are able to execute tricks which may be entirely convincing, in the sense that no one but another magician can tell how they were able to do it. For example, they may be able to bend a spoon (seemingly by psychokinesis, but actually using sleight of hand) while we watch, without seeming to touch it. The only difference, it might be said, is that magicians are, in a sense, "honest frauds", in that they openly declare that they are merely performing tricks, and that they are not really bringing rabbits into existence out of thin air, or cutting living women in half. At any rate, the fact that we can't explain how the fraud might have been perpetrated doesn't show that there was no fraud present. (Indeed, in the case of mediums, at least, many cases of fraud have been uncovered by investigators, casting a shadow of suspicion over the remainder.)

There is an important general point here which should be born in mind whenever the possibility of fraud is an issue. Often in dramatic cases of "paranormal" phenomena, eminent *scientists* are called upon to investigate and provide corroboration; and sometimes these scientists declare that they can see no alternative but to accept the genuineness of those phenomena. But the moral, "Employ a thief to catch a thief" applies. The best person to use as an expert consultant in such cases may be a magician or illusionist, not a scientist. Scientists, after all, are used to investigating the general structure of the world; whereas fraud will involve particular tricks and sleights of hand which aren't really in the scientists' domain of expertise. Indeed, illusionists have often been able to replicate so-called "paranormal" phenomena – such as seeming to bend a spoon without touching, apparently by psycho-kinesis – using the normal tricks of their trade.

3.4 Illusions of accuracy

Another point to notice in connection with all three alleged sources of evidence for the existence of the soul is that the evidence collected is by no means systematic, but is mostly anecdotal. Thus I am not aware of the existence of any data concerning the relative number of accurate to inaccurate reports of near-death experience, for example. Nor is there any evidence concerning the number of cases in which apparent recall of past lives has in fact proved historically *in*accurate, or the number of cases in which messages from the spirit-world have been mistaken. It is therefore possible that those who believe in such phenomena are under a mere illusion of accuracy, paying attention to confirming instances (which may in fact be the result of mere chance) while ignoring those which count against. This would, after all, be entirely understandable. Where people very much want to believe in something, it is a matter of common experience that they will often bend the evidence to suit their belief. (Compare the way in which gamblers may believe that they win at least as often as they lose, when the records show quite otherwise.) So until some hard statistical evidence is provided, the existence of anecdotal examples – no matter how dramatic – must remain unconvincing.

There is yet another way in which an illusion of accuracy may arise. For wherever the descriptions in question are sufficiently vague, their hearers will naturally (if they are motivated to believe in the existence of the soul) interpret the content of those descriptions in such a way as to make them come out true. This phenomenon will be familiar to students of Astrology, as already noted in section 2 above. If your horoscope for the week says, "Personal relationships will run smoothly", you may (if you are so inclined) take this to be accurate in the light of the fact that you get on well with your lover all week – ignoring the fact that if it had said

136

instead, "There will be trouble in your personal relations", you would equally have regarded *this* as verified, in the light of the argument you had with your mother on the Wednesday. So what we require, is not only some hard evidence as to the relative accuracy of the reports which constitute our sources of evidence for the existence of the soul, but also some measure of the degree of vagueness of those reports themselves. Until this has been provided, the fact that many people find such reports convincing is hardly to be wondered at.

3.5 Interim conclusion

I conclude that much of the empirical evidence which is alleged to support strong dualism isn't actually very convincing. Admittedly, the evidence for the existence of near-death and out-of-body experiences is quite robust (though we have yet to see whether these really support the existence of the soul). But the reports which can be given of past lives under hypnosis and the messages received from the "spirit world" via a medium, which are also supposed to constitute such evidence, may actually be fraudulent. Even if they aren't fraudulent, people may be under a mere illusion of accuracy, deriving either from failure to notice contrary evidence, or from the vagueness of the reports themselves. This is especially likely to be the case, given that many people have a deep need to believe in the existence of the soul. In addition, the constructive nature of memory may have an important part to play in a number of these phenomena – leading people to believe in the accuracy of a near-death experience, for example, and perhaps being responsible for the very existence of the phenomenon of infant memory of previous lives.

Let us suppose, however, that the possibility of fraud could somehow be ruled out, and that we could somehow be convinced that most of the reports in question are genuinely accurate, in a way that cannot result merely from chance or vagueness. Even so, it will only follow that we have reason for belief in the existence of the soul if there is no *other* explanation of the phenomena, which is equally good or better than the hypothesis of strong dualism. For the inference from the evidence to the truth of strong dualism isn't deductive (it doesn't *follow from* the accuracy of near-death experience, for example, that there is a soul which exists independently of the body), but is rather an *inference to best explanation* of the phenomena in question (see section 4.1 below).

In the section which follows we will compare the merits of various competing explanations of the data (supposing those phenomena to be genuine). We will pay particular attention to near-death experiences, since it is here that the evidence for the existence of the phenomena is most robust.

4 Alternative explanations

What I propose to do in this section, is to argue first, that in each case there is an alternative explanation to strong dualism available, which wouldn't involve the existence of a soul. I shall then argue secondly, that in each case it is the alternative explanation which is the better of the two. So even if we were to set aside worries about fraud and genuine accuracy, the various sorts of suggested empirical evidence fail to provide us with any reason for belief in strong dualism. First, however, something needs to be said about the category of inference to the best explanation in general.

4.1 Inference to the best explanation

As noted above, it is obvious that the existence of the soul cannot be *deduced* (i.e., validly inferred) from the evidence. Rather, if we come to believe in the soul on the basis of the evidence, it will have been by means of an inference to the best available explanation of that evidence. We find ourselves confronted with a set of data to be explained – reports of out of body experiences during brief periods of death, reports of childhood memories of previous lives, and so on. Our challenge therefore, is to come up with the best explanation which we can of that data.

Now one option here – as always in science – is to *dismiss* the data, or to explain it away. This is, in effect, the option which we have been exploring in section 3 above, where we discussed explanations in terms of fraud or the constructive nature of memory, for example. But even if we accept the data at face-value – even if we accept that near-death experiences really do occur, or if we accept that memory of past lives is genuine – we still face the question of explanation. Does the hypothesis of strong dualism provide the *best* explanation of these data? Or is there some other explanation which might fare better?

Philosophers of science have studied the sorts of tacit principles which scientists (as well as ordinary folk) employ for choosing between competing theories – that is, for making an inference to the *best* explanation of the data to be explained. While no one any longer thinks that it is possible to codify these principles, it is generally agreed that the good-making features of a theory include such features as:

- *accuracy* (predicting all or most of the data to be explained, and explaining away the rest):
- *simplicity* (being expressible as economically as possible, with the fewest commitments to distinct kinds of fact and process):
- *consistency* (internal to the theory or model):
- *coherence* (with surrounding beliefs and theories, meshing together with those surroundings, or at least being consistent with them):
- *fruitfulness* (making new predictions and suggesting new lines of enquiry); and
- *explanatory scope* (unifying together a diverse range of data).

One explanation will be better than another, then, to the extent that it is more successful overall along these six different dimensions of comparison. But as for how each of the dimensions should be weighted for importance, or how we should respond when one theory does better along one dimension, while another does better along another, there is probably nothing general which can be said. Individual cases need to be looked at on their individual merits. Certainly there is no simple choice-rule which we can be given in such cases which will survive the "retroactive prediction test". That is, there is no rule which will predict the choices which scientists actually made in past cases of successful scientific enquiry. Still, we have at least some guidelines to work with when considering competing explanations of the evidence.

4.2   *Explaining near-death experiences*

Consider, to begin with, the phenomenon of near-death experience. The obvious alternative explanation (to be elaborated on in a moment) is that these experiences are hallucinations of some sort, perhaps caused by a temporary lack of oxygen to the brain. Instead of the subject (i.e., their soul) really perceiving their own body from a position outside it, their brain may be constructing such an experience, as in a dream. The accuracy of the details of this experience may result partly from unconscious perception, similar to the way in which the ringing of an alarm-clock may be integrated into a dream. But they may also draw on the subject's prior knowledge, for example their knowledge of the appearance of their own body, or their knowledge of the color of shoe that their surgeon tends to wear.

Not only is this alternative explanation a possible one, but it is, in my view, a great deal better. This is partly because it is simpler, in terms of the types of entities and processes which it postulates; and because it is more readily consistent with our surrounding beliefs and theories. According to the hypothesis of hallucination, there is only one sort thing in existence which is relevant, namely the human body and brain. Moreover (as we shall see shortly), that hypothesis only utilizes processes which are already familiar to us from other areas, such as dreams and the way in which unconsciously perceived events can be integrated into a dream.

The strong dualist hypothesis, in contrast, supposes that there are two sorts of thing in question – namely, a non-physical soul as well as the human brain. It also has to suppose that there are ways in which the human soul can perceive events which don't require the mediation of physical sense-organs. Thus if the soul is seeing its own body from a position on the ceiling, it would have to be the case that the light reaching the ceiling is able to act on the soul directly (and how is *that* supposed to happen?) without passing through any physical mechanism such as the human eye. The hypothesis of hallucination is therefore a great deal more believable.

One of the strengths of the hallucination-hypothesis, moreover, is that it can explain, not only how and why a near-death experience takes place, but also many of the detailed features which are characteristic of such experience. But all this will require some setting up, and some elaboration.

The first point to notice is that some perception can continue even when subjects are completely immobile and unresponsive – to all appearances unconscious. It has been known for some time, for example, that the wrong mix of drugs during anesthesia can leave patients aware of what is happening to them (and sometimes in excruciating pain) although they are completely unable to move or signal their predicament. It is also well known that as unconsciousness sets in, hearing is the last sense to check out. It is not unlikely, then, that those who are seemingly unconscious during a cardiac arrest, say, may still be able to hear what is going on around them. But why would this lead them to undergo visual experiences with a content determined by what they hear? In order to answer this question we need to understand a little better what happens to the brain as death approaches.

In almost all forms of death, dying will be associated with a reduction in levels of oxygen in the brain, as the heart ceases to pump blood. "Cerebral hypoxia" (as it is called) has a marked effect on the level of activity of the brain-cells in the cortex. The important fact for our purposes is that hypoxia has a much greater effect on the inhibitory cells in the brain – i.e., those whose function is to modulate and reduce the activity of other cells. The result, somewhat paradoxically, is that hypoxia can lead to *increased* firing of excitatory cells, resulting in hallucinations and other forms of disordered experience. It is quite plausible therefore, that the content of these hallucinations, once real (visual) input has been turned off, might be heavily influenced by whatever other clues are available – e.g., the patient's background knowledge that they are suffering a heart attack, or from hearing remarks made by doctors and others. The result would be a partly-veridical visual hallucination of their situation. But why should these experiences be constructed from a perspective outside the body (e.g., from the ceiling)? This is not unexpected, since it is well known that memory images in general tend to be constructed using a "bird's-eye view". This might be essentially the same sort of phenomenon in operation here.

A similar explanation can be given of the "tunnel of light" which so often accompanies a near-death experience. There are many more cells in the visual cortex devoted to processing information from the center of the field of vision than are devoted to analysis of the periphery. If lack of oxygen, combined with lack of visual input, leads to random firing, it is predictable that the result may be a tunnel of light at the center of the visual field. What color light? Since white is a mixture of all other colors, one might predict that a tunnel of white light would result if all color-representing cells were firing randomly – and that tends to be just what happens.

As for the feelings peace, contentment and joy which so often accompany a near-death experience, this is probably the result of release of endorphins into the brain. It is known that this chemical produces exactly the feelings in question in other circumstances; and the release of endorphins are known to be caused, not only by cerebral hypoxia, but also by physical stress (injury, infection, and so on) – just the circumstances in which someone on the point of death is likely to find himself.

We have here a perspective, then, from which all of the elements which go to make up a near-death experience can be seen as predictable effects of changes taking place in the brain near the point of death – nothing non-physical or spiritual needs to be postulated. This perspective receives further confirmation from the fact that each of these elements can also be induced separately by drugs (e.g., hallucinogens) or by the application of appropriate meditation techniques.

Notice, too, that we have been able to provide an informative explanation of many of the details of a near-death experience, such as the inclusion of a tunnel of white light. In contrast, the explanations provided by the strong dualist are apt to seem almost vacuous at this point – the person experiences a tunnel of white light because the soul is undergoing experiences *as of* white light. (Notice that the explanation cannot be: because the soul is actually traveling down a tunnel of white light. Since the soul is non-physical it cannot really travel anywhere; and anyway there is no such tunnel in the vicinity of the operating theatre.) This is yet another reason why an explanation in terms of brain-activity is to be preferred.

4.3 Explaining remembrance of past lives

Consider, next, the phenomenon of apparent remembrance of past lives under hypnosis. Suppose that the data proved to be robust. That is, suppose that people could be shown to generate largely-correct memory-reports in these circumstances, and that hypnotic suggestion could somehow be ruled out. Would this support the existence of a non-physical soul, capable of being reincarnated from one body to another? Perhaps not. For an alternative explanation suggests itself. It may be that the effect of the hypnosis, and of the nature of the questioning by the hypnotist, is that the person can utilize long-forgotten information – perhaps gleaned from childhood history books or reports once read in a newspaper – in such a way as to unconsciously reconstruct that information into the form of a personal memory. This alternative explanation is preferable on grounds of simplicity and economy, since it only commits us to the existence of a single type of thing (the physical human being), and since it only appeals to phenomena which we know to occur anyway, such as information lying dormant in memory for many years.

This alternative explanation cannot be extended to account for infants' memories of previous lives, obviously. For here there is no earlier learning period in which the information might have been acquired. (Besides, infants don't know how to read!) What else might be proposed? If the memories in question turned out to relate only to the lives of relatives of the infant, then it might be suggested that personal memories can somehow become encoded genetically, and transmitted between generations. Everything we presently know about the processes of evolution, and about memory, suggests that this isn't the case. But strong data of the kind proposed might give us cause to revisit and revise these beliefs.

Alternatively again, *telepathy* might be proposed as an explanation. It could be suggested that these infants are capable of receiving the information about the life of the dead person from the mind of some other (living) person through a process of telepathy, or "thought transference", which then becomes transformed within the mind of the infant into a seeming personal memory. Admittedly, there is no sound independent evidence of the existence of telepathy. But *if* it turned out to exist, and *if* it turned out to be a physical process (perhaps resulting from weak electric fields generated and received by the human brain), then the resulting hypothesis wouldn't require us to believe in any non-physical entities or processes. This would make that hypothesis a good deal simpler than (and therefore preferable to) the hypothesis of a non-physical soul which can transmigrate between bodies. But this is premised upon two big "ifs", of course.

In section 3.2, I argued that the most plausible explanation of the phenomena in this domain involves the constructive nature of human memory, and the suggestibility of young children and of people undergoing hypnosis. There is currently no reliable data which cannot be explained in this way, and so no solid evidence of genuine memory of previous lives. *If* such evidence should turn out to be forthcoming, however – if, for example, the genesis of such memories in a young child could be observed in complete detail on-line to rule out all forms of suggestion – then we would have been given some reason to believe in the reincarnation of souls. But this, too, is a very big "if". (See also section 4.5 below.)

4.4 Explaining psychic messages

Consider, lastly, the evidence of messages from the dead provided via a medium. In section 3.3, I argued that these data are best explained away in terms of some combination of fraud, coincidence, and wishful thinking. But suppose that the data proved robust. Suppose that we could know, somehow, that these factors cannot account for all instances. Would strong dualism then remain as the only possible explanation? Would this then be powerful evidence supporting disembodied survival after death?

In fact one alternative explanation would remain, even supposing that we set aside worries about vagueness and the possibility of fraud. It is that the medium may, through telepathy, be drawing on the knowledge possessed by the living person who is present (i.e., the supplicant who is seeking information about a dead loved one), and unconsciously (as a result of their trance) recasting that information into the form of a message from the dead person. Admittedly this alternative explanation doesn't just appeal to processes which are already familiar and uncontroversial. For independent evidence of telepathy is scanty. But it is a great deal simpler than the hypothesis of strong dualism, in at least two respects.

First, our alternative hypothesis only commits us to the existence of a single type of thing, namely the physical human body and brain. (At least, this is so on the assumption that telepathy itself should turn out to be a physical process, if it exists.) Second, the original hypothesis of disembodied souls would have to appeal to telepathy (or something very like it) in any case. For it would have to be through telepathy that the disembodied souls of the dead would communicate their messages to the medium, since they cannot literally speak or write. Then given that we should have to believe in telepathy anyway, it will be simpler to suppose that it occurs between the medium and their supplicant (both of whom we already know to exist) rather than between the medium and the mind of a dead person. (Note that this point holds good *whether or not* telepathy is itself a physical process.) So in this case I conclude that the empirical evidence, even if robust, would fail to support the existence of the soul.

4.5 Any explanation is better than none?

In fact I am inclined to argue for a thesis which is a good deal stronger than those above. This is, that even supposing that we hadn't been able to think of alternative explanations of the phenomena in question, they *still* wouldn't have provided us with sufficient reason for belief in the soul. For although it is generally true that some explanation is better than no explanation at all, this principle fails where the explanation in question would conflict with many of our well-established beliefs and theories. In such circumstances it may be more reasonable to believe that there will turn out to be some alternative explanation, which is as yet unthought of.

If we were to accept the existence of a non-physical soul, and that there is causal interaction between souls and physical brains, then much of physics and biology would need to be revised, as we shall see in Chapter 5. For example, if an event in the soul can cause an event in the brain (as when your decision to say something sets in motion events which lead to the contraction of the muscles in your mouth and larynx), then the principle of conservation of energy will need to be modified. This states that in any physical process, energy is neither produced nor lost. But in this case physical energy would be being produced out of no physical cause. For similar reasons, biological beliefs about the causes of brain-cell firings would need to be modified. Besides being caused by such things as the activity of connected brain-cells, we should have to believe that they can be caused by an event, such as a decision, in a non-physical soul. Rather than make such far-reaching modifications to science, it seems to me that it would be more reasonable (if we couldn't think of any other explanation of the alleged phenomena) to suggest that some alternative explanation will one day be found, even if we don't know how.

This suggestion is really a generalization of a point already made in section 3.3 above, concerning the possibility of fraud. Even if we can't see how a fraud might have been perpetrated, that doesn't mean that none has occurred. Indeed, this is an area in which we have good inductive grounds for believing that there are many good explanations which we non-illusionists can't think of – because we know full well that there are illusionists who are capable of creating effects which we ordinary folk can't figure out. So we should believe that there is *some* explanation of the effect in question, even if we can't think what that explanation might be. The point now being made is similar, but more general. It is that, even if the evidence supporting the existence of the soul proved robust, and even if we couldn't think of any alternative explanation of it, *still* we should maintain that there is some such explanation to be found, even if we can't think what that explanation might be. For belief in the existence of the soul would conflict with important and well-established elements of our scientific world-view, as we shall see in Chapter 5.

The general moral is this. People have a natural tendency, when confronted by some body of data, to believe in the best explanation of that evidence *which they have been able to think of*. But there are many circumstances in which this natural tendency needs to be resisted. One is where there exists a possibility of fraud and clever trickery of one sort or another. Another is where the only explanation which we can think of conflicts with other things which we believe. (Recall that *coherence with surrounding beliefs and theories* is one of the good-making features of an explanation. The present point then is that severe-enough failure to cohere can mean that an explanation shouldn't be accepted, even if it is the only explanation currently available.)

Conclusion

In this chapter I have argued that Empiricists are probably correct – we cannot establish substantive matters of fact, such as the existence or non-existence of the soul, on the basis of thought alone. Rather, we need to consider the empirical evidence. My conclusion has then been, however, that there is no convincing evidence of the existence of the soul. Much of what evidence there is, is of poor quality. Even if we take the evidence at face value, there are more plausible explanations of it, not involving the hypothesis of a soul. So Empiricists as well as Rationalists should take the view there is insufficient reason for belief in strong dualism.

Questions for discussion

1. The Empiricists rejected the idea of knowledge by reason alone, and they also rejected innate knowledge and concepts. Why should the two issues be thought to belong together?
2. Is it possible to prove anything substantial about the world, just by thinking and without having to consult our experience?
3. Suppose you read in the newspaper of someone who claims to be able to foretell the future by direct insight, not by inference from current tendencies. What should your attitude be, and why?
4. Do the documented cases of childhood "memory" of a previous life provide substantial evidence of reincarnation of souls?
5. What is the best explanation of near-death and out-of-body experiences? – Hallucination? Or the separation of soul from body?

Further reading

Blackmore, S. (1992) *Beyond the Body: an investigation of out-of-body experiences*, Chicago: Academy Chicago Publishers.

Blackmore, S. (1993) *Dying to Live: near-death experiences*, New York: Prometheus Books.

Carruthers, P. (1992) *Human Knowledge and Human Nature: a new introduction to an ancient debate*, Oxford: Oxford University Press.

Ceci, S. and Bruck, M., (1995) *Jeopardy in the Courtroom: the scientific analysis of children's testimony*, Washington, DC: American Psychological Association.

Descartes, R. (1641) *Meditations on First Philosophy*. (Many translations available).

Edwards, P. (1996) *Reincarnation: a critical examination*, New York: Prometheus Books.

Hume, D. (1748) *An Enquiry Concerning the Human Understanding*. (Many versions available).

Leibniz, G. (1704) *New Essays Concerning Human Understanding*. (Many translations available).

Locke, J. (1690) *An Essay Concerning Human Understanding*. (Many versions available).

Stevenson, I. (1987) *Children who Remember Previous Lives*, Charlottesville, VA: University Press of Virginia.

5

⟤⟐⟐⟐⟤

The case for physicalism

This chapter will be concerned to argue for, to elaborate, and to defend physicalism. Physicalists maintain that all of the states and processes involved in the human mind are, at bottom, physical states and processes. Since physicalism is the denial of weak dualism (mental states are non-physical states), when dualism is referred to in this chapter it will be the weak version which is in question. If weak dualism is rejected, then so too, of course, must strong dualism be rejected. If mental states themselves are physical, then the *subject* of those states surely couldn't be *non*-physical.

1 Arguments for mind–brain identity

What the thesis of mind–brain identity affirms is that descriptions of our mental states, on the one hand, and some descriptions of our brain states, on the other, are in fact descriptions of the very same things. It holds that just as a particular cloud is, as a matter of fact, a great many water droplets suspended close together in the atmosphere; and just as a flash of lightning is, as a matter of fact, a certain sort of discharge of electrical energy; so a pain or a thought is (is identical with) some state of the brain or central nervous system.

The identity-thesis is a version of physicalism: it holds that all mental states and events are in fact physical states and events. But it is not, of course, a thesis about meaning: it does not claim that words such as "pain" and "after-image" may be *analyzed* or *defined* in terms of descriptions of brain-processes. (That would be absurd.) Rather, it is an empirical thesis about the things in the world to which our words refer: it holds that the ways of thinking represented by our terms for conscious states, and the ways of

148

thinking represented by some of our terms for brain-states, are in fact different ways of thinking of the very same (physical) states and events. So "pain" doesn't *mean* "such-and-such a stimulation of the neural fibers" (just as "lightning" doesn't *mean* "such-and-such a discharge of electricity"); yet, for all that, the two terms in fact refer to the very same thing.

In this section a number of arguments in support of mind–brain identity will be set out and discussed. All of these arguments are broadly empirical ones, drawing on our beliefs about the causal order of the world, and our place within it.

1.1 The closure of physics and the unity of nature

Almost everyone believes that mind and matter interact causally with one another. For example, stimulation of our sense-organs causes conscious experiences, and decisions cause bodily movements. An interactive-dualist will then have to picture the situation somewhat as represented in Figure 5.1. (The diamonds here represent mental events, and the triangles represent physical ones; the arrows represent causality, and "M" represents a bodily movement of some sort. Notice that on this picture there is a brain event among the causes of movement M *which has no physical cause*. This is a point we will return to in section 1.2 below. Notice, too, that the diagram is, of course, hugely over-simplified. Normally many different mental states will contribute to the causation of a given mental state, and many different complex patterns of brain states will contribute to the causation of any given brain state or bodily movement.)

One of the main objections to dualism has always been the difficulty of making sense of causal connections between mind and brain, as we saw in Chapter 2:2. Now, there isn't any problem of *principle* in understanding causal connections between physical and non-physical realms (as we argued in Chapter 2:2). For there is nothing in the concept of causation, as such, which requires all that

Mind: ⇒ ◊ ⇒ ◊ ⇒ ◊ ⇒ ◊ ⇒ ◊ ⇒
        ⇑   ⇓
Brain: ⇒ Δ ⇒ Δ ⇒ Δ ⇒   Δ ⇒ Δ ⇒ M

Figure 5.1 Interactive dualism.

causes be mediated by physical mechanisms. The real problem is to understand *how* such causation can occur, given what we already know or believe about the physical world, and about causation in the brain.

Consider, first, the physical world in general. Most scientists now believe that *physics is closed*, in the sense of permitting no interference from, or causation by, events at higher levels of description (e.g., chemical or biological). On this view, all atomic and sub-atomic events happen in accordance with physical laws (albeit probabilistic ones), and all events at higher, more abstract, levels of description must be realized in, or constituted by, those physical processes, in such a way as to allow no independent point of causal leverage. So while there may be chemical and biological laws, the events which figure in these laws must always, at the same time, fall under the laws of physics. (I shall say some more about this in section 2.2 below.)

On this conception, there is simply *no room* for a distinct and independent psychological level of nature, whose events are not physically constituted, but which can have an impact upon the physical behavior of the body. For in order for such a thing to be possible, it would have to be the case that non-physical mental events could have an impact on causal sequences at the physical level. But this would conflict with the causal closure of physics – it would mean that some physical events would be caused, not by other physical events or processes, but rather by non-physical mental events.

What reason do we have for believing in the causal closure of physics? This is not something which can be proved (least of all by thought alone, of course). But for some centuries it has been a successful methodological assumption of scientific enquiry. Scientists work under the assumption that processes in physics brook no interference from higher levels of causation. Whenever they come across physical phenomena which cannot presently be explained in physical terms, instead of postulating causation by *élan vital* (a supposed independent biological life-force), or causation by *ectoplasm* (a supposed independent psychic force), or whatever, they look deeper into the physical mechanisms. In many such cases this deeper look has proved successful; and in all such cases physicalistic scientific enquiries continue to make progress. This gives us good reason to think that the scientific methodology is correct, and that physics is indeed closed.

Closely related to the principle of the causal closure of physics is the principle of the *unity of nature*. On this conception, nature is *layered* into a unitary system of laws and patterns of causal organization, with the processes in any given layer being realized in the one below it. The bottom layer is fundamental physics, which *realizes* (or *constitutes*) all the rest. Chemical laws and processes are realized in those of atomic physics, bio-chemical processes are constituted by those of molecular chemistry, biological and neurological processes are realized in those of bio-chemistry, and so on. (Again, more on this in section 2.2 below.) In accordance with this layered picture of nature, we should expect the principles and processes of human psychology – or the 'laws' of operation of the human mind – to be realized in those of neurology. That is to say: we should expect mental events to be constituted by physical events in the brain.

The basic reason for believing in the unity of nature (like our reason for believing in the closure of physics) is that it is a highly successful working methodological assumption of much scientific enquiry. Although scientists are concerned to discover the laws and principles which operate at any given level of organization in nature – biological, say – it is also an important goal of science to try to understand how those same laws might be *constituted* or *realized* by patternings of events at lower levels. They seek to understand how the right sequences of events at the lower level – that of bio-chemistry, say – would give rise to the patterns observed at the higher one. (When successful, the result is a *reductive explanation* of the higher-level phenomenon. The difference between reduction and reductive explanation is discussed in section 2.2 below.) This methodological assumption, too, has proved immensely successful, giving us reason to believe that mental processes will somehow be constituted by processes in the brain.

These arguments may be summarized as follows:

(1) It is a successful methodological assumption of science that non-physical events cannot cause physical ones. (*The closure of physics.*)

(2) It is a successful methodological assumption of science that higher-level events and processes in nature must be realized in lower-level (ultimately physical) ones. (*The unity of nature.*)

(C) So we have reason to think that mental events must be realized in physical ones, probably in physical events in the brain.

The argument is broadly inductive in form, since it projects forward from the success of assumptions made by scientists in the past to a new case. But it seems none the worse for that. For in the light of our endorsement of Empiricism and rejection of Rationalism in Chapter 4, we should in any case be wary of attempts to *prove* the truth of physicalism. On the contrary, good inductive arguments are just what an Empiricist might be expected to look for.

1.2 The argument from causation in the brain

Now consider, more particularly, what we believe about the nature of the causal processes which take place in the human brain. There is still much to learn about the brain – about the functions and interactions of its parts, for example. But much is already known. It is known that the brain consists of nerve cells, of various known types. Much is known about how such cells function, and the physical causes which lead to their activity. Certainly there appear to be no "inverse causal black-holes" in the brain, such as would seem to be required by the interactionist picture. (That is, there are no places in the brain where brain activity begins to occur *for no physical reason*.) Indeed, I claim that enough is already known about the brain to justify the following principle: *each event in the brain has a sufficient physical cause*. In our picture, then, the chain of events in the brain leading to any given bodily movement ought to be *unbroken*, as in Figure 5.2. How can this be made consistent with interactive dualism?

As we noted in Chapter 2:2, we believe very firmly that some mental states and events are causally necessary for the occurrence of some physical ones. For example, I believe that if I had not been conscious of a pain in my foot (mental event), I should not have gone to the doctor (physical event). My awareness of the pain was, I believe, a causally necessary condition of my later visit to the doctor. But as we noted above, it seems most unlikely that we shall ever need to advert to anything other than physical–physical causality when we investigate the detailed causal nexus behind any given bodily movement. On the contrary, it seems likely that there will always be physical events providing us with a sufficient causal

Brain: $\Rightarrow \Delta \Rightarrow \Delta \Rightarrow \Delta \Rightarrow \Delta \Rightarrow \Delta \Rightarrow \Delta \Rightarrow M$

Figure 5.2 Causation in the brain.

152

explanation of the brain events giving rise to any particular bodily movement. For example, as we trace the causes of my legs moving me in the direction of the doctor's surgery, through events in the muscles of my legs and feet, through events in the nerves of my spinal column, into events in the cells of my brain, it seems most unlikely that the chain of physical causation will eventually run out. Indeed, according to the principle set out above, we already know enough about causation in the brain to know that it won't. So we shall never be forced to appeal to any non-physical event in order to provide a satisfactory causal explanation of the movements leading to my visit to the surgery.

Now the only way in which we can hold onto both beliefs – the belief that some mental events are causally necessary for the occurrence of some physical ones, and the belief that it is unnecessary to appeal to anything other than physical events in providing causal explanations of brain events – is by believing that some mental events *are* physical ones. Then somewhere in the chain of physical causes of my visit to the doctor there will be a brain event which is (is identical with) my awareness of a sensation of pain.

This argument for the general truth of the mind–brain identity-thesis may be summarized as follows.

(1)   Some mental states and events are causally necessary for the occurrence of some physical ones.

(2)   In a completed neuro-physiological science there will be no need to advert to anything other than physical–physical causality in the brain.

(C)   So some mental states and events are (are identical with) physical (brain) states and events.

The argument is valid. Although its conclusion only claims that *some* mental states are physical, it can easily be developed in such a way as to entail the stronger conclusion that all are. For almost every kind of mental state can sometimes be causally necessary for a physical one, we think. Sometimes a particular bodily movement would not have taken place if I had not made a particular decision; or if I had not entertained a particular thought; or if I had not been aware of a particular sensation; or if I had not had a particular after-image; and so on. Then since it seems extremely unlikely that some mental states are physical while some are not, it follows that all are.

1.3 Causal over-determination

An interactive-dualist may try to get around the difficulty by appealing to the notion of "causal over-determination". Very roughly, this is the idea that an event may have more causes than are necessary. For example, imagine someone being shot by a firing squad, each member of which has a loaded gun (contrary to normal practice). Suppose that every soldier's aim is true, that all fire at the same time, and that every bullet strikes the heart. Then it is true of every soldier, that even if the others had not fired, his action would still have caused the prisoner's death. (Each shot individually is causally sufficient for death.) But it is also true of every soldier, that even if he himself had *not* fired, the prisoner's death would still have been caused by the others. (No shot individually is causally necessary for death.) Similarly then: the dualist may propose that brain-events are caused *both* by prior brain-events (so the chain of physical causes is unbroken) *and* by prior mental events; where either type of event on its own is sufficient to produce the effect, but neither type of event on its own is necessary.

So we have: each shot is *causally sufficient* for death, in that death will follow from it, in the circumstances, even if the other shots aren't fired; but no shot is (individually) *causally necessary,* since even if it isn't fired, death will still be caused by the other shots. Perhaps, similarly, the events in the brain which cause bodily movements are caused *both* by earlier brain events *and* by certain mental events, such as a decision. The dualist's resulting conception of the relationship between mind and brain can then be schematized as in Figure 5.3 (where the arrows now represent causal sufficiency).

By deploying the thesis of causal over-determination, a dualist can hold onto one aspect of our common-sense beliefs in face of the likely discovery of unbroken causal chains of brain-events. Namely: the belief that our decisions are sometimes, in the circumstances, *sufficient* to bring about a bodily movement. Yet one aspect of common-sense would still have to be given up. Namely: the belief

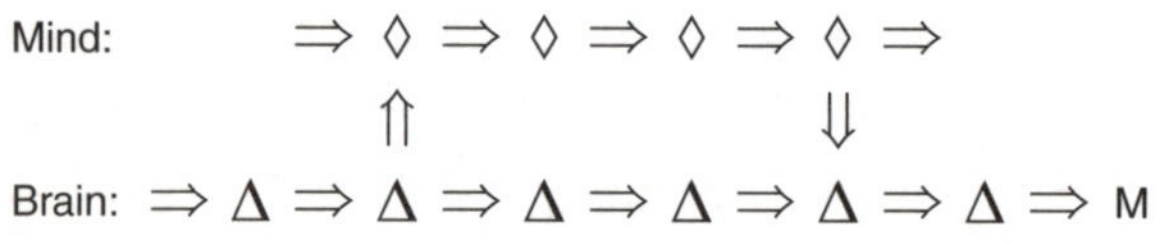

Mind: $\Rightarrow \Diamond \Rightarrow \Diamond \Rightarrow \Diamond \Rightarrow \Diamond \Rightarrow$

                   $\Uparrow$ $\Downarrow$

Brain: $\Rightarrow \Delta \Rightarrow \Delta \Rightarrow \Delta \Rightarrow \Delta \Rightarrow \Delta \Rightarrow \Delta \Rightarrow$ M

Figure 5.3 Causal over-determination.

154

that a decision is sometimes causally *necessary* for a bodily movement to occur.

People who take the over-determination view can believe the following: given that a subject is sitting at a keyboard and decides to start typing, then this is, in the circumstances, sufficient for typing to begin. But they can no longer claim that had the subject *not* decided in that way, then the bodily movement wouldn't have taken place. On the contrary, it would still have occurred, brought about by its other cause: a particular brain-event. But are we really prepared to give up this belief? Don't I believe almost as firmly as I believe anything, that if I had not decided to write this book (mental event) I should not now be typing at this keyboard (physical event)?

How, then, can a dualist explain the fact that decisions are causally necessary *and* sufficient for bodily movements, consistent with our beliefs about the brain?

1.4 Epiphenomenalism

One suggestion is that we should give up believing that our decisions make any real causal difference. Rather, those decisions are mere *epiphenomena*, produced as a by-product by the brain-events which are the true causes of our actions. Our picture of the relation between mind and brain will then be as represented in Figure 5.4.

An attractive feature of this account is that it can explain how we come to be under the *illusion* of agency, falsely believing that our decisions are *causally* necessary and sufficient for some of our movements. For a given mental event will, on this account, be *non-causally* necessary and sufficient for a given movement, since each of them has a common cause. In fact the epiphenomenalist-dualist can claim that each mental event will be correlated with a particular brain-event as a matter of causal necessity. In which case it will be causally impossible for the mental event to occur without the corresponding brain-event occurring.

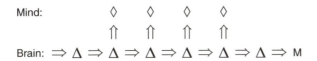

Figure 5.4 Epiphenomenalism.

So, given that the mental event occurs, then so too must the action occur which is caused by the underlying brain-event. (That is to say, the mental event is non-causally sufficient for the occurrence of the action.) And if the mental event *hadn't* occurred, then that would mean that the brain-event hadn't occurred either, and so nor would the movement happen. (That is to say, the mental event is non-causally necessary for the occurrence of the action.) On this account, then, it will be *true* that if I hadn't decided to write this book, I shouldn't now be typing. For the only way in which I could have failed to take that decision, would have been if the corresponding brain-event had failed to occur; and if that had failed to occur, then the bodily movement wouldn't have been caused.

Compare the froth on the wave which breaks a sandcastle on the beach (see Figure 5.5). Supposing that it is a law of nature that breaking waves produce froth on their leading edge, then we can say this: if the froth had not been there, the sandcastle wouldn't have been broken; and given that the froth is there, the sandcastle must be broken shortly thereafter. But it isn't really the froth which causes the sandcastle to break; rather, it is the wave which causes *both* the frothing *and* the breaking.

Similarly we can say: if I hadn't decided to type, then I wouldn't now be typing. (This is because, if the event of my deciding hadn't occurred, then that would have been because the brain-event which caused my movement hadn't occurred.) And we can say: given that I decide to type, in the circumstances, then typing occurs. (This is because, if the decision to type occurs, then that will have been caused by the brain-event which causes the relevant movements.) But my decision won't be the true cause of my typing, any more than the froth on the wave is the true cause of the sandcastle breaking.

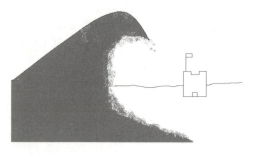

Figure 5.5 The wave and the sandcastle.

156

Although a theory of this sort can save our belief that certain of our bodily movements wouldn't have occurred if certain decisions hadn't been taken, it does so at the cost of explanatory redundancy. For the decision is no longer part of the true causal explanation of why the bodily movement took place. To say that our decisions are causally correlated with the events which cause our bodily movements, isn't the same as saying (what we intuitively believe) that our decisions themselves constitute the true causal explanations of our actions.

It seems that epiphenomenalism must conflict with our common-sense belief in the reality of agency – it conflicts with our belief that our decisions can make a causal difference to what we do. But another reason why epiphenomenalism is unacceptable is that, if it were true, it would remain a complete mystery why our decisions should march so neatly in step with our actions. Why is it that the brain event which causes me to sit down to type *also* causes me to think, "Now I will begin typing"? For, by hypothesis, it wouldn't have made the slightest bit of difference if that brain event had caused me to think instead, "Now I'll go swimming".

How would the underlying causal properties of the brain ever have evolved, for example? What would be the advantage if the brain-event which causes my arm to go up also causes me to decide, "Now I shall raise my arm"? For, by hypothesis, the latter has no causal effects in its own right. What difference would it have made if the brain-event had caused me to decide, "Now I shall open my mouth" or, "Now I shall sit down" instead? It would seem to be a quite remarkable cosmic coincidence that the evolutionary processes which caused our brains to have their causal powers in respect of bodily movement, *also* led them to cause content-relevant mental events. Then since it is good explanatory practice to minimize miracles, we have good reason to reject epiphenomenalism, and to endorse the thesis of mind–brain identity instead.

1.5 Mind–brain identity

In fact our belief in the reality of agency (that is, our belief that our decisions are often part of the true causal explanation of our actions) is very deeply held. If we are to give it up, then there had better be some powerful arguments for dualism to force us to do so. But in fact, as has emerged from Chapters 2 and 4, there are none. The only remaining picture of the relation between mind and brain,

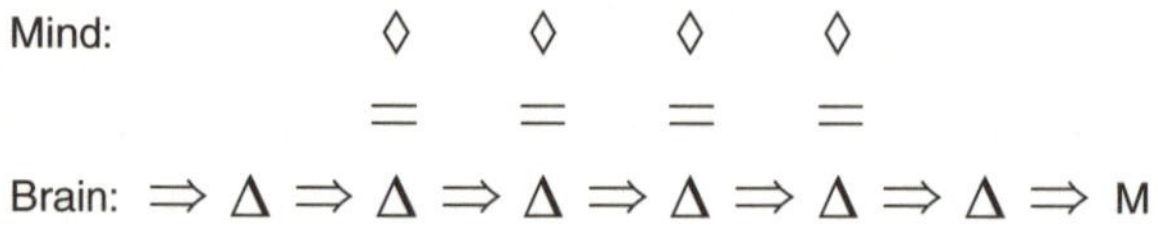

Mind: ◊   ◊   ◊   ◊

              =   =   =   =

Brain: ⇒ Δ ⇒ Δ ⇒ Δ ⇒ Δ ⇒ Δ ⇒ Δ ⇒ M

Figure 5.6 Mind–brain identity.

then, is one of *identity*, as represented in Figure 5.6. On this account, decisions are part of the true causal explanations of actions, because they are none other than (they are strictly identical to) the brain events which cause those actions.

The main argument for the thesis of mind–brain identity, then, can be represented as follows:

(1)   Our bodily movements are caused by brain-events.
(2)   Each event in the brain has a sufficient physical cause.
(3)   Our decisions are sometimes necessary conditions for some of our movements.
(4)   Our decisions sometimes form part of the true causal explanation of some of our movements.
(C)   So decisions *are* brain-events.

Premises (1) and (2) are intended to rule out classic interactive dualism; premise (3) rejects causal over-determination; and premise (4) rules out epiphenomenalism – thus leaving physicalism as the only remaining possibility.

Premise (1) seems undeniable in the light of modern scientific knowledge. Premise (2), also, seems sufficiently well-supported, given what is known about causal processes in the brain. Premises (3) and (4) form an important part of our common-sense view of ourselves and the world. We believe that mental processes can make a difference to the world. Then the only way in which we can hold on to this belief, together with the other premises, is to endorse the conclusion – which is the identity-thesis (or at least a limited version of it; see below). The argument as a whole seems rationally convincing in the absence of evidence to the contrary.

Here, as previously, it should be easy to extend the argument to justify the physical nature of *all* mental states, and not just decisions. This is because any mental state can play a part in causing a decision. I sometimes take a decision because of what I see, or what I feel, or what I want, or what I think. In which case these states, too, will form part of the true causal explanation of my action, and the same argument will lead to the conclusion that they, too, are physical.

Given its validity and the strength of its premises, the argument above could reasonably be taken as a proof of the identity-thesis, were it not for the myriad objections which can be raised against that thesis. (Some of these have already been presented in Chapter 1:3, in the guise of arguments for the truth of weak dualism.) In sections 3 and 4 below we shall consider a number of them, many of which involve apparent breaches of Leibniz's Law (identical things share identical properties). Despite the strength of the argument in its support, the identity-thesis will only be rationally acceptable if we can reply adequately to each (or at least to most) of the objections. (The qualification here is required because it can often be rational to hold onto a theory in the face of some difficulties or "anomalous data". Scientists do this all the time.)

2 Ramifications: types, tokens and other minds

In this section we will first clarify the thesis of mind–brain identity, distinguishing between two different versions of it, and relating it to different varieties of reductionism in general. We will then briefly explore to what extent the truth of that thesis enables us to make progress with the problem of other minds, left over from Chapter 1.

2.1 Type versus token identity

There is an important distinction to be drawn between *type*-identity and *token*-identity. The thesis of mind–brain *type*-identity holds that each general type of mental state – for instance, sensations of red, or pains in general – is identical with some general type of brain-state. So whenever a pain is felt it will be identical with a particular instance of some general type of brain-state, the same type of brain-state in each case. The thesis of mind–brain *token*-identity is much weaker. It holds only that each particular instance of pain is identical with some particular brain-state, those brain-states perhaps belonging to distinct kinds. It holds that each particular occurrence of a mental state will be identical with some particular occurrence of a brain-state, but that there may be no general identities between types of mental state and types of brain-state. Note that the arguments for the identity-thesis which we sketched above are indifferent between these two versions of it.

159

There is some reason to think that the thesis of mind–brain token-identity is the better theory. One argument would be this. We know that there is a considerable degree of plasticity in the human brain. For instance, although speech is normally controlled from a particular region in the left hemisphere, someone who has had that region damaged (especially when young) can sometimes recover their ability to speak, with practice. So a particular decision to speak may sometimes be identical with an event in one part of the brain, while sometimes it may be identical with an event in quite a different part. Now it doesn't immediately follow from this that the brain events are of different types: this will depend upon what counts as a "type" of brain-event. But there seems at least no particular reason to *assume* that the events will all be of the same type.

The case can be made even stronger if we recall that many creatures besides human beings can possess mental states. If not only mammals, birds and reptiles, but perhaps also non-biological systems such as robot–computers can possess mental states, then it is obviously false that there will always be the same one type of physical state in existence whenever there exists an instance of a given type of mental state. For the physical control-structures of these creatures will be very different from one another, and from the structure of the human brain. (One aspect of this topic – namely the question of "artificial intelligence" – will be pursued a bit further in Chapter 8.)

Supposing that the thesis of token-identity is the correct theory of mind–brain identity, then there must surely be something more to be said, at the physical level, about what is common to all the different kinds of physical event which are (are identical with) pains. Consider the following analogy. The true theory of clouds is very likely a version of token-identity thesis. For clouds can be made up out of many other kinds of droplet besides water droplets. Thus rain clouds, dust clouds, smoke clouds and clouds of industrial smog are all clouds. Yet there must surely be something common to all these different sorts of collections of particles which explains how they are all *clouds*. Indeed there is: what is in common is a *functional* property of the collections in question, having to do with their weight relative to the surrounding atmosphere, and the way in which they reflect light to give the characteristic appearance of a cloud. So the true theory of clouds is a version of token-identity thesis, coupled with an account of the function, or causal role, of the different physical tokens.

Similarly, then, for mental states: the best sort of theory of mental states may be a token-identity thesis, coupled with an account of the causal-roles of the different types of mental state which brings out what all the different tokens have in common. In Chapter 7 we will explore just this combination of views, when we come to consider various versions of *functionalism*. All accounts of this sort hold that mental states are to be individuated – or distinguished from one another – in virtue of their distinctive causal-roles or functions.

2.2 Reduction versus reductive explanation

Does the thesis of mind–brain identity commit us to *reducing* the mind to the brain? Are we required to say that the human mind is *nothing but* the activity of neurons and groups of neurons? The answer to these questions is negative, in fact. For a distinction closely related to the one just drawn between type and token identity, is the distinction between *reduction* (of properties), on the one hand, and reductive *explanation* (of tokens), on the other. We need only be committed to the latter. Let me explain.

Most philosophers and scientists today are physicalists. They believe that all things, events and processes in the natural world are, at bottom, physical things, events and processes. But few are *type-physicalists*, in the sense explained in section 2.1 above. Few believe that higher-level properties in chemistry, biology and psychology, for example, will line up type-for-type with properties in fundamental physics. On the contrary, most believe that the special sciences (chemistry, biology and the rest) are, in a sense, *autonomous* – dealing with laws and properties which cannot be reduced directly to those of physics (or indeed to any other science).

Admittedly, there have been *some* successful type-reductions of scientific laws and properties. A good example to consider is the reduction of the gas temperature–pressure laws to statistical mechanics. Boyle's gas law states this:

$$PV = kT \text{ (pressure} \times \text{volume} = \text{a constant} \times \text{temperature)}$$

So if the volume, V, of a gas is kept unchanged, an increase in temperature, T, will cause a corresponding increase in pressure, P. This law can in fact be derived from statistical mechanics on the assumption that gases are made up of particles in motion, together with the

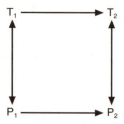

Figure 5.7 Classical reduction.

"bridge principles" that pressure is force per unit area, and that temperature is mean molecular momentum. For as the average momentum of the molecules (the temperature) is increased, so the force per unit area exerted on the surface of the container (the pressure) will also increase, if that surface area remains constant (as it must do if the volume remains unchanged).

The general form of such inter-theoretic reductions can be represented schematically, as in Figure 5.7. Here the top line represents a law of the reduced theory, involving the reduced theoretical terms T_1 and T_2, and the bottom line is to be derivable from the laws of the reducing theory, with predicates P_1 and P_2 drawn from some lower-level physical science. The bridge principles:

$$(T_1 \leftrightarrow P_1 \text{ and } T_2 \leftrightarrow P_2)$$

are then generally thought to license identities between the properties of the reduced and reducing theory.

There exist very few successful inter-theoretic reductions, in fact. The reason lies with the phenomenon of *multiple realizability*. It appears to be quite common for laws in the special sciences (chemistry, biology, neurology, psychology, and so on) to be multiply-realized in lower-level mechanisms. If there are a variety of different physical mechanisms, involving a variety of different physical properties P_i, any one of which is sufficient to realize a property in the special-science law $T_1 \rightarrow T_2$, then it will not be possible to *identify* the special-science property T_1 with any single physical property. This sort of situation is especially likely to arise in the case of biology and psychology, where we know that evolution can come up with a number of different mechanisms to perform the same function. (An example would be the wings of bats, birds and insects, all of which subserve flight, but all of which are structurally very different.) In which case we shouldn't expect to be able to find reductive accounts of psychological properties, including perhaps the properties involved in intentionality or mental representation, on the one hand, nor those involved in consciousness, on the other (these issues will be discussed at some length in Chapter 8).

What we *do* regularly find in science, however, is *reductive explanation*. A given higher-level process – in biology, say – is reductively explained when we can show that suitable lower-level event-sequences, happening in accordance with lower-level laws, are sufficient to *realize*, or *constitute*, the higher-level process in question. To put the same point rather differently: a successful reductive explanation shows how a particular instantiation (or type of instantiation) of a higher-level property is constituted by some lower-level property or process. But it does so without reducing the higher-level property as such, since there may be no lower-level process-type which is *always* instantiated whenever the higher-level property is instantiated.

Most physicalists believe in the unity of science, in the sense that they expect all higher-level properties and processes to be reductively explicable in principle. (Such physicalists thus think of the world as ordered into *layers* linked by *realization* relations, somewhat as depicted in Figure 5.8.) They think that it must be possible, in the end, to show how any higher-level property or process (of biology, psychology, or whatever) is realized in – or constituted by – some lower-level property or process (and ultimately by processes in fundamental physics). It must be possible to take a particular occurrence of a higher-level property and show how, on at least that occasion, it was constituted by some lower-level physical property or process. But physicalists don't have to say that biology is *nothing but* chemistry, or that chemistry is *nothing but* quantum mechanics.

It is thus possible to be a physicalist about the mind, while at the same time believing in the reality and irreducibility of mental properties, in exactly the sense that it is possible to be a physicalist about wings while at the same time believing in the irreducibility of the property *being a wing*. While in one sense the mind is *nothing but* the operation of the brain, for a physicalist – since each token mental state will be none other than some token brain-state – it may still be the case that if we want to understand the operations of minds in general, we shall unavoidably have to couch our explanations in

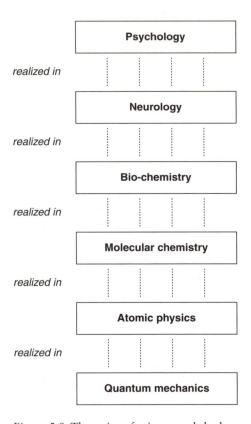

Figure 5.8 The unity of science and the layered world.

terms of mental properties; just as if we want to understand the operations of wings in general, we cannot appeal to the specific physical structures of specific wings.

2.3 *Mind–brain identity and the problem of other minds*

Can the thesis of mind–brain identity, if true, provide us with a solution to the problem of other minds? Recall from Chapter 1:2 that an argument from analogy to the existence of other minds was obstructed by the claimed uniqueness of my own states of consciousness. But if the identity-thesis is true, then my experiences aren't especially unique, after all. For then they are, in fact, physical states of the brain, and other people, too, presumably enjoy such states. So an argument from analogy could go through after all, as follows:

(1) I know of the existence of conscious mental states from my own case.
(2) All of my mental states are in fact brain-states.
(3) Other human beings possess brain-states similar to mine.
(C) So other human beings possess mental states similar to mine.

Of course this argument is not strictly valid, since it purports to be a species of inductive argument. But it does appear to be rationally convincing. Moreover premises (1) and (3) are pretty obviously true, while premise (2) merely states the identity-thesis. So if we could know that thesis to be true, the argument as a whole would carry conviction.

If the identity-thesis is true, then there is no longer any problem about knowing that other experiences exist: I can know this to be true on the basis of an argument from analogy. But can I know the particular experiences which people possess on particular occasions? If I see someone injured and groaning, I can know that they possess *some* conscious experience. But can I know that they are aware of the sensation with the distinctive qualitative feel which I describe, in my own case, as "pain"? Indeed, is the argument from analogy sufficiently strong to rule out the following sort of possibility: the conscious state which in their case is caused by injury and causes groaning has the qualitative feel which, were I to be aware of it, I should describe as a tickle? (Compare the case of *inverted color experience* which we used in outlining the problem of other minds in Chapter 1:1; see Figure 1.1.)

Recall the example of the black boxes found on the seashore, which we used in Chapter 1:2. Since the boxes all perform the same functions, we are entitled to conclude that they all contain states occupying the same causal roles, namely mediating between a specified input (e.g., a red button being pressed) and a specified output (e.g., a red light flashing). But the states occupying those causal roles may have only that in common: their causal role. In other respects they can be as different as you please.

Similarly, then, in the case of human beings: when I observe an injured person exhibit pain-behavior, I am entitled to conclude that there is some state in them occupying the same causal role occupied, in my own case, by the sensation of pain. In virtue of the likely truth of the mind–brain identity thesis, I am also entitled to conclude that the state occupying that causal role is very likely a mental as well as a physical one. But it seems left open that it might be

165

quite different in other respects (in particular, in respect of its qualitative feel) from the state which I call "pain".

But what of considerations of simplicity? Isn't it a great deal simpler to suppose that the same causal roles are occupied by the same feelings in all of us? Aren't simpler theories in general more reasonable? But in fact the difference in the degree of simplicity here is only marginal. For what really does the work, in our explanations of the behavior of ourselves and others, is the supposition that we all possess states which occupy distinctive causal roles. What explains how you can respond appropriately to the command, "Bring me a red flower", is the fact that you have learned to discriminate objects on the basis of some-experience-or-other, and to associate with that experience the term "red". Any hypothesis about the particular distinctive feel of your experience seems redundant to the explanation: I don't in fact need to employ any such hypothesis.

There seems no reason, at this stage, why it should be thought more likely that human beings all have the same feelings occupying the same causal roles, even given the truth of physicalism. For we already know that people differ from one another in all sorts of subtle ways. It is rather as if we had found a set of black boxes which not only share many of their features, but which are each of them, in many ways, unique. None of them look quite alike or has the same physical dimensions, and their responses to any given stimulus (e.g., the pressing of a red button) will often differ quite markedly from one another. Now in cases where we could be confident that all of the boxes had states occupying the same causal roles, could we also be reasonably confident that those states would be similar in other respects? Surely not. In the light of the many differences existing between the boxes, it seems just as likely that the physical mechanisms underlying any given causal role will be subtly different in each case. Equally, then, in the case of human beings: since we already know that they differ from one another in many ways, there is no particular reason to think that they will all have exactly similar brain-states (= feelings) occupying similar causal roles.

All of this is supposing that we only know of the *general* truth of the mind–brain identity-thesis. The situation would surely be different if we also knew some particular identities. If I knew that pains in myself were always identical with a particular type of brain-state, and then discovered that the states which occupy the same causal role in you are also of that type, then I would have to conclude that you, too, feel pain in those circumstances. There can, for the physicalist, be no differences at the level of mentality which don't reflect differences at the level of the brain. Unfortunately, however, we lack any knowledge of the required identities at this stage.

I conclude that the identity-thesis can only provide us with the general knowledge that other people possess mental states of some sort, occupying similar causal roles to our own. While this is an advance, it is not fully satisfying. For our common-sense view is that we can often know what other people are feeling on particular occasions. At this stage, however, the Cartesian conception of the meaning of mental state terms (outlined and defended in Chapter 1:4) remains unchallenged. Neither have we enquired whether it is possible to seek a scientific understanding of the nature of conscious feelings. These tasks will be taken up in Chapters 7 and 8 respectively.

3 Difficulties for mind–brain identity

In section 1 we presented an argument in support of the identity-thesis which would have been convincing if considered purely on its own terms. Over the next two sections we will consider all of the main objections which have been raised against that thesis, beginning with some of the less serious ones. They will get more serious as we go along.

3.1 Certainty

Our first objection derives from Descartes, who deployed a similar argument in support of strong dualism. It runs as follows:

(1) I may be completely certain of my own experiences, when I have them.
(2) I cannot have the same degree of certainty about the existence of any physical state, including my own brain-states.
(C) So (by Leibniz's Law) my conscious experiences aren't in fact identical to brain-states.

Although both the premises in this argument are true, the argument itself commits a fallacy, and is invalid. For as we noted in Chapter 3:1, Leibniz's Law only operates in contexts which aren't *intentional*.

It is obvious that the context created by the phrase "X is certain that
..." is an intentional one.

For example, the police may be certain that Mr Hyde is the
murderer, while they have no inkling that Dr Jekyll is the murderer, despite the fact that Jekyll and Hyde are one and the same
man. Oedipus may be certain that Jocasta loves him without
believing that his mother loves him, despite the fact that Jocasta is
his mother. So from the fact that I have complete certainty about
my own conscious states without having certainty about my own
brain-states, it doesn't follow that my conscious states aren't
brain-states. For just as one and the same woman may be presented to Oedipus in two different guises – as Jocasta, and as his
mother – so perhaps one and the same brain-state may be presented to me under two different aspects: in a third-person way (*as
a brain-state*), and via the qualitative feel of what it is like to be *in*
that state.

3.2 *Privacy*

This second argument is a variation on the first. It runs as follows:

(1) Conscious states are private to the person who has them.
(2) Brain-states aren't private: like any other kind of physical
     state, they form part of the public realm.
(C) So (by Leibniz's Law) conscious states aren't in fact identical
     to brain-states.

The term "private", here, is ambiguous, however: something can be
private in respect of *knowledge* (only I can know of it), or it can be
private in respect of *ownership* (only I can possess it). Taken in the
first way, the argument is the same as that in section 3.1 above, and
commits the same fallacy. But taken in the second way, premise (2)
is false.

It is true that only I can "own" my conscious states: no one else
can feel my pain, or think my thought. But it is equally true in this
sense that only I can own my brain-states. For other people can't
possess my brain-state either. Any brain-state which they have will
be, necessarily, their own brain-state, not mine. Conscious states are
certainly not unique in respect of privacy of ownership. The same is
true of blushes and sneezes as well as brain-states: no one else can
blush my blush or sneeze my sneeze. Indeed it seems that in general

the identity-conditions for states and events are tied to the identities of the subjects who possess them.

3.3 Value

A thought can be wicked. A desire can be admirable. But no brain-state can be either wicked or admirable. We may therefore argue as follows:

(1) Mental states are subject to *norms*: they can be good or bad, wicked or morally admirable.
(2) No purely physical states are subject to norms: no brain-state can be either wicked or morally admirable.
(C) So (by Leibniz's Law) mental states aren't identical to brain-states.

We might immediately be inclined to quarrel with premise (2). For can a particular stabbing not be wicked? What is a stabbing if not a physical event? But it may be replied that it is not the stabbing itself – considered merely as a physical event – which is wicked, but rather the intention behind it. In general, physical states and events are only subject to moral norms if they are intended (or at least foreseen). This is because norms imply *control* – or as it is some-times said, "Ought implies can".

This reply is sufficient to save the truth of premise (2), but at the cost of revealing the same fallacy in the argument as was involved in the argument from certainty. For if it is only things which are intended (or foreseen) which can be wicked, then the context created by "... is wicked" will be an intentional one. For example, if the fact that it is wicked of Mary to have a particular desire implies that she either intentionally adopted that desire, or at least foresaw that she would continue to possess it if she took no steps to eradicate it, then it is no objection to the identity-thesis that it is, on the other hand, not wicked of her to be in such-and-such a brain-state. For you can foresee e (that you will marry Jocasta) without foreseeing f (that you will marry your mother), even though e is identical to f. Certainly Mary neither intended nor foresaw that she should be in that particular brain-state.

3.4   Color

An after-image can be green. A pain can be sharp and piercing. But it is hardly likely that any brain-state will be either green or sharp and piercing. There will then be many arguments which take the following sort of form:

(1)   I am experiencing a fading green after-image.
(2)   No brain-states are green.
(C)   So (by Leibniz's Law) my after-image isn't identical to any brain-state.

One mistake in this argument is that it treats my after-image as though it were a particular individual thing, having greenness as a property. Now, it is true that the sentence, "I experience a green after-image" has the same grammatical form as the sentence, "I pick up a green book", which creates the impression that greenness is a property of the after-image in just the same way that it is a property of the book. But this impression is misleading. For the book in question might have had some other color, while remaining the numerically-same book. But can we make any sense of the idea that the very same after-image which I now have might have been red?

What is true, of course, is that I might now have been experiencing a red after-image rather than a green one. But can we make sense of the idea that it might have been this very same after-image (which happens to be green) which would then have been red? I suggest not. Rather, the greenness is essential to the identity of that particular after-image. This is because it is a mistake to treat the fading after-image as if it were a kind of object or individual thing. It is rather an event, or happening. The greenness is in fact *part* of the event of experiencing-a-fading-green-after-image, as opposed to being a property *of* it.

This reply on its own isn't sufficient to rebut the argument. For it seems certain that greenness is *not* a part of the event of undergoing-such-and-such-a-change-in-brain-state. So how can that event be identical with the event of experiencing-a-fading-green-after-image, if greenness really is part of the latter event? Must not identical events have identical parts? For example, if the battle of Waterloo is (is identical with) the battle which lost Napoleon the war, then if a particular cavalry charge is part of the battle of

Waterloo, it must also be part of the battle which lost Napoleon the war. For they are the very same battle (the very same event).

The second mistake in the argument is to think that an experience can be green – or that a mental event can have greenness as one of its parts – in anything like the same sense that a physical object can be green, or that a physical event can have greenness as one of its parts. Experiences aren't literally green in the way that grass is literally green. Rather, the "greenness" of my green after-image consists in my having an experience which is *like* the experience of *seeing* a green patch (and it is the patch which is green, not the experience). Then if having a green after-image is like seeing a green patch, and if the possession of that after-image is identical with some brain-state, it will indeed follow that the brain-state, too, is like the state one is in when one sees a green patch. But there is no difficulty about this. For the latter state will also be identical to some brain-state. It also seems entirely plausible that there should be some resemblance between the two brain-states.

The point can be put like this: green after-images are experiences *of* green, rather than things (or events) which *are* (or which contain) green. A green after-image is, as it were, an event of being-under-the-impression-that-one-is-seeing-a-green-patch. If this is so, then the after-image can be identical with a brain-state without breaching Leibniz's Law, so long as the brain-state, too, can in this sense be "of" green. If green after-images *represent* green, rather than literally *being* green, then there will be no difficulty here so long as it is possible for brain-states to represent things. This question will be pursued briefly in section 3.8 below, and then again at greater length in Chapter 8.

3.5 Felt quality

This objection arises out of the last one. Even if after-images aren't literally colored, still they do literally have phenomenal (felt) characteristics, which we describe by means of the color-terms ("sensation of red", "experience of green", etc.). There is the qualitative "feel" which is common to the experiences of having a green after-image and seeing green grass, for example. But can any brain-state have a distinctive feel? For example, think of a particular brain event – say one group of brain cells firing off impulses to another group – and ask yourself, "What is the distinctive feel of this event?" It is hard even to get a grip on the question. How can

171

any brain-event *feel like* a sensation of red, for example? Surely only another sensation can, in the required sense, have the *feel* a sensation of red.

The argument sketched above may be summarized as follows:

(1) All experiences have distinctive felt qualities.
(2) Brain-states don't have distinctive felt qualities.
(C) So (by Leibniz's Law) experiences aren't in fact identical with brain-states.

The problem, here, is to know that premise (2) is true. For if the thesis of mind–brain identity is correct, the felt quality of an experience *is* some brain-state or property of a brain-state. The difficulty we have in seeing that this is so may relate entirely to the different perspectives which we take on this one-and-the-same state. We can think about that state in a third-person way, in terms of spatial extent, electrical potentials, chemical reactions and so on; or we can think of that state in a first-person way, in terms of the way that it feels to a subject who is *in* that state.

There is nothing here, as yet, to convince us that the felt properties of experiences aren't properties of the brain. Yet it is one thing, of course, to accept that these two sorts of properties may really be identical (or, in the light of the arguments of section 1 above, to accept that they *are* identical), and it is quite another thing to understand *how* this can be so. Our task at this point is just to show that there isn't any good reason *not* to accept the arguments of section 1, and so no good reason *not* to believe in physicalism. In Chapter 8 we will return to consider whether it is possible to give some satisfying *explanation* of how felt qualities can be physically constituted.

3.6 The explanatory gap

This objection again arises quite naturally out of the last one. For some have claimed that there is an unbridgeable explanatory gap between all physical facts, on the one hand, and the facts of felt consciousness, on the other. (This idea was first developed by the American philosopher Joseph Levine.) No matter how detailed a story I am given about the operations of the brain, I shall always remain capable of thinking, "Surely all *that* might be true while *this* sort of feeling was different or absent". (It is this thought which suggests the possibility of zombies, indeed.) Some have claimed that the truth of physicalism *requires* that conscious states should be reductively explicable in physical terms. They can then argue as follows:

(1) If the thesis of mind–brain identity were true, then it would have to be possible to *explain* the felt qualities of our experiences in physical terms.
(2) No such explanation is possible: there is an explanatory gap between physical facts and feeling facts.
(C) So the thesis of mind–brain identity isn't true.

This argument is valid. But we can explain why reductive explanation of felt qualities is impossible, however (at least when those qualities are conceptualized in a certain way), consistent with the truth of mind–brain identity – in effect, denying premise (1). We just have to recall that we may possess some *purely recognitional* concepts of experience, as was argued when we were defending the Cartesian conception of the meaning of mental state terms in Chapter 1:4. For if so, then no story about physical events and causal roles will be capable of engaging with these concepts, leading us to think, "Ah, in those circumstances *this* state would have to be present". On the contrary, nothing will be capable of evoking an application of one of these concepts except the actual presentation of the appropriate sort of felt quality. But for all that, the quality recognized may actually be a physical one, just as the thesis of mind–brain identity affirms.

We will return to consider the challenge of providing a reductive explanation of the felt qualities of consciousness in Chapter 8. For the moment, we can note that although the explanatory gap might show something distinctive about our *concepts* for felt qualities of various types (namely, that they are purely recognitional concepts, lacking conceptual connections with concepts of other sorts), the existence of such a gap shows nothing about the non-physical status of the felt qualities themselves.

3.7 Complete knowledge

Someone could know all physical and functional facts about the brain without knowing what the different experiences feel like. In order to see this, consider the example of color-deprived Mary, first introduced into the now-extensive literature by the Australian philosopher Frank Jackson.

We are to imagine the case of Mary, who has lived all her life in a black-and-white room. At the point where we take up the story, Mary has never had any experience of color; but, we may suppose, there is nothing wrong with her visual system – she still has the *capacity* for color vision. Now, Mary is also a scientist, living in an era much more scientifically advanced than ours. So Mary may be supposed to know *all there is to know* about the physics, physiology, and functional organization of color vision. She knows exactly what takes place in someone's brain when they experience red, for example, and has full understanding of the behavior of the physical systems involved. So she knows all the objective, scientific, facts about color vision. But there is one thing she *doesn't* know, surely, and that is what an experience of red *is like*. On being released from her black-and-white room there is something new she will *learn* when she experiences red for the first time. Since knowledge of all the physical and functional facts doesn't give Mary knowledge of *all* the facts, Jackson argues, then there are some facts – namely, facts about subjective experiences and feelings – which aren't physical or functional facts, and which cannot be explicable in terms of physical or functional facts, either.

The thought is: if there is information about feelings which could not be conveyed by any amount of information about the brain, then feelings cannot themselves be brain-states. The argument is as follows:

(1) Even complete knowledge of physical states wouldn't give someone the knowledge of what an experience *feels like*.

(2) But if experiences *were* physical states, then complete knowledge of the physical states *would* imply complete knowledge of experiences, including knowing what they *feel like*.

(C) So experiences aren't physical states.

Although this argument, like the argument from certainty in section 3.1, involves an intentional term (the context created by the phrase "X knows that . . ." is an intentional one) it doesn't seem to commit the same fallacy. This is because the premises speak of *complete* knowledge, knowledge from all points of view. Oedipus certainly couldn't have complete knowledge of Jocasta without knowing that she is his mother. (So if he does know everything about her, but doesn't know that she is his mother, then she *isn't* his mother.)

All the same, the argument is fallacious. In the sense of "complete knowledge" in which premise (1) can plausibly be thought to be true, premise (2) is false. (Conversely, in the sense of "complete knowledge" required for premise (2) to be true, premise (1) is false.) In order to see this, notice that there are two ways of counting items of knowledge – either in terms of the worldly facts known about, or in terms of the beliefs or sentences which represent those facts. If Oedipus knows that Jocasta is beautiful and knows that his mother is beautiful, then we can *either* say that there is just one item of knowledge involved (the knowledge, namely, of the beauty of a particular woman), *or* we can say that there are two items of knowledge involved (one for each of his distinct beliefs).

Notice, now, that for premise (1) to be plausible, items of knowledge have to be counted in the first of these ways. For if items of knowledge were counted in terms the distinct ways of thinking of a subject-matter, then it would be *impossible* to have complete knowledge of *anything*! For any one fact can always be represented in *infinitely* many distinct ways. For example, the fact that a particular brain-cell fires can be represented by the sentence, "The brain-cell exactly 1.11111 millimeters below this point in the skull is firing", or by the sentence, "The brain-cell exactly such-and-such a distance below this point on the ceiling is firing", or by the sentence, "The brain-cell exactly such-and-such a distance from this point in the roof is firing", and so on, and so on.

Having "complete knowledge" of one's brain-states surely couldn't require one to know all facts about the brain under all possible modes of presentation, or all ways of thinking of those facts. (If it did, then premise (1) would just beg the question against the identity-theorist. For among all these ways of thinking of a brain-state, according to the physicalist, will be the way of thinking given in terms of what it feels like to be in that state.)

But now, if "complete knowledge" is read as meaning "knowing all facts in terms of *some* (not all) ways of thinking of them", then premise (2) is false. From the claim that someone knows all of a certain range of facts represented in *some* way, it doesn't follow that they know those same facts represented in *all* ways. If the identity-thesis is correct, then among these other ways of thinking will be first-person ways of thinking, grounded in the way experiences (= brain-states) feel to subjects who have them.

So we can allow that there are some things that color-deprived Mary won't know about color vision, even if she knows all facts about the brain. For there are some concepts which you can only have if you have undergone certain kinds of experience – namely, recognitional concepts of the *feels* of those experiences. So there are some thoughts which will be unavailable for Mary to think – namely, thoughts employing those recognitional concepts. Then there will be some thoughts which Mary can't know to be true, either. But if the identity-thesis is correct, then some of these thoughts will be *about* facts which Mary *does* know to be true. What Mary would gain, if she could acquire color vision, would be some new concepts and ways of thinking of the very same brain-events which she would already have had scientific knowledge of.

3.8 *Intentionality*

Recall from Chapter 1:3 the claim that mental states are unique in being *intentional* (i.e., representational). Our argument was as follows:

(1)   Some mental states are intentional, or representational, states.
(2)   No merely physical state (e.g., of the brain) can be intentional in its own right.
(C)   So (by Leibniz's Law) some mental states aren't identical with brain-states.

This argument is valid, and premise (1) is obviously true. So everything turns on the acceptability of premise (2).

There is a general philosophical problem about representation. Much of the philosophy of mind over the last twenty years has been concerned with the question: how is it possible for anything to represent – or be about – anything else? It is by no means easy to *understand* how an arrangement of cellular connections could represent anything. This is a topic we will return to in Chapter 8. Here we will do just enough to show that there need be no convincing reason to believe that premise (2) is true.

Perhaps the claim that physical states can be representations-in-their-own-right cannot be made *entirely* convincing in the absence of a solution to the general problem of representation. But we can at least get an inkling of how intentionality can be embodied in a physical system in advance of a solution to that problem. For by looking at systems which are, manifestly, purely physical – namely, computers and computer-controlled machines – we can begin to see how they can display some of the distinctive features of intentionality. If we can see the beginnings of intentionality embodied in a physical system such as a computer, then there is no reason in principle why full-blown intentionality (beliefs, desires and the rest) shouldn't be embodied in the biological computer which is the human brain.

One distinctive feature of intentional states is that they represent things in one way rather than another. For a crude analogue of this, imagine a computer linked to a video-camera and mechanical arm. The computer is programmed to scan the input from the camera, and to grab with its arm any yellow object. In order for the grabbing-operation to be successful it must also be able to interpret from the input the shapes, sizes and spatial positions of those objects. But the computer doesn't select objects on the basis of their shape or size, but only on the basis of their color.

Now suppose that the only yellow objects which are ever presented to the machine are in fact lemons, its purpose being to select lemons from a passing array of fruit. Of course lemons do also have a characteristic shape, but the computer is indifferent with respect to shape. It initiates a grabbing motion only in response to the yellow color. Then there is almost a sense in which the machine might be said to desire the yellow objects which it grabs, but not the lemon-shaped objects, even though the yellow objects are all lemon-shaped.

I don't want to say that such a machine would literally have a desire for yellow objects, of course. Although quite what is missing here, which would be present in the case of a genuine desire, is not easy to see. Perhaps (as we suggested in Chapter 2:4) we can only make sense of something having a particular desire against a wider background, a network of other desires and beliefs. Or perhaps only a being which is alive, which has needs (and which may consequently be said to have "a good") can have desires. Some of these possibilities will be explored in Chapter 8. The important point for our purposes here is that we have found an analogue for the intentionality of desire in the concept of "differential response". Just as Oedipus will respond differently to one and the same woman presented to him now as Jocasta, now as his mother; so the machine will respond differently to one and the same bit of fruit presented to it now as a yellow thing (its shape being obscured), now as a lemon-shaped thing (its color being obscured).

The other distinctive feature of intentional states, is that they can be directed at non-existent objects. It is apt to seem unintelligible how any physical system could do this. Here again my strategy is to construct, by way of reply, a crude physical analogue for this aspect of the intentionality of the mind. Thus consider the sort of behavior which might be displayed by a Cruise missile. It is programmed to take photographs of the terrain beneath it at various points along its route, to scan those photographs for landmarks in order to check its position, and adjust its direction accordingly. Now suppose that as a result of an error, it is programmed to find a distinctively-shaped lake at a particular point on its route, but that no such lake exists. As a result, the missile circles round and around the area, until finally it runs out of fuel and crashes. Here we might almost say, "The missile was searching for a lake which didn't exist."

Note that the intentionality displayed in the Cruise missile's "desire" isn't merely derivative from the thoughts and intentions of the computer-programmer. True enough, that "desire" was caused to exist by the programmer. But its intentionality – its directedness on a non-existent object – is actually displayed in the behavior of the missile itself. For it has entered a cycle of behavior which we know will only be terminated if it succeeds in photographing a lake with a particular distinctive shape; but we also know that no such lake exists.

I tentatively conclude that there is no reason in principle why a merely physical system shouldn't display the various features characteristic of intentional states. So we have been given no reason for supposing that beliefs and desires aren't themselves physical (brain) states. The point is, arguing that intentional states *can't* be physical states is one thing (and that argument can be seen to fail); achieving a detailed *understanding* of *how* intentional states can be physical ones is quite another (and that is something I don't pretend to have provided, either here or in Chapter 8).

3.9 Free will

Many people believe that humans have free will, in the sense that they can make decisions which aren't determined by prior causes. But it looks certain, in contrast, that each brain-event will be determined by prior causes. We may therefore argue thus:

(1) The decisions people make can be free, not determined by prior causes.
(2) All brain-events are determined by prior causes in the brain or central nervous system.

(C)   So decisions (or at least the free ones) aren't identical with brain-events.

This argument is valid. The real question is whether the two premises can be adequately supported. This is a large topic, which we must set aside for the moment. We will return to it at some length in Chapter 8. (Remember that we don't necessarily have to be able to reply to *every* objection to the identity-thesis in order for the latter to be rationally acceptable. Some of these objections can be left as *anomalies* which we don't presently know how to solve.)

3.10   *Spatial position*

Recall from Chapter 1:3 the following argument:

(1)   All brain-states must occupy some particular position in space.
(2)   It is nonsense (meaningless or self-contradictory) to attribute any particular spatial position to a mental state.
(C)   So (by Leibniz's Law) conscious states can't be identical with brain-states.

This argument is valid. Premise (1) is obviously true. So everything depends upon the truth of premise (2). I shall not waste time quibbling that some mental states (e.g., pains) are apparently attributed spatial positions. For the identity-thesis extends to all mental states without exception. In any case it is unlikely that some mental states are identical with brain-states while some are not. I shall focus on the hardest case for the identity-theorist; namely, thoughts.

Identity-theorists might be tempted to respond to the above argument by conceding that our ordinary concept of thought makes attributions of spatial position to them nonsensical, but by rejecting that ordinary conception as mistaken. They may insist that every thought (properly conceived of) does in fact have a place, namely the place of its identical brain-state. But for them to take this line might be a mistake. For then the thesis of mind–brain identity would no longer represent a empirical discovery, but would be something which we have stipulated as true through a change of meaning.

We might be entitled to reply to the identity-theorist as follows, indeed. "If you mean the word 'thought' as we usually do, then your thesis is false; indeed necessarily false. But if, on the other hand, you wish to give the word a different meaning for your own

179

special purposes, then you are perfectly entitled to do so. But don't pretend that you have made a momentous discovery, or that you are saying anything which conflicts with what the weak dualist believes. All you have done is to give a new definition". (It is rather as if someone were to give new definitions of the words "red" and "green", in such a way that it then makes sense to ascribe those words to numbers; and were then to announce, as if they had discovered something terribly important, "Contrary to what has always been believed, every even number is red and every odd one green".)

A more promising strategy for the identity-theorist is to suggest that we have again been misled by the grammatical form of phrases like "my thought of my mother" into conceiving of a thought as if it were a special kind of individual thing or object. For obviously, if a thought were really a physical object like a grain of sand or a brain-cell, then it would have to occupy some precise position in space. So perhaps we need to be reminded that a thought is an action, and an action is a species of event (a "happening"). Then the general question becomes: what are the criteria for attributing spatial positions to events?

Often the place of an event can be pinned down no more precisely than the place of the subject of that event. In such cases requests for more precise specifications will seem nonsensical. Thus the place of the event of Mary-growing-older is wherever Mary is. And the question, "Is the event of Mary-growing-older taking place two inches behind her right eye?" seems just as nonsensical as the parallel question about the event of Mary-thinking-of-her-mother. Yet, for all that, the process of ageing is a purely physical one.

Now we only need to be reminded of these facts to realize that we do in fact attribute spatial positions to thoughts; namely: whenever we say where the *thinker* of that thought is. The fact that it sounds nonsensical to request more detailed specifications of the spatial positions of thoughts needn't show that thoughts themselves are non-physical. Thinking, like ageing, may be a physical process whose subject is the whole human being.

The position of an event isn't always simply the position of its subject, however. An event can also take place in *part* of its subject. Thus the position of Mary's-left-big-toe-turning-blue isn't simply wherever Mary is. It is, more precisely, wherever her left foot is. For if Mary is lying on a river-bank with her left foot in the cold water, then the event takes place in the water; whereas Mary herself is *not* (or is only partly) in the water.

It seems likely that the physical event which is, according to the identity-theorist, the event of Mary-thinking-of-her-mother, takes place in some particular region of her brain. So we still have a problem, if the closest we can get to the spatial position of Mary's thought is the spatial position of Mary. If the brain-event can be two inches behind her right eye, while it is incorrect to describe the thought of her mother as occurring two inches behind her right eye, then the thought and the brain-event cannot be identical.

The correct way for an identity-theorist to respond, is by denying that it is nonsensical to ascribe precise spatial positions to thoughts. The only real evidence which the weak dualist has for this claim, is that most of us would be left gaping, our minds completely blank, if asked whether or not Mary's thought is two inches behind her right eye. But this doesn't show that the question is literally meaningless, nor that it is self-contradictory. It only shows, first, that it is not the sort of question which itself points you in the direction in which you have to look for an answer. (Contrast: "Where is the dam cracking?" It is part of the ordinary notion of a crack, that in order to find them you have to search in specific locations.) Secondly, that we can have no idea where to look for an answer until we have acquired some further information.

Suppose you were asked, "In what specific region of her body is the event of Mary-catching-a-cold taking place?" This, too, would have a tendency to make your mind go blank, partly because it isn't part of the ordinary concept of a cold that in order to establish whether someone has a cold you have to search in specific locations within the body. But on reflection you may realize that what you are really being asked is: "In virtue of changes in what parts of Mary's body is it becoming true that she has a cold?" This is a question which you can understand, at least. But if you know nothing of viruses, or of medicine generally, you may not even know what *sorts* of things would be relevant to the discovery of the answer. Yet when you are told that colds are viruses, and that viruses enter the body at specific locations, then you *do* know what would constitute an answer. Note, moreover, that it would be hardly very plausible to say that the term "a cold" had changed its meaning for you when you acquired this information.

The question about the specific location of Mary's act of thinking about her mother is essentially similar. The first step in dispelling the puzzlement which it causes is to realize that what we are in fact being asked is: "In virtue of changes in what specific region of Mary is it becoming true that she is thinking of her mother?" The next step is to learn that each mental event is identical with some brain-event. Then we know that in order to answer the question, we should first need to discover *which* brain-event is identical with Mary's thought, and then discover *where* that brain-event is occurring. Yet we don't need to regard our acceptance of the identity-thesis as altering the meaning of the term "thought", any more than our acceptance that colds are viruses alters the meaning of the term "a cold". We may thus reasonably deny the claim made in premise (2) of the argument above.

4 The necessity of identity

In this section we shall deal with a particularly important difficulty for the thesis of mind–brain identity, which turns on the claim that a statement of identity, if true, is true necessarily: it is a truth about all possible worlds. For then if, as seems plausible, the thesis of mind–brain identity is merely contingent (i.e., *not* a truth about all possible worlds), it will follow that it is not true at all. This argument was first developed by the American philosopher Saul Kripke. It closely parallels the one we considered (and dismissed) in Chapters 2:1 and 3:4 in support of strong dualism.

4.1 The argument

Thus far in this chapter we have tacitly assumed that the thesis of mind–brain identity is not only empirically grounded but contingent. We have assumed that, although it may be true in the actual world, there are other possible worlds in which it is false. Now what is certainly the case is that it is not a *conceptual* truth: it is not true in virtue of the meanings of the terms involved. But as we saw in Chapter 3:4, some necessary truths aren't conceptual truths. Some truths are truths about all possible worlds without being true in virtue of meaning. For example, consider once again the identity between Jekyll and Hyde (supposing them to have been a real historical character). The truth of, "Jekyll is Hyde" is certainly not merely a matter of meaning; for the police had to discover it by empirical investigation. But it is, for all that, a necessary truth. Since it is in fact true that Jekyll is identical with Hyde, things could not have been otherwise. For if Jekyll is Hyde, then there is only one thing involved rather than two. It is not as if there were two logically distinct things, which happen to be related to one another in a particular way in the actual world (being identical with one another), but which could exist unrelated in some other possible world. Rather, there is only one thing, which must remain identical with itself in all possible worlds in which it occurs.

In general, where we have a true identity-statement which involves two names for the same thing, we cannot say, "This thing is identical with that thing in the actual world, but there are other possible worlds in which they aren't identical". For if the identity-statement is true, then there is really no "this" and "that". There aren't two things in question, but only one. Therefore, it is impossible to conceive of a world in which that thing isn't identical with itself.

Confining ourselves just to the case of pain, then, opponents of the mind–brain identity-thesis can now argue as follows:

(1) If each pain is identical with some brain-state, then the things which are, in this world, the pains, are identical with those brain-states in all possible worlds in which they exist. (*Necessity of identity.*)

(2) Each pain in this world is, in some other possible worlds in which it exists, *not* identical with any of those brain-states.

(C) So it isn't the case that each pain is identical with some brain-state, even in the actual world.

Since this argument is valid, and since premise (1) is true, the identity-thesis will have been refuted if we can establish premise (2).

Now premise (2) can in fact be made to seem extremely plausible. I can imagine a world in which the very same pain which I feel at the moment isn't identical with any brain-state. I can, for example, conceive of turning into a pillar of salt (like Lot's wife in the bible story) while the pain goes on; or I can imaging being transformed gradually into a partial humanoid robot, with hard-ware rather than wet-ware encased in the relevant portions of my skull, again while my pain exists unchanged; and so on. Alternatively, in connection with any particular candidate brain-state, I can imagine my current pain existing while *that* brain-state doesn't occur (even though some other one does). Then since this exercise can be repeated for all other candidate brain-states, and all other pains, we have apparently done enough to establish premise (2).

We have arrived at a powerful-looking argument against the identity-thesis. On the one hand it seems that the very same mental states which I now enjoy might continue to exist, or might have existed, in the absence of any of the relevant brain-activity. But on the other hand it seems that if these mental states are in fact brain-states, then they will have to remain brain-states (i.e., remaining identical with themselves) in all possible worlds in which they occur. It therefore seems that the identity-thesis must be false.

Notice that the argument here would work equally well if premise (2) were replaced with premise (2*), claiming that it is possible to have the relevant brain states without the presence of pain, thus:

(2*)   Each of the brain-states which is correlated with the presence of pain in this world, can occur in other possible worlds *without* the existence of any pain.

What this premise tells us, in effect, is that philosophical zombies are possible. Since it is possible for me to be physically just as I am without feeling any pain (a zombie), my pains cannot be identical with any physical states. For if they *were* identical, then (by the necessity of identity) they would have to exist whenever the relevant brain states exist, and zombies would be impossible.

4.2   Criticism of the argument

I shall now defend the claim that premise (1) of the argument above is only true in respect of *metaphysical* (as opposed to *conceptual*) necessity; but that the most that we have reason to believe with respect to premise (2) (and also (2*)) is that it is *conceptually* possible that the feel of pain in question isn't identical to the candidate neural event in question. So the argument is, after all, invalid. In so far as we have sufficient reason to believe its two premises, it commits a fallacy of equivocation (that is, a fallacy of ambiguity, or a shift in meaning). For premise (1) is a metaphysical truth, whereas premise (2) (and also (2*)) is a merely conceptual one.

Recall that the moral of the story of Jekyll and Hyde, discussed in Chapter 3:4, was that not all necessities and possibilities are conceptual ones. Something can be conceptually possible (conceivable) while being metaphysically *im*possible; and something can be metaphysically necessary which isn't conceptually so. Indeed, precisely this sort of situation will arise whenever we conceive of what is in fact one and the same thing or event in a number of distinct ways. Then with the distinction between conceptual and metaphysical necessities firmly in place, we need to enquire after the status of the premises of the above argument. In particular, is the possibility that the feel of pain might exist, or might have existed, independently of its associated brain-state a genuinely metaphysical possibility, or is it merely conceptual?

All of the kinds of data which seem to establish the truth of premise (2) have to do with *conceivability experiments*, in fact. Thus, I can *conceive of* turning into a pillar of salt while the pain continues; or I can *imagine* being transformed into a partial humanoid robot while my pain exists unchanged; and so on. The most that such thought experiments can establish is that it is *conceptually* possible that the pain in question isn't identical with the given neural event. But then that isn't enough to generate an argument against physicalism, any more than the conceptual possibility that Jekyll isn't Hyde is any argument against their actual identity.

Similarly, the argument giving rise to premise (2*) is also a mere conceivability experiment. We can, indeed, *conceive of* me existing physically exactly as I am now, while nevertheless lacking any experienced pains. So it is, indeed, conceptually possible for zombies to exist. But it doesn't follow that this is also metaphysically possible – it doesn't follow that there is really any world in which someone physically indistinguishable from me lacks pain. Indeed, if the thesis of mind-brain identity is true, then such a thing *isn't* possible, just as it isn't really possible to have a world in which Jekyll exists but Hyde doesn't.

If Jekyll *is* Hyde, then Jekyll will remain Hyde in all possible worlds in which they exist – the identity, if true, is metaphysically necessary, despite the fact that it is easy to *conceive of* Jekyll existing while Hyde does not. Similarly, then, in respect of mind and brain. If this pain *is* a particular neural state, then this pain will remain that neural state in all possible worlds in which it exists, despite the fact that we can *conceive of* the pain continuing, or of it having existed, in the absence of that neural state; and despite the fact that we can *conceive of* zombies. There is no good argument here against the thesis of mind–brain identity.

Conclusion

In section 1 of this chapter we presented arguments for thinking it likely that all mental states are identical with brain-states. In section 2 we saw that this thesis is most plausible when confined to *tokens* (as opposed to *types*) of mental state, and we saw that the thesis provides a partial solution to the problem of other minds. Then in the sections following we have replied to all (or at least most of) the various objections to the identity-thesis. Since there is good reason to believe the identity-thesis to be true, and no good reason (as yet) to believe it false, the case for that thesis is rationally convincing. We should therefore embrace the thesis of mind–brain identity, and declare ourselves to be physicalists about the human mind.

Questions for discussion

1. How strong are the arguments for thinking that all mental states are identical with brain-states? Is this the only way in which we can believe that the mind makes a causal difference?
2. If mental states were merely non-physical a-causal *epiphenomena* of the brain, then how could we ever tell?
3. Must physicalists about the mind be committed to saying that the mind is *nothing but* the brain?
4. Is there something about color experience which Mary couldn't know, while locked in her black-and-white room, which she would learn as soon as she comes out? If so, what (if anything) does this show?
5. Can you conceive of turning into a pillar of salt (like Lot's wife) while your headache continues? If so, what consequences would this have for the identity-thesis?

Further reading

Armstrong, D. (1968) *A Materialist Theory of the Mind*, London: Routledge.

Davidson, D. "Mental events", in Foster, L. and Swanson, J. (eds.) (1970) *Experience and Theory*, London: Duckworth. Reprinted in Block, N. (ed.), (1980) *Readings in the Philosophy of Psychology*, vol. 1, London: Methuen; and in Davidson, D. (1980) *Actions and Events*, Oxford: Oxford University Press.

Jackson, F. (1986) "What Mary didn't know", *Journal of Philosophy*, vol. 83. Reprinted in Block, N. *et al.* (eds.) (1997) *The Nature of Conscious-*

ness, Massachusetts: MIT Press and in Rosenthal, D. (ed.) (1991) *The Nature of the Mind*, Oxford: Oxford University Press.

Jackson, F. (1982) "Epiphenomenal qualia", *Philosophical Quarterly*, vol. 32. Reprinted in Lycan, W. (ed.) (1990), *Mind and Cognition*, Oxford: Blackwell.

Kripke, S. (1980) *Naming and Necessity*, Oxford: Blackwell, lecture 3.

Levine, J. (1983) "Materialism and qualia: the explanatory gap", *Pacific Philosophical Quarterly*, vol. 64.

Lewis, D. (1966) "An argument for the identity theory", *Journal of Philosophy*, vol. 63. Reprinted in Lewis' (1983) *Philosophical Papers*, vol. 1, Oxford: Oxford University Press; and in Rosenthal, D. (ed.) (1979), *Materialism and the Mind-Body Problem*, Harlow: Prentice Hall.

Nagel, T. (1974) "What is it like to be a bat?", *Philosophical Review*, vol. 83. Reprinted in Block, N. (1980) (ed.), *Readings in the Philosophy of Psychology*, vol. 1, Methuen; in Hofstadter, D. and Dennett, D. (eds.) (1981), *The Mind's I*, Brighton: Harvester Press; and in Nagel's (1979) *Mortal Questions*, Cambridge: Cambridge University Press.

Place, U. (1956) "Is consciousness a brain process?", *British Journal of Psychology*, vol. 47. Reprinted in Borst, C. (ed.) (1970) *The Mind-Brain Identity Theory*, London: Macmillan in Chappell, V. (ed) (1962), *The Philosophy of Mind*, Harlow: Prentice Hall; in Flew, A. (ed.) (1964), *Body, Mind and Death*, London: Macmillan; and in Morick, H. (ed) (1979), *Introduction to the Philosophy of Mind*, Brighton: Harvester Press.

Smart, J. J. C. (1959) "Sensations and brain processes", *Philosophical Review*, vol. 68. Reprinted in Borst, C. (ed.) (1970), *The Mind-Brain Identity Theory*, London: Macmillan; in Chappell, V. (ed) (1962), *The Philosophy of Mind*, Harlow: Prentice Hall; and in Rosenthal, D. (ed.) (1979), *Materialism and the Mind-Body Problem*, Harlow: Prentice Hall.

6

❖

After-life for physicalists

I have argued that a strong form of physicalism is the truth about ourselves. The answer to the question, "What am I?" is probably, "A wholly physical thing". Since we concluded in Chapter 5 that our mental states – our thoughts, experiences and feelings – are identical with physical events in the brain, there is no scope for people themselves to be other than physical things. In this chapter we shall consider the various possible criteria of identity (over time) for physical selves, and we will raise the question whether it is possible, as physicalists, to hope for some kind of life after death.

This issue is important, because for most people it is their belief in an after-life, grounded in religious conviction, which provides one of their main reasons for believing in the existence of the soul. If it can be shown that physicalism, too, is consistent with belief in an after-life, then this final argument for the existence of the soul will have been undermined. The chapter will conclude, however, with a less welcome reflection: given our best understanding of the nature of personal survival, it may be that many of us won't even survive as far as normal biological death.

1 Resurrection

Traditional views of the after-life come in three forms: disembodied existence, resurrection, and reincarnation. Our arguments against strong dualism and in support of physicalism have ruled out the first of these three. The other two may remain possible. In this section we will consider resurrection, and in the two sections following, reincarnation.

1.1 General points

The connection which apparently exists between questions of personal identity and after-life can be brought out as follows. We have to ask, of whatever entity is supposed to survive my death, "Would that be *me*?" (We will return to consider challenges to the correctness of this assumption in section 3 below.) If the after-life – whatever it consists in – is supposed to be an object of hope or fear for me, in the way that I have hopes and fears for my old age (and as opposed to the way in which I have hopes and fears for my children), then it seems essential that the thing which continues to exist after my death should be myself (as opposed to merely a *part* of myself, such as my kidney; and as opposed to something merely *resembling* myself, such as my child). We have to ask, "Would the person whom I now am be the very same person as the person who will continue to exist (or after an interval come to exist) after my death? Should we be numerically identical?"

There are a number of different considerations which we can use as a touchstone in discussing questions of personal identity. The first, already hinted at, is self-interest. In considering whether some future person would be identical with yourself, it will at least aid intuition if you ask whether or not you would be concerned for the welfare of that person in the way that you are concerned for your own future happiness. However, this test needs handling with care. For as we shall see, it is problematic exactly how to characterize the nature of self-interest, as opposed to other-interest. (Certainly it isn't a matter of strength of feeling, anyway. I may care more for my children than for myself.)

Another consideration is moral and legal responsibility. It is one of the first principles of justice that people shouldn't be blamed or punished for things which they didn't do themselves. (This is my view anyway. But others apparently think differently. In some versions of Christianity, God is supposed to have punished the descendants of Adam and Eve for the original sin, which they themselves didn't commit.) So in considering whether one of us could be identical with some person who continues to exist after normal biological death, ask yourself whether it would be fair to punish the later person for the misdeeds of the former.

1.2 Human identity

Turning now to the question of resurrection: if the criterion of bodily-identity is spatio-temporal continuity, as we suggested in Chapter 3 that it might be, then for most of us there can be no question of resurrection. For we shall either be buried, to have our bodies decompose and be eaten by worms, or cremated. So, relatively soon after our death there will be no body. In which case it is impossible for any later body to be spatio-temporally continuous with the body of the person who died. The only class of exceptions would be those who have had their bodies frozen or otherwise preserved. If God or the scientists can ever cause these bodies to be brought back to life, then there would emerge a living human being who is indeed spatio-temporally continuous with a person who had earlier died.

If the criterion of identity for the human organism is spatio-temporal continuity, then resurrection will only be possible for the rich. However, recall that in the case of at least some physical objects, their identity-over-time can reach across periods of non-existence. For as we saw in Chapter 2:2, the criterion of identity for human artifacts allows them to survive across temporary disassembly. When my motorcycle is lying around in pieces in the garage, there is no motorcycle. For a collection of unrelated motorcycle parts isn't a motorcycle. Yet when I put those parts back together again, what I do is rebuild my motorcycle, not create a new one.

Analogously then: suppose that on the Day of Judgment God brings together all the original bits and pieces which had made up my body – all the molecules and atoms which constituted the cells and biological structures – and puts them back together in the way that they had originally been arranged during my life. (Since God is supposed to be omnipotent there can be no real obstacles in the way of him doing this.) Would he then have rebuilt me? Would the resulting human organism be the very same physical body that I am now? In order to answer these questions we need to consider the extent to which living organisms are like artifacts. In particular, is their criterion of identity such as to allow them to survive temporary disassembly?

An example suggesting a negative answer is as follows: suppose that a great oak tree dies and decomposes, with all of its constituent atoms and molecules passing back into the soil from which it had grown. Then some years later an acorn germinates on the very same spot and begins to grow. Now suppose that by chance the acorn possesses the same genetic code as the original tree, and that by some miracle all the atoms and molecules from the original tree get taken up out of the soil as the seedling grows. Let the result be a tree as similar in appearance to the original as you like, made up out of the very same pieces arranged in the very same way. Should we say that this wasn't really a new tree, but rather the very same oak which had earlier died and decayed? Have we imagined a case of tree-resurrection? – unlikely perhaps, but nonetheless logically possible? It seems to me clear that we have not. I should want to say that we have, in this story, two trees rather than one, despite the close similarities in appearance and physical construction.

It is easy to find examples to pull us in the opposite direction. Think, for instance, of the concepts of "beaming up" and "beaming down" in the television series *Star Trek*. In order to transport people backwards and forwards between the star-ship *Enterprise* and nearby planets, they use a machine which breaks the human body up into its atoms and molecules, and then accelerates those particles in a high-energy beam which can travel through solid objects, arranging for them to be reconstituted exactly as they were at some designated spot. Here we feel no difficulty with the idea that it would be the very same human organism which would emerge at the end of this process, despite the fact that – as in the example of the oak tree – there has been an interval during which no living organism exists as such. (A beam of living-organism-parts is not a living organism.)

We apparently have conflicting intuitions about whether a living organism can survive temporary periods of non-existence. How are they to be reconciled? I conjecture that the ground of our intuition in the oak tree example is the fact that living organisms undergo a characteristic process of birth, growth, degeneration and death. We are thus accustomed to counting them by counting life-cycles: to every such process of birth-to-death corresponds a single living organism. Then because, in the oak tree example, we have two such processes, we are inclined to judge that there are two distinct trees. In the "beaming down" example, on the other hand, there is nothing recognizable as normal birth and death. Since the process of beaming down doesn't form a separation between two distinct life-cycles, there is nothing to incline us to say that it divides two distinct living organisms, either.

Resurrection is like beaming down, and unlike the oak tree example, in that it doesn't involve two complete cycles of birth-to-death. For the process of resurrection itself, as we imagined it, is quite unlike any normal birth. Indeed it is very closely similar to the reconstitution out of atoms which would occur at the end of the process of beaming up or down. So I conclude – albeit tentatively – that resurrection is a logical possibility, even for those whose bodies have disintegrated.

1.3   An objection

An apparent difficulty for the whole idea of resurrection by reconstitution out of parts is as follows. As everyone knows, most cells in the human body are replaced, perhaps many times over, during the course of a normal life-time. So come the Day of Judgment there will be enough of my original bits and pieces lying around in the world for God to resurrect two of me. Well suppose – for reasons best known to himself – he does just that. The resulting people cannot be identical with one another; for they are distinct living organisms, who may go on to lead quite different lives. Since there exists absolutely no reason for identifying one rather than the other of them with the original me, I cannot be identical with either. Yet each of them satisfies the criterion of reconstitution out of parts. The structure of this example is represented in Figure 6.1, where A is the original me, and B and C are the two distinct bodies created on the Day of Judgment.

Similar cases can occur in connection with artifacts. For not only can artifacts survive across temporary disassembly, they can also survive through a considerable extent of replacement of parts. (Thus many of the parts of my antique car have been replaced by new ones over the years. Yet for all that, it is the very same car which I bought all those years ago.) Consider the example of the ship of Theseus, first debated by the ancient Greeks. Theseus owns a wooden ship which he is keeping in dry-dock over the winter. Each night a thief comes and steals a single part of the ship – now a plank, now a length of rope, etc. – and each morning Theseus discovers the theft and replaces the stolen part. By the spring the thief has enough parts to build a ship of his own, which he does. Who then owns the original ship of Theseus? If we go by spatio-temporal continuity over replacement of parts we shall answer, "Theseus". But if we go by reconstruction out of original parts we shall answer, "The thief". Yet they cannot both have the original, since they now have different ships. (Remember from Chapter 3:1 that identity is transitive and symmetric.)

192

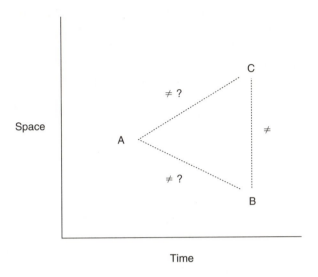

Figure 6.1 Two non-identical things can't both equal a third.

What do examples of this sort show? In my view, not a great deal. In particular, it doesn't follow that resurrection of the body is impossible. All that is really shown is that we don't have a criterion of identity – either for human beings or for artifacts – which will cover every conceivable kind of circumstance. But this is no very serious matter, since many of our concepts are incompletely defined in this way. Many of our concepts are such that there exist conceivable circumstances in which we should have no idea what to say; yet this need not prevent us from making true judgments with them in ordinary circumstances. For example, suppose that we come across a particular chair, which we can see and touch and sit upon. But next moment it vanishes completely. Later it reappears again. Then it vanishes again. Now is this a real chair or not? I think that nothing in our ordinary concept of "chair" determines what we are to say in extraordinary circumstances such as these. But this need not prevent me from judging truly that I am now sitting on a chair as I write these words.

The issues raised by examples like that of double-resurrection and the ship of Theseus are essentially a matter of "tidying up" our concepts. If examples like these arose often, we should have to extend and refine our criteria of identity for human beings and artifacts in order to be able to cope with them. We might, for example, say that artifacts are identical if and only if *either* (a) they are spatio-temporally continuous over replacement of less than a majority of parts, *or* (b) the one is reconstituted out of a majority of parts from the other. (This would give the original ship to the thief.) In tidying up our concept of organism-identity we might give priority to atoms and molecules which came from the organism later in life rather than earlier (or vice versa). But so long as these examples don't (or don't often) arise, there is no particular reason why we should bother. So let us trust that God won't act as we imagined on the Day of Judgment, and rest content with a simple account of resurrection in terms of reconstitution out of original parts.

1.4   Is bodily identity sufficient?

It would appear that resurrection of the body is logically possible. In which case belief in the reality of an after-life, grounded in religious faith, need provide no motive for rejecting physicalism. For the religious believer can think that God will arrange for the resurrection and reconstitution of the body and brain at some point in the future (just as Christians have traditionally believed).

But would bodily resurrection be sufficient, by itself, to ensure personal survival of death? Is bodily identity a sufficient condition of personal identity? I shall argue that it is not. I shall argue that mere bodily resurrection, in the absence of any degree of psychological connectedness (see Chapter 3:2 for details), wouldn't constitute a form of personal after-life. On the contrary, in order for the resurrected individual to be the very same person as myself, it is at least necessary that they should be psychologically connected with myself.

Consider the following example: suppose that scientists have a way of freezing dead bodies to preserve them from decay, and are confidently predicting that in ten years time they will have developed the technology to be able to bring those bodies back to life again. But they also tell you that the freezing process must involve the complete destruction of all memory and personality-traces from the brain. So the human being who is revived, ten years hence, will remember nothing of your life, and will have none of your desires, interests or ties of affection. That person's mind will be, in these respects, a blank sheet. Now would you, in these circumstances, be prepared to pay good money to have your corpse frozen and later revived? I certainly would not. For the process only ensures that there will live, at some time after my death, a human being who has exactly my physical appearance, and whose body is

194

made up of the very same cells which currently make up my body. Why then should I take any particular interest in that?

Perhaps it might be rational to have one's corpse frozen, gambling that the scientists may yet discover some means of reviving it which will ensure that psychological connectedness is retained. But suppose we know that this cannot be done. Suppose we know that there is something about the freezing process itself, and the way in which memory and personality are encoded in the brain, which means that freezing must inevitably destroy all traces of each; rather in the way that once having switched off a computer which lacks an automatic back-up program, there is no way of recovering any files which have not been saved.

From a third-person perspective there would be every reason to regard the revived human being as a new person. For they would have to establish new interests, new personal relationships and a new life. Thus there would be no point in paying to have a dead loved-one frozen, in the hope of being reunited with them in ten years time. For the revived individual wouldn't remember you, and would have none of the qualities of character which made you care for them in the first place. (If your attraction were largely physical then there might be some point in it. But of course there would be no guarantee that the revived person would take any reciprocal physical interest in you.) Moreover, it would seem totally unfair – or at any rate pointless – to hold the revived person responsible for any evils committed by the original. For not only would they remember nothing whatever of those incidents, but they would have none of the desires, motives and qualities of character which had caused the original deeds to be committed.

From a first-person perspective, too, there would be no reason to regard the revived individual as yourself. For none of the motives which you now have for desiring your own survival will carry across the loss of psychological connectedness. A proper demonstration of this point must wait upon an analysis of the motives for survival, to be undertaken in the next section. But reflect here upon the fact that all of those things which make your life worth living – your personal relationships and friendships, projects and plans, interests you have developed and pleasures you have cultivated – would be lost to you with the loss of psychological connectedness.

Thus far the case may seem convincing. But a counter-consideration is this: suppose someone told you that your corpse would be frozen and later revived (without psychological connectedness), and that the revived body would then be tortured or used in painful medical experiments. Wouldn't you feel fear? If so, doesn't this suggest that you would in fact regard the revived individual as identical with yourself, despite the lack of psychological connection? (This argument is due to the English philosopher Bernard Williams.)

However, the capacity to feel fear isn't a very reliable guide on matters of personal identity, since it is possible to feel fear on someone else's behalf. Thus if I were told that someone I love were about to be tortured, I should of course feel fear for them. Now it is true that one has no particular reason to feel attached to the resurrected individual; so the fear one feels cannot be exactly analogous to the fear that one can feel on behalf of a loved one. But we can still explain how it can arise independently of any belief in our identity with the revived person.

We naturally imagine the threatened torture "from the inside". For this is what imagining an experience is: to imagine what it would be like to be tortured is to imagine, from the inside, what it would feel like to be tortured. This may by itself be sufficient to cause fear, since it is a familiar fact that imagining an experience can provoke the emotions appropriate to the real thing. (This is why fantasy can be fun.) But the effect will be compounded when I add to my image the thought, "And it will be *this* body which feels all that pain". For I am used to thinking that anything which happens to this body happens to myself. But if I hold clearly before my mind the loss of psychological connectedness, then I no longer take this seriously. I then no more literally fear the torture of the revived individual than I would fear for myself on being told that the car I am just getting out of will be blown up in ten minutes time. (Though this, too, can send a shiver down the spine; for it is so close to me.)

I conclude that resurrection of the body is logically possible. But it will only count as a version of after-life – that is to say, as a way of continuing the life of the very same person who had earlier died – if the resurrected individual retains something of the memory and personality of the original. In the next section we will consider whether memory and personality might by themselves be sufficient for personal survival, independently of bodily identity. We have concluded that bodily identity isn't sufficient by itself for personal survival; we shall now ask whether it is even necessary.

2 Reincarnation

Can physicalists consistently believe in the possibility of reincarnation? It might seem obvious that they cannot. For reincarnation will only take place if people can exist, successively, in different bodies. How could this be possible unless the people themselves are something distinct from their bodies (e.g., non-physical souls)? Now although believers in reincarnation have generally been dualists – indeed the theory is often called "the theory of transmigration of souls" – I don't see that they *had* to be. One could equally well, as a physicalist, believe in reincarnation by believing in a divergence between the criteria of identity and individuation for people.

2.1 Divergent criteria

An analogy will make clear what I have in mind. Consider the criteria of identity and identification for a particular school class, or form. At any given time, a class is identified by identifying its members. Thus if someone asks, "Who are 5.v?" your reply should either list the members of 5.v, or identify them in some other way ("The children in the classroom next door"). Moreover, truths about 5.v at any given time, are truths about (most of) its members at the time. Thus, "5.v want to go to see the new production of *King Lear*" reduces to, "Most of John, and Mary, and Peter, and Susan, . . . want to go".

The criterion of identity for a class *over* time is quite different. Often it will be given in terms of a fixed position within the age and ability range of the school, so that two distinct groups of children can in successive years constitute one and the same class. Thus if a teacher is asked, "Are you teaching the same English class again this year" she may reply, "Yes, I have got 5.v again", despite the fact that 5.v have undergone a total change in membership. So to summarize: the criterion of identification-at-a-time for a school class is the set of its members, whereas the criterion of identity-over-time allows a number of different sets of children to constitute, successively, one and the same class. (Something similar may be true of governments and football teams.)

When I speak of the possibility of a physicalist version of belief in reincarnation, I have in mind a similar divergence. As physicalists, we believe that the subject of thoughts and experiences is a physical thing. So we have no option but to give the criterion of individuation

197

for people in physical terms. We have to say that a person x at time t = a person y, also at time t, if and only if x and y are one and the same human being (or: one and the same human brain). But we can, quite consistently with this, give the criterion of identity (over time) for people in terms of the notion of psychological connectedness. We can allow that so long as the later human being has quasi-memories of the life of the earlier, and has sufficiently similar desires, interests and ties of affection (all of which are causally descended from the states of the earlier human), then those human beings will constitute different stages in the life of one and the same person. This would make it possible for a person to exist successively *as* (rather than "in") a number of distinct human beings, which would be a form of reincarnation.

However, to say that such a view is consistent is not the same as saying that it is true. To say that the criteria of identity and individuation *could* diverge, is not the same as saying that they do. So we need to consider how plausible it would be to say that I should survive, provided that there exists a person who is sufficiently strongly psychologically connected with myself.

2.2 An example

Let us sharpen up our intuitions on an example (due to the English philosopher Derek Parfit). Suppose that scientists have built a machine which they claim will enable people to travel at the speed of light. (Our problem is whether this is really a case of personal travel.) Thus suppose that Mary is wanting to visit her relatives, who are colonists on a planet in another solar system. The scientists tell her that instead of having to travel by rocket, which would take many years, she can step into their machine here on Earth and (so they claim) step out of a similar machine on the colonized planet a few hours later.

What the machine does is conduct a complete scan of the state of every single cell in her body, recording all this information on to a computer (the nature of the scan being such that the cells are all destroyed by the process). The information is then transmitted in the form of a radio signal to a machine on the colonized planet, which will build a replica of her which is exact right down to the last detail. Because the replica is so exact, the person who steps out of the machine at the other end will have all of Mary's quasi-memories and quasi-intentions, as well as her beliefs, interests and

198

general personality. Moreover, that person's body will resemble Mary's exactly. It is, however, a distinct body. For unlike the example of "beaming down" discussed in the last section, no material is actually transmitted by the machine. So the new body is neither spatio-temporally continuous with the old, nor is it made up out of the same physical bits and pieces.

Our question is this: would the person who steps out of the machine on the colonized planet be Mary? Would this be an example of reincarnation without souls?

2.3   Practical considerations

From a third-person perspective there is every reason why the new body should be treated as a reincarnation of Mary herself. Consider her relatives, for example: ought they to welcome the new body as herself, or reject it as an impostor and be grief-stricken because Mary has ceased to exist? Well, the new body would have all of the qualities, both physical and psychological, which they had come to know and love (or hate, as may be) in the old. There would be the same shared knowledge of family history and the same ties of affection. Given all this, why should they take any interest in the fact that the person possessing these qualities is made up of new matter? Why should they feel the slightest bit distressed at the destruction of the old body back on Earth? For they surely never were attached to that very body as such.

Also from a third-person perspective, consider the question of responsibility and punishment. Suppose that Mary had committed some evil deed prior to entering the machine on Earth. Now, the question whether it would be fair and just to punish the new human being for the misdeeds of the old, perhaps has to wait on an answer to the question of personal identity. For the notion of "just punishment" appears to imply that the person punished is identical with the person who committed the crime. But we can at least see that blame and punishment would have exactly the same *point* here as in the normal case. For the new human being would quasi-remember the crime (it would certainly feel to her as if she had done it); and all the motives and bad qualities of character which had led her to commit the crime in the first place would still be there in the new body.

Viewed from the first-person perspective, after the fact, there would also be every reason to regard the example as a genuine case

199

of reincarnation. For the person stepping out of the machine on the colonized planet will not in any way feel herself to be a new person. On the contrary, her present existence will seem to her to be entirely continuous with the life of the human being on Earth. She will quasi-recall many of the events of that life, including getting into the machine on Earth; that event being separated from her present existence by what seems to her to have been a brief period of unconsciousness (like waking after a night's sleep). She will quasi-recall her feelings then, and the thoughts and discussions which led up to the decision to get into the machine. She will now set about executing the plans and intentions which she quasi-recalls having made earlier. Why should she herself take any interest in the fact that her consciousness is now supported by a new body?

From the first-person perspective of the person before the fact, the issue is perhaps not so clear. When I imagine myself in the position of someone about to step into such a machine, I find that I can easily induce in myself either one of two contradictory attitudes. If I focus my thoughts on the *result* of the process, and slur over what takes place in between, then I imagine myself looking forward to the prospect of seeing loved ones again, and feeling apprehensive at the reputedly harsh conditions on the colonized planet. But if I focus my attention on what will happen most immediately – the destruction of all the cells in my body – then I find myself thinking, "So that will be the death of me", and I feel afraid. Then thoughts about the person who will exist on the colonized planet seem merely to be thoughts about someone who will exactly resemble myself, and I am concerned for *his* sufferings not at all.

Well, how *ought* a person about to step into such a machine regard the prospect? Should they fear it as they fear death, believing that they will cease to exist with the destruction of their body? Or should they regard it merely as a convenient form of personal travel? In order to answer these questions we need to look more closely at the nature of self-interest. We need to consider whether or not our normal desire for survival – however that should best be characterized – would be just as well served by the existence of the replica on the colonized planet. It will help us in this task if we recall the distinction between those desires and projects which are self-referring (like my desire that I myself should be rich) and those which are impersonal. (This distinction was first drawn in Chapter 3:2.) We can then subdivide our discussion accordingly.

2.4 *Impersonal motives for survival*

Many of us have impersonal (non-self-referring) desires, which are for states of affairs which don't necessarily contain ourselves. For example, political activists working for the revolution may know perfectly well that it will, very likely, not come during their lifetime. But what they want is that there should *be* a revolution, not that they should live to see a revolution. Similarly, people who want to save the whale may not particularly want that they themselves should save the whale, but simply that the whale should be saved. Someone who loves both Shakespeare and the Japanese language, and whose project is to translate the works of Shakespeare into Japanese, may not particularly desire that they themselves should do the translation. What matters to them is that Shakespeare should be translated, and if they thought that someone else could perform the task better they might gladly hand it over. Closer to home, when I desire the happiness of those whom I love, my desire is simply that those people should be happy. If my love is genuine, then my desire must to some extent be disinterested: I must want them to be happy irrespective of whether or not I live to see it.

Where someone has impersonal desires, at least part of their motive for survival will derive from the fact that their own continued existence will normally be a necessary condition of (or at least may contribute to) the achievement of what they desire. Thus political activists have a motive for survival, in so far as they think that their activity may make the revolution more likely. (However, if an activist is particularly single-minded – this desire dominating all others – then they may gladly lay down their life for the cause if it turns out that it is their death, rather than their continued existence, which will bring the revolution closer.) The translator, too, has a reason for living in so far as he believes that the job will not get done properly unless he himself does it. Disinterested love will also provide a motive for survival, since our continued existence will often contribute considerably to the happiness of those whom we love.

From the perspective of our impersonal desires, what matters in survival is psychological connectedness (and sometimes physical resemblance). Bodily identity won't matter at all. Thus in the case of the political activist what matters, from the point of view of their desire for revolution, is that there should continue to exist someone with the desires and qualities of character necessary to engage in revolutionary activity. That there should continue to exist a living body identical with the body of the activist will in itself be of no help in furthering the cause. Indeed, the really single-minded activist will fear brain-washing – where the effect is permanent loss of the desire for revolution – in the same way and to the same extent that they fear death. Similarly, what matters to the translator is that there should continue to exist someone with the desires, interests and literary sensibility necessary to perform the task. In the case of the disinterested lover, what matters is that there should continue to exist someone who has that love, and who has the qualities (both psychological and physical) which may be loved in return.

I conclude that in so far as our interest in normal survival derives from impersonal desires, then it is best characterized as the desire that there should continue to exist someone psychologically connected with myself (and perhaps also physically similar to myself), rather than as the desire that there should continue to exist someone whose body is identical with mine. So from this point of view radio-transportation should be regarded as a means of personal travel. At any rate, to the extent that someone contemplating getting into the machine has impersonal desires, to that extent they should regard the future existence of the replica as being just as good as ordinary survival.

2.5 Personal motives for survival

Of course many (perhaps the majority) of our desires are self-referring. When I want to be happy, or rich, or famous, what I want is that I myself should be happy, or rich, or famous. (Note, however, that some self-referring desires may be based upon impersonal ones. When I desire not to have a migraine tomorrow, at least part of the underlying motive may be that severe pain would interfere with my translation work, or would make those whom I love suffer with me.) In these cases the notion of personal identity forms part of the content of the desire itself: to want to be rich is to desire that some future person who is identical with myself should be rich. So we have to ask just how the content of such desires should best be characterized. Should we say that they are desires for things to happen to a particular living body? Or are they best characterized in terms of psychological connectedness (and perhaps also physical resemblance)?

We can see that psychological connectedness should at least be included as a necessary ingredient in the content of self-referring desires, if we notice that such connectedness will often be just as much presupposed, for the satisfaction of those desires, as is ordinary survival. This is so for two reasons. The first derives from the causality of desire. As we noted in Chapter 3:2, desire is a causal notion: to conceive of something as a desire is to conceive of it as a state apt to cause the thing desired. My desire to be rich disposes me to try to become rich, and hence is apt to cause its own satisfaction. So if I want to be rich, I should realize that the loss of that desire (the loss of one aspect of psychological connectedness) will make it that much more likely that I shall never be rich. For without the desire I shan't make the attempt.

The second point is that without the continued existence of the desire, success will not be satisfying. If I have lost the desire for riches, then even if I were to become rich by chance this wouldn't satisfy any desire which I would then currently have. So from both points of view, if I want to be rich, then I should also desire that I continue to possess that desire. (I may also have other desires, of course – for instance, the desire to be humble – which may lead me to want to *lose* that desire.)

It seems that from the point of view of my self-referring desires, I should desire the existence of someone psychologically connected with myself (possessing those very same desires), in the same way that I desire my own ordinary survival. This completes the argument sketched at the end of section 1 above, that psychological connectedness is at least a necessary condition of personal survival. But it is still left open that bodily identity may also be necessary. For we haven't shown that the self-referring desire for riches isn't *also* the desire that some body identical with my own should be rich. I shall present two arguments intended to establish the further claim that self-referring desires *aren't* well-characterized as desires for things to happen to a body identical with (i.e., which is none other than) mine.

The first argument is based upon the frequency of dualistic beliefs. Since many people believe in disembodied existence, or at least feel no difficulty with the idea of such existence; and since they entertain hopes and fears for what might happen to them in that existence; then it is hardly very plausible to construe all their desires for the future as desires for things to happen to a particular body. If people hope that the disembodied after-life will not be lonely, then this cannot be construed as involving the hope that some body identical with theirs will not be lonely, without accusing them of explicit, and obviously foolish, self-contradiction. It is more charitable to them to understand the content of what they hope purely in terms of psychological connectedness.

The second argument is this: when I reflect upon, and spell out to myself, the content of many of my self-referring desires, what I think of are particular events and experiences taking place against a background of desires and interests similar to mine; the thought of a particular individual body does not enter in at all. Thus suppose that I am hungry, and find that what I particularly want is a hot fish curry. What exactly does this desire involve? Just this: that I think with longing of eating such a curry. When I think of this, I imagine enjoying it; so it is presupposed that I retain my liking for curry (and indeed my hunger). But at no point does the thought occur to me, "And the human being who eats the curry is to be the physical body identical with my own". Similarly with the desire to be rich: here I think of all the things which riches can bring, such as large houses and holidays in Sri Lanka; and I imagine these against a backdrop of desires and interests similar to my own. I don't especially imagine the riches being possessed by a body identical with mine.

2.6 Interim conclusion

Self-referring desires are best characterized as desires for things to happen to a person who is suitably psychologically connected with yourself. Then the desire for normal survival should also be characterized in psychological terms. So from all points of view – from the point of view of a third party, from a first-person perspective after the fact, and from a first-person perspective before the fact – the replica on the colonized planet should be regarded as identical with the person Mary who stepped into the machine back on Earth. We have therefore conceived of a case of reincarnation without souls.

Although the doctrine of reincarnation isn't a traditional part of Christian belief, Christians, too, should take an interest in our conclusion. For it means that they no longer have to believe that God must gather together enough of their original physical bits and pieces in order for their after-life to be secured. Since psychological connectedness is (we have argued) sufficient for survival, God can create a physically-new (and perhaps better!) body, provided he ensures that the details of its brain-structure give rise to the right kinds of psychological connectedness with yourself. Christians are therefore free to interpret the traditional doctrine of resurrection of

204

the body as meaning that God will re-create a body of the appropriate *sort* (similar to, but not numerically identical with your original body), which will have the right kinds of psychological connectedness to you in order to *be* you.

3 Double difficulties or secondary survival?

We argued in the last section that the best conception of the nature of ourselves allows our criteria of identity and individuation to diverge, with the criterion of identity-over-time being given in terms of psychological connectedness. In the present section we will consider, and try to resolve, a number of different objections to this idea.

3.1 An initial counter-example

Consider the following development of the radio-transportation example. The machine which scans Mary's body here on Earth doesn't destroy it immediately; but fatally weakens it. Mary would therefore step out of that machine again, knowing that she has only a few days to live, but also knowing that an exact replica of her has been created on a distant planet. Surely this wouldn't give her much consolation! So far as she herself would be concerned, she will soon cease to exist; and the continued existence of the replica on the distant planet will merely be the continued existence of someone else (although admittedly, someone who exactly resembles herself). The situation can be seen represented schematically in Figure 6.2.

Note, however, that the replica would not in fact be directly psychologically connected with the weakened Mary who steps out of the machine back on Earth. Rather, they would both of them be psychologically connected with a common ancestor, namely the person Mary before she stepped into the machine. For the replica would have no quasi-memories of Mary's life since then; nor would Mary have any quasi-memories of her existence on the distant planet. More importantly, although both of them would have exactly similar desires and intentions, those states wouldn't be directly causally linked: Mary's current desire to write a detective novel wouldn't be apt to cause the other's similar desire to be satisfied; nor would any intention which Mary now forms cause the other to perform actions once Mary is dead. So Mary couldn't possibly take the kind of interest in the future existence of the replica which she would take in her own normal survival.

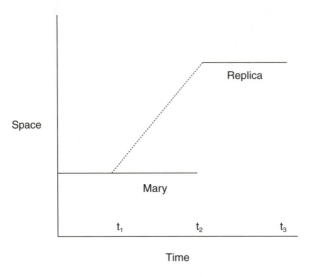

Figure 6.2 Mary survives briefly while a replica is created.

One way of responding to the objection, therefore, would be to drop the claim that an overlapping series of psychological connections can give identity. We could insist instead that personal identity requires direct psychological connectedness. (We will return to examine this suggestion in section 4 below.) Another, weaker, way of responding would be to insist that personal identity requires the possibility of forwards causal influence. We could still give our account of personal identity in terms of overlapping psychological connections, but write into the account a "no backtracking" clause. This would state that if A at t_1 and B at t_2 are to be identical, then the psychological connections linking A and B must all of them exist between the two times t_1 and t_2 – it cannot be the case that we have to look back to times *before* t_1 in order to establish the psychological connectedness, if the two of them are to count as one and the same person.

3.2 Duplication

The second objection also involves a slight development of the original example. As before, Mary intends to visit a distant colonized planet. But suppose that there are two such planets, with a replica-building machine on each of them. Now due to an error on the part of the machine-operator here on Earth, the record of Mary's cell-states is transmitted to *both* planets, so that two exact replicas of her are built, while the original is destroyed. Each of these replicas would resemble her exactly, and each would be equally strongly psychologically connected with the original on Earth. So what are we to say? Does Mary survive as both of them? Does she survive as one rather than the other of them? Or doesn't she survive at all?

Clearly the two replicas aren't numerically identical with one another. They are different physical beings occupying different regions of space on different planets. Although they are psychologically exactly similar, complete similarity will only last for a moment. As soon as they attain consciousness they will start to have different experiences and perform different actions. The one may step out on to a harsh stony planet to be greeted ecstatically by their relatives. The other may step out into lush tropical vegetation, to be met by a barrage of questions from surprised strangers. The one may live happily ever after in the bosom of the family, while the other becomes totally embittered and turns to a life of crime. It would obviously be absurd to punish the one for the crimes of the other, claiming that these are one and the same person.

Now, if the two replicas aren't identical with one another, then they cannot possibly both be identical with the original Mary on Earth. For the transitivity and symmetry of identity together imply the following general principle:

if x = y and x = z, then y = z.
(If the original Mary = replica 1, and the original Mary = replica 2, then replica 1 = replica 2.)

So if Mary *were* identical with both of them, then they would have to be identical with one another; but they aren't. In fact the situation is the same as the one we represented earlier in Figure 6.1, now adapted and reproduced here as Figure 6.3.

Moreover, since each of the two replicas has precisely the same claim to be identical with the original Mary – both of them resembling her exactly – it cannot be the case that she survives as one rather than the other of them. For if she were identical with one but not the other, then there would surely have to be some relevant difference between them; but there isn't: they are exactly alike.

If Mary isn't identical with both of the replicas, and she isn't identical with only one of them, then the only remaining alternative is that she isn't identical with either. Then, supposing that the

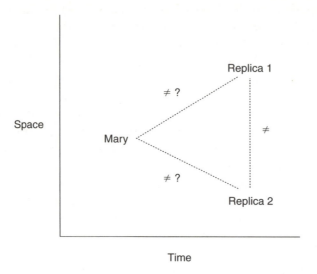

Figure 6.3 A case of duplication.

original body back on Earth was destroyed by the scanning process, it must follow that Mary herself doesn't survive. So when the machine-operator made the error which resulted in the existence of two exact replicas, he brought it about that Mary herself ceased to exist.

This conclusion can now be turned into a strong argument against the claim that psychological connectedness is a sufficient condition of personal identity-over-time. For what emerges is that if we employ a psychological criterion of identity, then the question of the identity of x and y may depend, not just upon facts about them, but also upon events taking place in some quite different part of the universe. Thus the identity between Mary and the replica on the planet containing her relatives may depend upon what happens on a planet many millions of miles away. For if the machine-operator had not made his error, then Mary would, on our account, have survived after all. Even given that error, if the machine on the other planet had malfunctioned – so that the replica there had never attained consciousness – then, too, Mary would have continued to exist. For either way, it would have been true that the replica on the planet with the relatives was more strongly psychologically connected with Mary herself than is any other person.

We surely believe, in contrast, that the question of the identity of x and y must depend only on facts about those two individuals, and

208

the relations between them. For numerical identity certainly isn't an explicitly comparative notion. One cannot, for example, speak of an object x being more, or less, identical with an object y than is some other object z. But then neither does it depend upon any implicit comparison, in the way that the concept of "leadership" may depend upon such a comparison. (In order to decide whether or not someone is the leader of a particular group, you may have to compare their role with that of others.) Rather, we surely think that the question of the identity of an object x with an object y is an all-or-nothing, non-comparative, one.

It seems intuitively obvious that identity isn't a comparative relation. For what more intimate relation could there be between any "two" objects than the relation of identity? Since if x and y are identical there is only one object involved rather than two, how could the fact of their identity depend upon facts about other individuals? Then since the proposed account of personal identity in terms of psychological connectedness is comparative (requiring that x should be more strongly psychologically connected with y than is any other person, if x and y are to be identical) we appear to have sufficiently refuted that account.

3.3 The depth of the problem

It is important to see that we cannot avoid the difficulties raised by the possibility of duplication through some kind of "tidying up" of the suggested criterion of personal identity. For the similarities with the problems of duplication raised in our discussion of resurrection in section 1 above are only superficial. Those problems arose because we were allowing the criteria for bodily identity – like the criteria for artifact identity – to be multiple. We suggested that identity of body could be given *either* by spatio-temporal continuity over complete replacement of parts, *or* by reconstruction out of original parts. This then opened up the possibility of duplication, identity with one object being given by one criterion, and identity with some quite different object being given by the other. The problem was then merely to provide a precise formula to bring about the correct balance between the two criteria, in such a way as to yield an unique judgment in all cases.

Our difficulties in the present connection are much more fundamental. They arise out of the very nature of the relation we have chosen to use in constructing our account of personal identity. Since psychological connectedness is a "many–many" relation, whereas identity itself is a "one–one" relation, there are bound to be problems if we use the one to define the other. Let me elaborate.

By a many–many relation, I mean a relation which can hold between more than one thing and more than one thing. For example, "is a sister of" is the name of a many–many relation, since someone can have more than one sister, as well as be sister to more than one other person. By a one–one relation, on the other hand, I mean a relation which can only hold between one thing and one thing. For example, in monogamous societies, "is a spouse of" is the name of a one–one relation, since someone can only have one spouse at a time.

It is obvious that psychological connectedness is a many–many relation. For instance, it is possible for more than one person to quasi-remember events from the life of any given individual, and for one person to quasi-remember events from the lives of more than one. Yet it is equally obvious that identity is one–one. This follows from the transitivity and symmetry of identity:

if $x = y$ and $x = z$, then $y = z$.

Given this disparity, the only possible way in which we can make use the relation of psychological connectedness in giving an account of personal identity, is by making the definition quantitative and comparative: relying upon the phrase, "the greatest quantity of psychological connections" to secure the uniqueness of identity, and insisting that if two different people are equally closely connected with a single original, then *neither* of them is in fact identical with that original.

We seem to have refuted the proposal defended in section 2 above, that personal identity should be defined in terms of psychological connectedness. For any such definition must be comparative, whereas identity itself *isn't* comparative. This then appears to refute the claimed possibility of reincarnation. Despite the various practical considerations raised in section 2, relating to the kind of interest which we take in the survival of ourselves and others, it seems that the concept of identity is such as to force us to require some element of bodily identity as a necessary condition of personal survival.

3.4 Survival without identity

In section 2 we argued for a conception of personal identity in terms of psychological connectedness, which would make reincarnation possible; but thus far in the present section we have raised a serious objection to that idea. Let us review our options.

First, we could accept that body (or brain) identity is a necessary condition of personal survival; indeed, this seems forced on us if we are to work with a conception of personal identity which is non-comparative. But this option conflicts with all of the arguments of section 2, to the effect that bodily identity is of no particular importance to us. If we take this option, then we should have to say that we will often in fact be satisfied with something rather less than strict survival.

Secondly, we could give our account of personal identity solely in terms of psychological connectedness, as urged in section 2. But if we did this, then we would have to accept that questions of identity can be comparative. In any case there might still be a conflict with the practical interest which we take in survival, since in cases of duplication we should have to say that the original person ceases to exist altogether. But would we in fact regard duplication as being just as bad as normal death?

For example, suppose that Mary is suffering from a rare respirtory disease which means that, if she remains on Earth, she has only a few weeks to live. Her employers offer to pay for radio-transportation to a distant planet, where the difference in atmosphere will mean that she can look forward to many years' of healthy life. Initially, of course, she is delighted at the news: she will think of this as a way to survive her disease. But then she learns that, as a condition of the offer, her employers are insisting that she must consent to a duplicate also being created on a third planet, where workers with her particular skills are scarce. Is she really going to think that this makes the whole thing pointless, on the grounds that, if *two* replicas of her are created, she will cease to exist anyway? Surely not. Surely both she and others would regard such an offer of duplication as being as good (or almost as good) as normal survival.

Our third option is to stop thinking of personal survival as involving identity. We could give our account of the notion of survival in terms of psychological connectedness, which fits well with the arguments of section 2. But if we no longer have to try to guarantee the uniqueness of identity, we can avoid making that account a majoritarian one. We might simply say this: *a person x is a survivor of a person y if and only if they are sufficiently strongly psychologically connected*. We thus allow that in cases of duplication the original person survives as two distinct people (without of course being identical with either of them).

I shall argue shortly, in sections 3.6 and 3.7 below, that we ought to take this third option. There I shall argue (following Parfit) that we should change the terms in which we conceptualize the survival of ourselves and others. But first I want briefly to examine a fourth alternative, which has been developed and defended by the American philosopher David Lewis. This would allow us to continue thinking of survival as requiring identity (as well as being intrinsic and non-comparative) while still allowing us to think of each of the replicas as survivors of the Mary who gets into the machine on Earth.

3.5   Conceiving of people as 4-D worms

According to Lewis, people should really be thought of as four-dimensional creatures, rather than the familiar three-dimensional ones. We thus shouldn't think of people as being wholly present at any one time, existing in the region of space which they occupy at that time; but rather, on this account, we should think of people as being spread out in both space *and* time. People (and other physical objects) should be thought of as space–time *worms*, consisting of the set of three-dimensional matter-filled spaces which they occupy throughout the times during which they exist. In order to match our intuitions about personal survival in ordinary cases of radio-transportation, then, the *same* worm can be thought of as existing across discontinuities in space, provided that the right kinds of psychological connections are in place to provide a link across the spatial gap.

Ignoring these spatial discontinuities for simplicity of representation, we can see the case of Mary's duplication pictured in Figure 6.4. What emerges is that there are two distinct people involved, both of whom happen to share a space–time segment. So it isn't that *one* person *becomes* two. Rather, one space–time *segment* (Mary back on Earth) forms a *part* of each of two distinct four-dimensional worms. What we can call "Mary-on-Earth" is really just a shared *portion* of two distinct people – Mary A, and Mary B.

This proposal would involve radical changes in the way in which we think and reason in our daily lives. I normally think of myself as

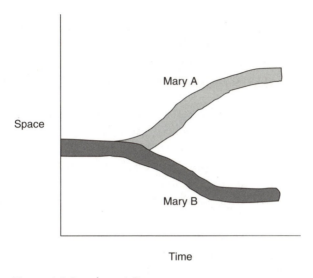

Figure 6.4 People as 4-D worms.

being wholly present right now; and when I think of my past, or my future, I am thinking of people who are similarly wholly-present at the times I am thinking about, but who are, nevertheless, *me* – they are related to me by the relation of identity-over-time. So, when I reason about what to do – whether I should go to the mountains or go to the beach, for example – I am reasoning about which place I should arrange for *myself* to be in at some future time. According to the four-dimensionalist, in contrast, it isn't me *qua* person who thinks about anything; rather, it is a person-segment which does the thinking. In thinking about "its" past and "its" future, that segment is really thinking about other distinct *segments* of the very same person – that is to say, of the same space–time worm. In reasoning whether to go to the mountains or the beach, I should really be reasoning about *which* person (which space–time worm) I (this segment) want to be a *part* of. My thought should have the form: do I want to be part of a person whose other parts are in the mountains this weekend, or do I want to be part of a person whose other parts are at the beach?

Now, I have no objections of principle to the idea of reforming our conceptual system. Indeed, I shall be urging such a reform in section 3.6 below – I shall be arguing that we should stop thinking of personal survival as requiring identity, and should think rather in terms which would permit each of two distinct people to be

213

survivors of a single original. But any such reforms need to be *motivated*. My own proposal is motivated by practical considerations, as we shall see. It keeps our basic three-dimensionalist conceptual scheme, but suggests that our concepts of "survival" and "continued existence" should be weakened somewhat, by dropping any implication of numerical identity from them. Then, the argument is that such a reform would better serve the kinds of interest which we take in the survival of ourselves and others.

The alternative proposal being canvassed here, is that we should drop our three-dimensionalist conceptual scheme, and replace it with a four-dimensional one. This would involve a major upheaval in the way in which we think and reason about ourselves and others. Its only advantage is that it would enable us to continue thinking of survival as involving identity – to say that A survives as B would now be to say that both A and B are segments of the very same space–time worm. For this to have a point, there would have to be some powerful reason why we should *want* to conceptualize survival in terms of identity. But in fact no such reason exists. As we shall see, the truth is merely that we have fallen into thinking of survival in terms of identity because it is somewhat *easier* to think that way in relation to the sorts of cases which we normally have to confront.

3.6   *Practical considerations in survival*

Let us set four-dimensionalism to one side, then, and return to the familiar three-dimensionalist framework. How *ought* we to regard cases of duplication from a third-person perspective? In a case of radio-transportation, for example, how should Mary's relatives respond to the knowledge that there now exist two exact replicas of her? It is impossible to believe that they would be stricken with grief. Yet on any three-dimensionalist conception of survival as involving identity, Mary herself ceased to exist when her original body back on Earth was destroyed. The existence of two replicas would be disturbing, of course. (Imagine meeting both of them together for the first time!) But once they get used to the idea, Mary's relatives should surely be equally interested in and concerned about *both* of them.

An analogy may help here. Suppose that you have spent a good deal of time with someone over a period of months, and have grown to care for them very much. But then you discover that you have in fact been in the company, on alternative occasions, of a pair of identical twins who are physically and psychologically extremely similar. Although the discovery would be disorientating, you ought surely to realize, as you adjust to the idea, that you in fact care for them both. The similarity with the example of duplication should be clear: in this case you *believed* that you loved one person where in fact there were two; and in the other, your relatives did in the past love one person, where *now* there are two.

From the point of view of blame and punishment, as well, we should surely respond as though both replicas were survivors of the original. For suppose that the person back on Earth turns out to have been a vicious criminal. Are we really going to allow the two replicas to wander around free, on the grounds that the person who committed the crimes no longer exists? Surely not: for both will have the same desires, beliefs and vicious qualities as the original. Indeed both will be chuckling gleefully at the thought that the error made by the machine-operator has given them a lucky escape from prosecution. Here we would obviously be mad to let considerations of identity stand in the way of an early arrest. (If this involves changing our conception of "just punishment", then so be it.)

From the point of view of the replicas themselves after the fact, they too would surely regard themselves as survivors of the original. Obviously they won't feel as though they have just come into existence. On the contrary, their lives will seem to them to be continuous with that of the original: each will quasi-remember many events from life on Earth, and will quasi-remember getting into the radio-transportation machine; moreover each will find themselves with the same familiar desires, interests and affective ties as the original.

Their situation would bring its own problems with it, of course. For each would presumably try to claim the same job as the original Mary, and would try to move in with the same spouse. So some sort of compromise would have to be worked out, which might cause unhappiness. Indeed the mere existence of someone who is (initially at least) exactly similar to yourself, may be difficult to adjust to psychologically. But none of this is likely to change their view of themselves as having once lived on Earth, and as having survived the process of radio-transportation.

But how ought one to regard the prospect of duplication prior to the fact? If Mary knows that the radio-transportation machine is faulty, so that there is no way to visit her relatives on the one planet without a duplicate being created on the other, then how should she decide? Would the outcome be one in which she has ceased to exist, to be feared as she fears death? Or would it be almost as good as normal survival? It will help here if we once again consider separately the situation as it should be regarded from the point of view of a person's impersonal and self-regarding desires.

From the point of view of most impersonal desires the situation is mostly straightforward: two heads are better than one. For example, the dedicated political activist should regard the prospect of there being two people who possess their political skills and desire for revolution, as actually being *better* than normal survival. Similarly, the person whose major desire is to see Shakespeare properly translated into Japanese should realize that there would be more chance of the task being carried out successfully if there were two people who shared their desire, their linguistic skills and literary sensibility, who could divide the labor between them.

In the case of an impersonal desire for the welfare of a loved one the situation is marginally more complicated. In some respects the existence of two lovers would be an advantage: think, for example, how much more successfully they could nurse the loved one through a serious illness. But it may also be a source of distress to the loved one, if there were to exist two different (but exactly similar) lovers, between whom they would have to divide attention. So in this respect duplication may be less welcome than ordinary survival. But it would still be a great deal better than ordinary death. For if the worst came to the worst, the two duplicates could always draw lots for one of them to absent themselves from the scene, leaving the other to care for the loved one alone.

From the point of view of our self-referring desires the issue is difficult. For such desires will normally be expressed using the personal pronoun "I", which seems to require identity and hence uniqueness. If I want a holiday in Sri Lanka, then I want that I myself should have a holiday in Sri Lanka; and this seems to be the same as wanting that the future person who will be identical with myself should holiday in Sri Lanka. However, I doubt whether uniqueness is really an essential component of my desire. When I think of what I should really want from such a holiday, I imagine – from the inside – lying under coconut palms on white beaches and eating crab-curry in the local restaurants; all against a background of desires and interests similar to my own. At no point do I think, "And there should be no other person who is similarly psychologically connected with myself, who is also enjoying such experiences." So why should I regard my desire as having been *frustrated* if duplication were somehow to occur along the way (as I would have to do if self-identity were an essential ingredient in it)? In fact when I spell out to myself what I should really want from a holiday in Sri Lanka, I find that I am indifferent to the thought of duplication occurring in the interim.

I conclude that from the point of view of the various kinds of practical interest which we take in survival, whether of ourselves or others, we should regard duplication as being nearly as good as normal survival. Now against this must be set the fact that we do undoubtedly think of survival in terms of identity. It is deeply embedded in our habits of thought and speech that one person can only be a survivor of another if they are uniquely related (i.e., numerically identical). Thus we say, "If Mary has survived then *she* is lucky", and take this to imply, "If Mary has survived then the living person who is identical with Mary is lucky". But if, as we have seen, identity itself doesn't matter, then what we ought to do is stop thinking and speaking in this way. We should stop thinking of survival in terms of identity, and instead use a notion of survival which will allow one person to survive as two.

3.7 Conceptual pragmatism

I claim that we are mistaken in thinking of our survival as requiring identity. But this isn't a mistake of fact. Rather we have got into the way of using the wrong concept. It is easy to understand how this should have happened. For since cases of duplication have never in fact occurred, we have never had occasion to distinguish between personal *survival* over time and personal *identity* over time. They have always gone along together in the past, and in some respects it is simpler to talk in terms of identity. But as we approach the time when duplication may become technically feasible, the situation will change. Even now, reflecting on imagined cases of duplication, we can see that we are, strictly speaking, employing the wrong concept of personal survival; although this hardly matters for everyday purposes.

The general thesis underlying this line of thought might be called "conceptual pragmatism". It consists of two parts: (a) there are always more concepts available to us in a given area of discourse than we need; and (b) our selection of concepts from the range of alternatives should be governed by the purposes for which we wish to employ them.

A concept is a mode of classifying things: our different concepts represent different ways of dividing up the world. So thesis (a) tells us that there are always more ways of classifying things than we actually use, or need to use. This is obviously true. Think of the many different ways in which we might divide up the color-spectrum, for example, and hence the many different ways in which we might classify things in terms of their colors. Some of these modes of classification will come very much more naturally to us than others, of course, given the causal structures underlying human perception. But it remains true that there are many alternatives available. For instance, we might classify together the shades of color between mid-blue and mid-green (perhaps called "bleen"), if it suited our purposes to do so. (Suppose we lived in an area where the only edible plants had leaves whose colors fell within that range.)

There is no such thing as the right way to divide up the color spectrum, unless this means, "the way which is most in accord with the purposes for which we classify things in terms of their colors". For that spectrum certainly doesn't come to us already divided up, in such a way that we are constrained in our choice of concepts to respect the divisions which already exist within it. The same goes for items of furniture and foodstuffs: since there is no such thing as the correct set of concepts to use in classifying these things, we have to make a choice.

Wherever there are alternatives available, the only sense in which a choice can be correct or incorrect is that it can accord or fail to accord with our purposes. Now sometimes, but not always, our purposes will be scientific. In that case there will be a sense in which we shall want our modes of classification to correspond to the natural divisions in reality. That is to say: to the divisions which would figure in the various causal laws of a completed science. But more often our purposes will be social, as when we choose concepts for classifying colors, foodstuffs and items of furniture. Here our modes of classification may cut right across those which a scientist would wish to employ. So as thesis (b) above claims: the concepts which we actually employ, from the wider range of possibilities, should be determined in accordance with our purposes.

Once we realize that there will always exist alternatives to the modes of classification which we presently employ; and once we realize that our selection from the range of alternatives should be governed by our purposes; then the possibility opens up that we may find ourselves, upon reflection, to have been employing the wrong concepts. For we will often just have *fallen into* a way of classifying things, without anyone ever having consciously selected that concept in the light of our purposes. A practice will somehow have grown up, and selections may have been made for all sorts of irrelevant historical reasons. This is especially likely to have happened wherever the alternative concepts differ only in the judgments which they would deliver in various imaginable, but non-actual, circumstances.

This is exactly the situation in which we find ourselves with respect to the concepts of personal survival and personal existence over time. Both of these concepts, as presently employed, imply identity: "x is a survivor of y" implies, "x is identical with y", and, "x continues to exist" implies, "There is still (at some later time) a person who is none other than x". But the concepts which would best subserve the sorts of interest which we take in the survival of ourselves and others do *not* imply identity. Therefore, we ought to change our modes of classification. We ought to understand the term "survive" in such a way that two distinct people can both be survivors of a single original. We ought to allow that a person continues to exist, at any particular time, just so long as there exists at that time *some* survivor of them (perhaps more than one). Since our interest in selves certainly isn't a scientific one, it is irrelevant whether or not the concept of a person or *self*, so construed, would correspond to any natural division within reality (that is to say: to any division which would be recognized by a completed science).

I conclude that there is a sense in which reincarnation is possible, after all. For the best conception of personal survival is one which is defined purely in terms of psychological connectedness. This would allow one physical human being to be a personal survivor of another, provided that they are sufficiently strongly psychologically connected. (Just what should count as "sufficient", here, is an interesting and important question – see section 4 below.) Since this preferred conception doesn't imply that a survivor of a person must also be identical with them, the possibility of duplication doesn't constitute a genuine objection to the idea of reincarnation (so understood).

4 Limits of individual survival

We have argued for the use of a concept of personal survival which would leave room for the possibility that we might, through reincarnation, survive normal bodily death. This is a welcome result, since it means we can hope that either God or the scientists might bring it about that death will not be the end of our existence. But we come now to a somewhat less welcome consequence. Namely: that some of us might not even survive long enough to *reach* bodily death.

4.1   Does each of us survive unto death?

The simplest sort of example would be this. Imagine that military scientists have developed a technique of radical brain-washing – to be called "brain-wiping" – which not only destroys all quasi-memories, but also all developed desires, interests and traces of individual personality. Then a person after brain-wiping will not, on our account, be a survivor of the earlier person. For the two of them will not be directly psychologically connected, nor will they be linked by a series of overlapping connections. On the contrary, the brain-wiping represents a clean break. (Note, however, that a person *would* normally survive ordinary amnesia; for this only involves the loss of personal memory, leaving many other psychological connections intact.) But it is no real objection to our account that people therefore wouldn't survive brain-wiping. For this is also a consequence of the thesis argued for in section 1, that bodily identity isn't sufficient for personal survival. For the only connection between the people before and after brain-wiping would be the body.

The issues raised by cases of severe senility are more interesting. For an extremely senile individual may be able to recall nothing of their earlier life, and share none of their earlier desires and interests. There may thus exist no direct psychological connections between Mary in middle age and Mary as a senile old lady. The two will, however, be linked together by a series of overlapping connections. For the senile Mary will be able to recall events from moment-to-moment and day-to-day; and these will stretch back in a chain of connections which will eventually reach Mary in middle age. Then has Mary survived into senility or not? (Similar questions arise in connection with babies. For I can recall nothing of my earliest years; nor do I share any desires or interests with that individual. Yet we are presumably linked together by a chain of overlapping psychological connections.)

What is at issue here is this: ought we to choose to think in terms of a concept of survival involving only direct psychological connectedness? Thus:

(D) Person x at t_1 survives as person y at t_2 if and only if x and y are sufficiently strongly psychologically connected.

Or should we choose to think in terms of a concept which is modeled more closely on the account of personal identity sketched in Chapter 3:2, allowing a person to survive across a series of overlapping psychological connections? Thus:

(O) Person x at t_1 survives as person y at t_2 if and only if either (i) x and y are sufficiently strongly psychologically connected, or (ii) y is, by repeated applications of clause (i), a survivor of someone who is, again by clause (i), a survivor of x.

We need to decide which of these two concepts would best subserve the kinds of interest which we take in survival.

From a third-person perspective there is no reason to regard one person as a survivor of another, if there exists only indirect psychological connections between them. Thus suppose that you have been friends with a person x at time t_1 (at kindergarten, say), but then do not see them again until the much later time, t_3 (in a retirement home). During the interim x has altered out of all recognition, changing first into person y at t_2, and then into z at t_3. Person y still retains many psychological connections with x, as z does with y; but z has lost all trace of psychological connectedness with x. Now when you meet z in retirement, what motive have you for regarding that person as being (a survivor of) your friend at t_1? I suggest none. For z will recall nothing of your previous friendship, and will have lost all of the interests and personal qualities which formed the basis of your friendship with x. Moreover, supposing x to have committed some evil deed, it would seem pointless to blame or punish z. For that person will remember nothing of it, and will have lost all the desires and vices which led x to commit that act.

From a first-person perspective after the fact, why should z on looking back regard the things done by x as forming part of his own life? For he will in fact remember nothing of it, having to be told about those events by other people. Now of course this information will hold a certain fascination, since it may furnish explanations of features of z's own character. (As when I find an explanation of my nervous twitch in the fact that I was battered as a baby.) But this interest seems all-of-a-piece with the kind of interest which we take in the lives of our parents and ancestors: we know that things which happened to them may have had indirect effects upon ourselves.

From a first-person perspective before the fact there seems little reason to regard someone as a survivor of oneself, with whom one is only indirectly psychologically connected. This is certainly true from the point of view of our impersonal desires. For those desires themselves, and the personal qualities which might have made fulfillment of them more likely, will all have been lost in that future person. So far as my self-referring desires go, why should I take an interest in someone merely because someone in whom I *do* take an interest takes an interest in them? Thus x will take a personal interest in the existence of y, and y will take a similar interest in z; but why should that provide x with any reason to think of z as being a survivor of himself? In fact when I look forward to the senile individual whom I (my body) will one day become, I find it impossible to take any personal interest in him.

(Note that if x desires that *all* of y's desires should be satisfied, and one of those desires is the desire that all of z's desires should be satisfied, then x will, after all, have to take an interest in z. But which of us desires that literally all of our future desires should be satisfied? – For we know that many of them may be for things we should now abhor.)

I conclude that we should think of our existence as people in terms of a concept of survival which requires some degree of direct psychological connectedness. Then the existence of many of us, as people, will be rather briefer than our existence as human beings; and the life of a single human being may be constituted by the lives of a number of different people.

4.2   Is survival a matter of degree?

Psychological connectedness is, of course, a matter of degree. In the case of a very young child it will gradually increase in extent from day-to-day and month-to-month; and in the case of the very old it will gradually fade away. Moreover, people's personalities – their interests, desires and memories – will often alter a great deal during the course of a lifetime, sometimes quite radically. We therefore face a choice, we can either select a concept which allows that survival, too, is a matter of degree; saying that x will survive as y *to the extent that* they are psychologically connected. Or we can insist that survival (like identity) should be an all-or-nothing matter; in which case we shall need to choose the precise degree of psychological connectedness necessary for survival. We shall then say that x will survive as y, if and only if, they are psychologically connected *to such-and-such an extent.*

There is in fact no reason to choose a concept which would make survival an all-or-nothing matter. For the interest which we take in survival isn't all-or-nothing. Rather, our desires for the future are generally multifarious, as is the nature of our attachment to other people. So when I imagine a whole series of progressively more extensive brain-wipings, causing greater and greater loss of psychological connectedness, I am conscious of a *gradual* loss of interest in the welfare of that future person, and (in my own case) of steadily increasing fear at the prospect of my own (partial) loss of existence. There certainly doesn't come any particular point at which, having been happy to regard the person as surviving until then, I suddenly think, "But *that* would be the end of him".

When it comes to choosing a measure of the precise *extent* of personal survival, to be constructed somehow out of the extent of psychological connectedness, we might be tempted to go for fragmentation into a number of different concepts. For here the different kinds of interest which we take in survival can pull in different directions. From the point of view of the interest which people will take in their own survival, we should perhaps choose a concept which relies upon the subject's own evaluations. Most of us have a rough hierarchy of desires and interests. Some of our projects, memories and ties of affection are more important to us than others, and should accordingly be given greater weight in determining the degree of survival. But some of them we may wish we did not have at all, as when I want to be rid of my desire for wealth, and these should accordingly be given no weight.

From the point of view of blame and responsibility, on the other hand, the subject's own evaluations are of little relevance. What matters is the extent of the changes which may have taken place in their moral character – the virtues and vices which they may have lost or acquired, and the changes in those of their desires which have moral significance. It is these things which should accordingly be given greater weight in determining the degree to which the person has survived.

223

In fact, however, we don't have to let our concept of degrees of survival fragment in this way. We can allow for the different points of view from which we may wish to employ the concept, by writing a reference to them into the concept itself. Thus: x's degree of survival as y is given by the extent to which they have the sorts of psychological connections *which are important for the purposes in hand*. Then if the purposes in hand are those of x himself, we may judge one thing; but if the purposes in hand are those of determining an appropriate punishment, we may judge another.

(There would be nothing unique in our employment of a concept of this sort. Concepts which can vary in application according to our purposes are very handy things to have, and it is arguable that we already possess quite a few of them. For instance, if a tank-commander asks for a flat field on which to practice maneuvers, you may point to one and say truthfully, "That one is flat"; but if the local bowls club come asking for a flat field, you may point to the very same one and truthfully say, "That one is *not* flat". The word "flat" seems to mean something like, "is close enough to being absolutely flat for the purposes in hand".)

Once we start thinking of our survival as people as a matter of degree, then we shan't only find application for the idea in imaginary examples, but also in real life. We shall say that the person I am now is only a partial survivor of the person I was as an adolescent; and that the person I shall be at retirement will only be a partial survivor of the person I am now. This isn't at all an unnatural way of thinking of our lives. (There are many examples in literature where people's lives are described in precisely these terms.) As a matter of fact, I felt entirely distanced from the person I was as an adolescent, even before starting to think systematically about these issues. I should have said, "Looking back, it feels like the life of a stranger". Indeed, we can now see that those Christians who talk about "being born again" may be speaking more literally than they know. For given that there is a considerable change of beliefs and values at the point of conversion, the person after that time will very likely be only a partial survivor of the earlier. They will be partially (and literally) a new person.

Conclusion

The final important obstacle in the way of acceptance of physicalism should now have been overcome. People who believe in the existence of the soul because they believe in an after-life, grounded in religious faith, should see that their religious beliefs are just as consistent with physicalism as with strong dualism. Physicalists can believe in an after-life through belief in the resurrection of the body. Or physicalists might believe in a form of reincarnation, provided they believe that there will be a later body which is sufficiently strongly psychologically connected with themselves.

(Admittedly, many religions do use the language of "soul" and "spirit". But this needn't be interpreted in such a way as to involve a commitment to strong dualism. Rather, it can be interpreted as referring to the *spiritual side of our nature* – for example, to higher emotions, altruism, and impersonal love. There is nothing in physicalism which need prevent recognition of our nature as spiritual beings, in this sense.)

An equally important upshot of our discussions, however, is that we should change the way in which we conceptualize our own survival. We should stop thinking of survival as requiring identity, and as being an all-or-nothing matter. We should, instead, think of survival as given in terms of (some degree of) direct psychological connectedness. This allows that one person might survive as more than one. It also allows survival to be a matter of degree – someone can, on this account, quite literally be a *partial* survivor of an earlier self. Indeed, this is probably the situation we are all in with respect to our existence as children.

Questions for discussion

1. Can the human body survive across periods of non-existence?
2. Suppose you knew that your brain was about to be "wiped clean" of all traces of memory and personality: should you have hopes or fears for what will happen to your body afterwards?
3. What kinds of reasons are there for wanting to survive? Are they in any way tied to the existence of a particular body?
4. Might we be employing the wrong concept of personal survival? Would the right concept be one where it would be possible for one person to survive as two different people?
5. People sometimes say, "I am not the person I once was". Is there any literal truth in what they say?

Further reading

Carruthers, P. (1987) "Conceptual pragmatism", *Synthese* vol. 73.

Dennett, D. (1979) "Where am I?", in Dennett, D. (ed.) *Brainstorms*, Brighton: Harvester Press.

Lewis, D. (1979) "Survival and Identity", in Rorty, A. (ed.), *The Identities of Persons*, Berkeley: University of California Press. Reprinted in Lewis, D. (ed.) (1983) *Philosophical Papers*, vol. 1, Oxford: Oxford University Press.

Martin, R. (1998) *Self-Concern: an experiential approach to what matters in survival*, Cambridge: Cambridge University Press.

Parfit, D. (1971) "Personal Identity", *Philosophical Review*, vol. 80. Reprinted in Glover, J. (ed.) (1976), *The Philosophy of Mind*, Oxford: Oxford University Press and in Perry, J. (ed.) (1975), *Personal Identity*, Berkeley: University of California Press.

Parfit, D. (1984) *Reasons and Persons*, Oxford: Oxford University Press, part 3.

Perry, J. (1979) "The importance of being identical", in Rorty, A. (ed.), *The Identities of Persons*, Berkeley: University of California Press.

Shoemaker, S. (1984) "A Materialist's Account", in Shoemaker, S. and Swinburne, R. (eds) *Personal Identity*, Oxford: Blackwell.

Williams, B. (1956–7) "Personal Identity and Individuation", *Proceedings of the Aristotelian Society*, vol. 57. Reprinted in Gustafson, D. (ed.) (1964) *Essays on Philosophical Psychology*, London: Macmillan and in Williams, B. (ed.) (1973) *Problems of the Self*, Cambridge: Cambridge University Press.

Williams, B. (1970) "The self and the future", *Philosophical Review*, vol. 79. Reprinted in Glover, J. (ed.) (1976), *The Philosophy of Mind*, Oxford: Oxford University Press in Perry, J. (ed.) (1975), *Personal Identity*, Berkeley: University of California Press and in Williams, B. (ed.) (1973) *Problems of the Self*, Cambridge: Cambridge University Press.

7

⏤◈⏤

The case for theory-theory

In this chapter we return to the question of how we conceive of our mental states, as well as to the question of how we have knowledge of the mental states of other people. Much of the chapter develops and motivates a position on the former question which is now "orthodox" among philosophers of mind. On this theory-theory account, mental state concepts get their life and sense from their embedding in a common-sense causal theory of the mind and its operations. (The "theory-theory" is so-called because it is the *theory* that common-sense concepts are embedded in a *theory*.) The chapter also shows how theory-theory can provide us with a satisfying solution to the problem of other minds.

1 From Cartesian conception to philosophical functionalism

Nothing in our critique of strong dualism, nor in our defense of physicalism, has yet challenged the thesis argued for in Chapter 1:4, which we called the "Cartesian conception" of the meanings of terms referring to mental states. This holds that those meanings are wholly concerned with the subjective feel of the corresponding states – concepts of mental states are, in effect, *recognitional* concepts for the way those states feel to us when we have them. The Cartesian conception has been almost universally rejected throughout the 20th and 21st centuries, however. For a substantial portion of this time – especially in the middle part of the 20th century – philosophers have gone to the other extreme of analyzing mental state terms purely behaviorally. This section charts the movement from the Cartesian conception through behaviorism to its later descendants, functionalism and theory-theory. Much of the remainder of the chapter will then be taken up with elaborating and defending the latter, and exploring its implications for the problem of other minds.

1.1 Against the Cartesian conception

Historically speaking, one major reason for the rejection of the Cartesian conception in the middle part of the 20th century had to do with a set of arguments against the possibility of private concepts, developed by the influential Austrian philosopher Ludwig Wittgenstein, who taught and wrote at the University of Cambridge. These are generally referred to in the singular as "the private language argument". According to these arguments, concepts which refer just to the private feelings of a thinker – in such a way that applications of those concepts can neither be checked by others nor compared with any sort of objective standard – are impossible; there can exist no such concepts. I am very doubtful, however, whether any of these arguments are successful. Certainly the issues which they raise are difficult and complex. They will therefore not be pursued any further in the present book.

There are a number of reasons why the Cartesian conception of the meaning of mental state terms should still be unacceptable, however, quite apart from any argument from the impossibility of private concepts. The first is that it leaves us with no room for the intuitive distinction between conscious and unconscious mental states. If the concepts *thought* and *emotion*, for example, consist in introspective recognitional capacities for the distinctive sorts of feel which such mental states have, then the very idea of an *un*conscious thought or an *un*conscious emotion (which would, of course, be states lacking any introspectible phenomenology) should be unintelligible. But they are not. Ever since Freud's influential writings, at least, the idea that we can have thoughts and emotions which aren't conscious ones has been part of every person's common-sense world-view. There is now robust scientific evidence that almost all types of mental state (including perceptual states) admit of unconscious analogues.

A second point is that the Cartesian conception makes it difficult to see how we could think that some mental states can even *continue to exist* in the absence of consciousness. Thus, as we have noted before, I can say of someone who is asleep that she believes she has been betrayed, and is still angry and bitter about it. In saying this I might surely say something true. But I don't think that the person must be undergoing certain characteristic introspectible feelings in her sleep, as I would do if I thought that all mental states consisted in private *feels* for which I possess recognitional concepts. Rather, I am describing states which are somehow dormant in her during sleep, but which might have a causal impact on her thinking and behavior when she wakes.

The third objection to the Cartesian conception is that we can have concepts of mental states which we have never enjoyed; in which case it is hard to believe that our conception of such states can consist in just a bare recognitional capacity for their subjective "feels". For example, I have concepts of beliefs and desires which I have never had, such as the belief that there is a red dragon on the roof. Indeed, I have unlimitedly many such concepts, since I have the concepts *belief that P, belief that P and Q belief that P and Q and R,* and so on. The combinatorial powers of my language puts me in position to understand unlimitedly many that-clauses, each one of which can form a component in a distinct belief-concept. Yet it is hard to see how I could have recognitional capacities for unlimitedly many such states. For how can I have a bare capacity to recognize the feel of a state which I have never enjoyed, let alone have unlimitedly many such capacities?

The only way forward that I can see for the Cartesian conception, here, is to borrow a claim which has been defended by some people, namely that conscious propositional episodes of judging, wondering whether, and so on, consist in deployments of imaged sentences in "inner speech"; and to couple this with the claim that we can immediately recognize such images in virtue of the way that they feel to us. This enables the account to harness the creative powers of language to explain our capacity to recognize in ourselves an unlimited number of propositional episodes, and makes it seem plausible that there will, indeed, be a feeling distinctive of thinking that there is a dragon on the roof, say – namely the distinctive feel of *imaging the sentence*, "There is a dragon on the roof".

Thus I can, on this account, recognize in myself the new act of wondering whether there is a dragon on the roof (never before encountered), because this action consists in the formation of an image of the sentence, "Is there a dragon on the roof?" (which is a state *a bit like hearing* that sentence); and because I can recognize this image in myself in virtue of being capable of recognizing the distinctive feels of its component parts.

While such a view can avoid the objection as originally stated, it is premised on a hugely controversial thesis: namely, that all propositional thinking is conducted in images of natural language sentences. Moreover, there remain a number of other difficulties with this way of developing the Cartesian conception. Notice, to begin with, that I should have to do a good deal of inductive learning from my own case before I could be capable of explaining and predicting any behavior, on this account. I should have to learn, in particular, that whenever I am aware of the distinctive feel of an intention, where the feel is similar to that of hearing an utterance of the form of words "P", that I thereafter generally find myself performing actions describable as "P". Since these feelings don't wear their causal efficacy on their sleeves, I should also have to reason to the best explanation, having discovered reliable correlations between feelings of various types, to arrive at a theory of the causal sequences involved.

Notice, too, just how *opaque* an explanation of action would seem at this early stage. It would have the normal form:

> *This* feel and *this* feel caused *that* feel. [This belief and this desire caused that intention.] And *that* feel caused me to do P. [That intention caused my action.]

The suggestion that one could get from here to anything recognizable as belief–desire psychology is about as plausible (that is, immensely *im*plausible) as the claim that we can get from descriptions of sequences of sense-data (that is, visual experiences described merely in terms of colors and patterns of light and shade) to full-blown descriptions of physical reality.

Philosophers and psychologists alike have long since given up believing that children learn to construct the world of three-dimensional physical objects, and then arrive at something resembling common-sense physics, by establishing inductive correlations among sense-data and reasoning to the best explanation thereof. Indeed, the most recent evidence is that human babies interpret the world three-dimensionally almost from birth; and that the basic principles of a simple contact-physics are in place by the age of about three months, with an understanding that one solid object cannot pass through another, that an object placed behind a screen should still be there when the screen is removed, and so on. No one any longer thinks that the infant acquires these principles by theorizing from a set of initially uninterpreted sense-data. On the contrary, most now accept that some core set of those principles must be innate, acquired through some process involved in biological maturation, rather than being learned from experience.

The idea that children have to construct a folk-psychology from their first-person acquaintance with their own feelings should seem equally indefensible. For in both domains, note, the classifications made by the folk have to reflect, and respect, a rich causal structure. In the physical domain children need to understand how objects can move and be moved, how they react on contact, how solids differ from liquids, and so forth. In the mental domain, similarly, children need to understand how beliefs and desires can be formed, and how both can be influenced by perception; that beliefs can represent the world incorrectly; how beliefs and desires lead to intentions through processes of practical reasoning, and how intentions lead to actions in relation to the perceived environment; and so on and so forth. In which case, even if we were to agree that all mental states *have* introspectively accessible feels, fit to be objects of immediate recognition, it still remains true that such feelings are useless for purposes of explanation until supplemented by much additional causal knowledge. Such knowledge cannot plausibly be arrived at from such a meager initial basis through some combination of inductive learning and theorizing. (I shall return to this point briefly in section 2 below, and I shall be arguing for the innateness of the core principles of our common-sense psychology in section 3.)

1.2 The case for behaviorism

The problem of other minds is still with us. As we saw in Chapter 5:2, even if we accept that mental states are physical states of the brain, I still cannot have knowledge by analogy, on that basis, of the particular mental states which other people undergo. So long as we adhere to the Cartesian conception of the meaning of mental state terms, there can be no (conceptually) valid arguments from the observed physical circumstances and behavior of other human beings to descriptions of their states of mind. So either way we lack sufficient reason to believe in the existence of any other specific mental states besides our own. Now with the Cartesian conception rejected, we need to investigate how well the proposed replacements for it may fare with respect to the problem of other minds.

It is worth reminding ourselves just how counter-intuitive the skeptical conclusion is, that we can have no specific knowledge of any other mental states besides our own. Imagine that you see a friend fall heavily in a skiing accident. You approach to find him with an obviously-broken leg, groaning loudly, with his face contorted in apparent agony. Naturally you would have not the slightest doubt that he is really in pain. Just try, in a case of this sort, holding on to the thought, "This might merely be the behavior of a unconscious zombie, or he may just be feeling a slight tickle in his scalp rather than a pain in his leg"! It is almost psychologically impossible to do. Of course, this doesn't by itself show that the thought in question is false, since we may somehow be caused to believe something which we really have no reason to believe. But it does bring out just how difficult it would be to live with the conclusion that we have no knowledge of other people's mental states.

Since we are actually quite certain of the mental states of other people, on some occasions, and since all our judgments concerning those states are based upon observations of their behavior, this gives us a powerful motive for saying that those judgments are, themselves, judgments *about* behavior. This is the thesis of the philosophical behaviorists, whose most prominent members in the middle part of the 20th century included the Oxford philosopher Gilbert Ryle and (on some interpretations, at least) his Cambridge counter-part, Ludwig Wittgenstein. Behaviorism aims to solve the problem of other minds by providing an analysis – a definition, a translation – of all words referring to mental states into purely behavioral terms. On this view, there simply is nothing to our mental states over and above behavior and dispositions to behave.

The philosophical behaviorist can claim, and with some justice, that our thesis of the logical independence of mental and physical states (see Chapter 1:4) was granted far too readily. Certainly the truth of this thesis doesn't follow from the obvious facts that someone can be in pain without showing it, and can be exhibiting pain-behavior without really being in pain. Nor does it follow, from the fact that descriptions of actual behavior are neither necessary nor sufficient for the correct application of a mental state term, that the meanings of such terms can't be cashed purely behaviorally. All that really follows, is that a behavioral analysis would have to be complicated, to take into account not only actual behavior, but also "dispositional" or "hypothetical" behavior. For it may still be true of the person who is in pain but doesn't show it, that he would acknowledge being in pain *if* we asked him, or that he would have groaned *if* he hadn't been aware of us watching him, and so on. It may still be true of the person who exhibits pain-behavior without really being in pain, that he would confess to be practicing for a performance in a play *if* we asked him, or that he wouldn't be behaving as he is *if* there were no one watching him, and so on. It is in such terms that behaviorists may hope to frame their definitions.

So although we might initially be inclined to object against the behaviorist, that a person can surely feel a twinge of pain which they don't express at the time, and which they immediately forget about so that it never emerges in any way in their behavior, this is really no difficulty. For it may still be true that *if* someone had asked, "How do you feel?" they would then have replied, "I feel a twinge of pain." This is all that the behaviorist claims to need: the fact of the person feeling that twinge, simply consists in the fact that they would have given such a reply if asked.

What does begin to emerge is just how complicated a behaviorist analysis of words like "pain" would have to be, however. It would have to proceed roughly as follows: someone is in pain if and only if, either (a) they exhibit characteristic pain-behavior (think how complicated a detailed spelling-out of this would be) and wouldn't later say "I was only pretending" etc. in one of a range of hypothetical circumstances; or (b) they don't exhibit pain-behavior but would say "I am in pain" if asked, and wouldn't later say "I was lying" etc.; or (c) they don't exhibit pain-behavior and wouldn't say "I am in pain" if asked, but would have exhibited pain-behavior if the circumstances had been different (i.e., if they had had no motive for pretending); ... and so on. But naturally mere complexity cannot show philosophical behaviorism to be false: the mind is indeed complicated.

Behaviorism does have its attractions, then. It allows humans to be included smoothly within the natural order by avoiding postulation of anything "ghostly" inside the organic machinery of the body. It is thus able to reject any sort of ontological dualism between non-physical minds and physical bodies. Behaviorism also promises a complete defense of our knowledge of the mental states of other people (perhaps *too complete* – see section 1.4 below). For knowing about others' minds is reduced to knowing about their behavioral dispositions. Furthermore, it seems to be right, as behaviorists were quick to point out, that people can correctly be described as knowing this or believing that, irrespective of what is going on inside them at the time – indeed, even when they are

233

asleep. This makes perfectly good sense if beliefs are really just behavioral dispositions.

1.3 Reductive versus holistic behaviorism

Despite the strength of the above arguments, there are in fact devastating objections to behaviorism, if it claims to spell out the nature of each type of mental state into purely behavioral terms (call this "reductive behaviorism"). These objections arise most obviously in connection with the attempt to give behavioral analyses of beliefs and desires. For a belief only disposes to action in the presence of certain desires. Also, a desire only disposes to action in the presence of certain beliefs.

For example, there really isn't any behavior which is characteristic of someone who believes that the ice on a particular pond is thin. If they desire death by drowning, then their belief may lead them to go skating. If they desire someone else's death, it may lead them to say, "That is a good place to skate." If they possess neither of these desires, then they will presumably do something else instead; but precisely what they do will depend upon their other beliefs and desires. Moreover, all this is only "may" and not "must". Even if they desire death by drowning they aren't guaranteed to go skating. On the contrary, their abhorrence of cold water may send them heading for the bathroom with a bottle of sleeping-tablets.

It looks as if a behaviorist analysis of belief will require clauses referring to various hypothetical desires. The clauses will specify the behavior which may be expected of someone holding that belief, who also has the desire in question. (For example: someone with belief P will do x if they have desire D, and will do y if they have desire E.) But then when we come to the behaviorist analysis of desire, this will in its turn require clauses referring to various hypothetical beliefs. (For example: someone with desire D will do x if they believe P, and will do z if they believe Q.) We should then be forced to move in circles.

It is doubtful whether the sort of circularity which is involved here must be vicious, however, nor that it must totally undermine the behaviorist program. For there are other areas in which groups of concepts are similarly intertwined, in such a way that it is impossible to explain any one of them without mentioning the others. For example, the concepts of space and of physical objects are interrelated in just such a fashion.

You can't explain the concept of a physical object to someone without introducing the idea of occupancy of space. Indeed, the criteria of identity and individuation for physical objects palpably involve the concepts of spatial position and change of spatial position. But then, on the other hand, you can't explain the concept of space without bringing in talk of physical objects. For it is arguable that space itself just *is* relations obtaining between physical objects, so that if there were no physical objects there wouldn't be any space either. At any rate, you certainly can't form any conception of particular places (e.g., the spatial position of London) except as relative to the place occupied by yourself ("London is over *there*"), or the places occupied by physical things with which you are already familiar ("London is due south of Leeds").

Philosophers describe concepts which are intertwined in this kind of way as being related "holistically". Other examples come from science, where a group of new concepts may be introduced at the same time as a new scientific theory, in such a way that each one of those concepts can only be defined in terms of other concepts belonging to that theory. So although it is by no means clear what account should be given of holistic relations in general, perhaps it can be said that holistically related concepts get their sense from their role within some wider theory, or interlocking group of beliefs. Then the only way to get to understand those concepts, is to become immersed in the theory.

In any case, whatever is the proper explanation of the phenomenon, it would seem that holistic circles cannot be vicious ones. For we do, after all, possess concepts of space and of physical objects, as well as the concepts special to various scientific theories. Nor does it follow that holistically circular definitions must be totally useless. On the contrary, they display the connections between the holistically related concepts, grasp of which will form an important part of understanding them. It is thus open to behaviorists to defend their analyses of the concepts of belief and desire against the charge of vicious circularity, by claiming that those concepts are related holistically, being embedded in our common-sense theories for explaining human action (sometimes called "folk-psychology").

1.4 Problems for behaviorism

Although behaviorism does have some attractions, and although it did have some supporters for a while during the middle part of the

20th century, its deficiencies quite rapidly became apparent. For how can knowledge of my *own* mind consist in knowledge of my behavioral dispositions? This hardly leaves room for the idea of first-person authority about my own thoughts and feelings. (Hence the old joke about the two behaviorists who meet in the street: "You're feeling fine", says one, "But how am I feeling?") I surely have an awareness of some of my own mental states – say my pains, my experiences of red, and of what I am presently thinking – which cannot be analyzed as mere knowledge of my own dispositions to behave in this way or that in a range of hypothetical circumstances.

The point that some of our mentalistic discourse is dispositional rather than episodic has to be conceded to the behaviorist. When I say that someone is friendly, or grumpy, or irascible, I *am* ascribing to them states which are dispositional ones. But then again, some of our mentalistic discourse is episodic rather than dispositional. Surely a sudden realization, or a vivid recollection, or a momentary feeling of revulsion cannot be treated as mere dispositions. There are, it would seem, mental *events*. Moreover, the fact that beliefs, knowledge and desires can be long-standing rather than fleeting and episodic (and can be retained during sleep) is by no means a decisive argument that they are dispositions to behavior. Their durational nature is equally compatible with their being underlying states with a lasting causal role or potential.

Return to the point which everyone admits: that it is possible to feel a twinge of pain which goes unexpressed at the time, and which the person then completely forgets about. As we saw, the behaviorist will claim that the having of such a twinge merely consists in the fact that certain hypothetical sentences become true of the person at the time – such as, that if anyone were to ask the person how he feels, he would reply, "Just now I feel a twinge of pain". But this account seems to get everything back-to-front. How can the pain itself merely *consist in* the disposition to make such a reply? Surely the pain is, rather, the positive state which is the *cause of* that disposition. Surely he is disposed to make that reply *because* he is in pain (rather than his disposition *being* the pain).

Another example: suppose someone wakes up one morning and thinks to herself, "It must be time to get up" – this thought remaining unexpressed in either speech or action, because she straight away falls asleep again. Now the behaviorist will have to say that the person didn't actually do anything at the time, since no observable behavior took place. All that really happened is that she acquired, when she woke up, a certain disposition-to-behave (e.g., to say, "That it must be time to get up" in response to the question, "What are you thinking?") which in fact remained unactualized.

One way of articulating precisely why we find this sort of account so strange, is by asking how it is possible for a hypothetical sentence to be true ("If asked ..., then she will say ...") unless there is some categorical fact which makes it true ("She is doing ..."). For how can a person or thing have a dispositional property (a disposition-to-behave) unless there is some positive fact about her (or it) which explains, or constitutes, that disposition? Thus how can it be true that a particular glass is brittle, say ("If struck with moderate force, then it will break") unless there is some categorical fact about the glass which explains or constitutes its brittleness (presumably to do with its molecular structure)?

The behaviorist may reply that the positive change which takes place in the person when she wakes up, which constitutes her acquisition of the disposition to behave, will be a change which takes place in her brain. Of course we don't know in detail what this change is, but then neither do we know exactly what it is about the glass which makes it brittle. Yet this reply seems inadequate. For we would ordinarily believe that the positive change which takes place in someone, which explains the truth of the hypothetical sentence, "If asked ..., then she will say ...", is nothing other than her act of thinking to herself that it must be time to get up. Surely it is that act which *explains* the disposition, rather than the act itself *being* the disposition.

These points converge on the following objection: we need to insist that thinking is an activity, which we are sometimes aware of engaging in at the time when we engage in it. We also know that we sometimes engage in that activity privately. Then it cannot be right to analyze words which refer to activities ("think", "imagine", etc.) in such a way that in certain circumstances (i.e., private thinking) they merely refer to behavioral dispositions. We need to insist that when someone thinks something privately to herself, she is actually doing something positive at the time. When someone engages in a private train of thought, it cannot be right to say that what really happens is that she merely acquires a whole series of dispositions-to-behave which remain unactualized.

Although I have focused here on the behaviorist's treatment of unexpressed pains and acts of thinking, the objection is really quite general. Our ordinary view is that mental states are the causes of (rather than being identical with) our behavior and behavioral dispositions. Thus when someone screams and groans in pain we normally think that the pain itself isn't the behavior, but is the cause of the behavior. When someone isn't exhibiting pain-behavior but is disposed to do so (would do so *if* we were to ask him about his feelings, perhaps) we don't think that the disposition is itself the pain. Rather: if it is true that he would answer, "I am in pain" if asked how he is feeling, then this is *because* he *is* in pain. So mental states cannot in general be identified with behavioral states – whether actual or dispositional – since they are, rather, *the causes* of behavior.

1.5 *Functionalism*

In response to difficulties like these, most philosophers sympathetic to behaviorism began to shift to some form of functionalism instead. They were now proposing that mental states should be analyzed in terms of their normal causal role, mediating between a specified input – e.g., injury – and a specified output – e.g., pain-behavior. In effect, the guiding idea behind functionalism is that some concepts classify things by what they *do*. For example, transmitters transmit something, while aerials are objects positioned so as to receive air-borne signals. Indeed, practically all artifact-concepts are functional in character. But so, too, are many concepts applied to living things. Thus wings are limbs for flying with, eyes are light-sensitive organs for seeing with, and genes are biological structures which control development. So perhaps mental concepts are concepts of states or processes with a certain causal role, or function. This idea has been rediscovered in the ancient Greek philosopher Aristotle's writings (particularly in *De Anima*). Its introduction into recent philosophy of mind is chiefly due to the American philosopher Hilary Putnam, as well as the Australian philosopher David Armstrong.

Functionalism has seemed to be the answer to several philosophical prayers. It accounts for the multiple realizability of mental states, the chief stumbling-block for a "type-identity" theory, as we saw in Chapter 5:2. It also has obvious advantages over behaviorism, since it accords much better with ordinary intuitions about causal relations – it allows mental states to interact and influence each other, rather than being directly tied to behavioral dispositions. Finally, it remains explicable that dualism should ever have seemed an option. For although we conceptualize mental states in terms of causal roles, it can be a contingent matter what actually *occupies* those causal roles; and it was a conceptual possibility that the role-occupiers might have turned out to be composed of some sort of *mind-stuff*.

Multiple realizability is readily accounted for in the case of functional concepts. Since there may be more than one way in which a particular function, *Φ-ing*, can be discharged, things of various different compositions can serve that function and hence qualify as *Φ-ers*. Think of *valves*, for example, which are to be found inside both your heart and (say) your central heating system. So while mental *types* are individuated in terms of a certain sort of pattern of causes and effects, mental *tokens* (individual instantiations of those patterns) can be (can be identical to, or at least constituted by) instantiations of some physical type (such as C-fiber firing), perhaps differently in different cases.

Compare the mind with any complicated machine, such as the motor car. We have concepts, such as "gear-box" and "carburetor", for describing the various parts of a car. These concepts are functionally defined, their meanings being given in terms of the causal roles of the parts within the overall functioning of the machine. Thus gear-boxes can be made out of many diverse materials, and present a wide range of appearances. All that is essential, is that they should occupy the characteristic causal role of a gear-box. But of course there can be no saying what the function of a gear-box is without mentioning any other parts of the engine, since it only has its function when in conjunction with those other parts. Moreover, its function should be described in "for the most part" terms, since engines do not always work as they ought.

Similarly, then, with the mind: we believe that human behavior characteristically results from the causal interaction of many different mental states, some of these interactions taking place at some distance from the behavior itself. We believe that these mental states, in turn, are caused in complex ways by other mental states and by the impact of the physical environment on the body. (See Figure 7.1 for an initial partial sketch of what a functional account of the mind might look like. Terminological note: a higher-order belief is a belief which is *about* some other mental state, for example another belief.) Small wonder then, that there can be no describing the function of any given mental state without mentioning other such states. Small

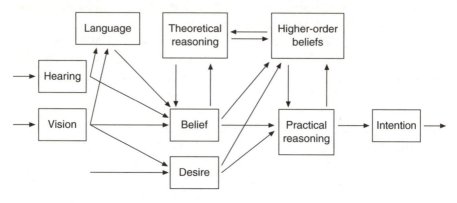

Figure 7.1 The (partial) functional organization of mind.

wonder also, that mental states do not always occupy precisely the causal roles which they normally would – for example, someone can be in a state which would normally cause pain-behavior without actually exhibiting any.

(I note in passing that there is a sense in which functionalism can be seen as a vindication of the bundle theory of the mind. For on this account there isn't anything *mental* which underlies and possesses, or which serves to guide and control, the various different mental functions. Rather, there is just the network of interacting mental states themselves. The only sense in which Descartes was right in insisting that thoughts require a thinker, is that the various mental functions do all need to be realized in a human body or brain. But Hume was right that there is no *mental* self – no ego – over and above the network of thoughts and feelings, and the principles in terms of which they interact with one another.)

According to functionalism, mental states are states with a certain causal role, characterized in terms of how they are produced, and in terms of their effects on both other such states and behavior. Functionalism doesn't by itself explain the asymmetry between knowledge of self and knowledge of others. So it does need to be supplemented by some account of how it is that knowledge of one's own present mental states can be both peculiarly direct and especially reliable. Most functionalists have responded that among the causal roles of many mental states will be a tendency to cause a higher-order belief that a state of that very sort is occurring. (How adequate this response is will be discussed in a moment.)

One of functionalism's chief sources of appeal has been the plausible treatment it provides for knowledge of the mental states of others, however. Our attribution of mental states to other people fits their situations and reactions and is justified as an inference to the best explanation of their behavior. This view places our knowledge of other minds on a par with theoretical knowledge, in two respects. First, the functional roles assigned to various mental states depend upon systematic relations between such states and their characteristic causes and effects. So it seems that we have a common-sense theory of mind, or a "folk-psychology", which implicitly defines ordinary psychological concepts. Secondly, the application of that theory is justified in the way that theories usually are, by success in prediction and explanation.

It is important to distinguish, however, between the *justification* for our beliefs about the minds of others and *what causes us to have* such beliefs. While our theory of mind can be justified by our predictive and explanatory successes in a vast number of particular applications, we don't, in general, apply that theory *because* we have seen it to be justified. Rather, we apply it because we have grown up applying it; thinking in terms of other people's mental states comes as "second nature" to us. Indeed, as we shall see briefly in section 3 below, it may well be an aspect of our normal, innate, human cognitive endowment to apply such a theory of mind. It may be, in fact, that we cannot help but think about each other in such terms.

1.6 Problems for functionalism

So far I have been painting a rosy picture of functionalism. But, as usual, there have been objections. The two main problems with analytical functionalism (that is, functionalism as a thesis about the correct *analysis* of mental state concepts) are set out here.

The first objection to functionalism is that it is committed to the existence of a distinction between *analytic* and *synthetic* truths, which many people think (following the writings of the influential American philosopher W. V. Quine) to be unviable. An analytic truth is supposed to be one whose truth is dependent solely on the meanings of the terms involved. A synthetic truth is supposed to be one whose truth depends upon something other than mere meaning, such as some state of the world. What Quine argued is that there is no principled distinction to be drawn here. There is no privileged set of truths which we should hold true *come what may*, no matter what else changed in the course of our experience. Rather, our beliefs form a complex inter-connected web, which faces the tribunal of experience as a whole; and adjustments can in principle be made anywhere within the web, depending on what produces the most satisfying overall fit with the evidence.

Consider, for example, our belief that whales are mammals. This seems like a good candidate to be an analytic truth – it is so deeply obvious that it is hard for us to imagine how we might give it up. But just a few centuries ago, people found it equally obvious that whales were fish – after all, whales live and breed in water, just as fish do; they swim using their fins and tails, just as fish do; and so on. Yet is it hardly very plausible that the *meaning* of the term "whale" changed when people discovered that whales are mammals. It looks like I say something *true* when I say, "People once falsely believed that whales were fish"; yet this *wouldn't* be false if (given what *they* meant by "whale") whales *were* fish. Similar points could be made in connection with other alleged analytic truths, such as that the stars in the sky are shining objects, for example – for the Greeks believed that the stars were holes in the canopy of heaven. But we don't think that they *meant* something different by "star". On the contrary, we say that they had a false belief *about* stars.

Whatever one might think of the analytic/synthetic distinction in general, it is certainly hard to decide quite *which* truisms concerning the causal role of a mental state should count as analytic (true in virtue of meaning), rather than synthetic but just *obviously* true. So it is actually hard to see how to carry out the functionalist project of providing *analyses* of each of our mental state terms. Consider, for example, our conviction that beliefs are often the result of a process of conscious reasoning. Is this part of the *definition* of the term "belief"? It is certainly one of the obviously-true things which we believe about ourselves. But if it is part of the definition of belief, then we might be forced to say that animals lack beliefs, if they never engage in conscious reasoning processes as we do. Indeed, some philosophers have claimed just this. Yet if someone insists that, on the contrary, animals do have beliefs, only beliefs which aren't caused in all of the same sorts of ways that ours are, then it is hard to see what might be said to convince them of their error.

The second commonly-voiced objection against functionalism is that it is incapable of capturing the felt nature of conscious experience. While it might be acceptable to say that a conscious belief that *P* is merely a belief one of whose functions is to cause the higher-order belief that one believes that *P*, the parallel move is surely *un*acceptable in respect of conscious experience. A conscious experience isn't merely an experience which is apt to cause me to believe that I am having it. Rather, there is something distinctive which it is *like* to be aware of having that experience; a conscious experience will have a distinctive *feel* which one is aware of. Being aware of a pain isn't just a matter of believing myself to be in pain, as a functionalist would have it (see Figure 7.2). Still less is it just a matter of believing that I am in a state whose normal cause is tissue damage and whose normal effect is pain-behavior – which is what you get when you plug the functionalist definition of "pain" into the above account.

Objectors have thus urged that one could know everything about the functional role of a mental state and yet still have no inkling as to what it is like to be in that state – to be aware of its so-called *quale*. While this is no objection to physicalism (as we saw in Chapter 5:3), it *is* an objection to functionalism. For functionalism purports to tell us how we conceptualize our mental states (namely, in terms of causal roles, or functions); whereas at least part of our conception of a conscious experience would seem to consist in our awareness of its characteristic feel. Moreover, some mental states seem to be conceptualized *purely* in terms of feel; at any rate, with beliefs about causal role taking a secondary position. For example, it seems to be just the feel of pain which is essential to it, as we saw in Chapter 5:4. Indeed, we seem to be able to imagine pains which occupy some other causal role; and we can imagine states having the causal role of pain which aren't pains (which lack the appropriate kind of feel).

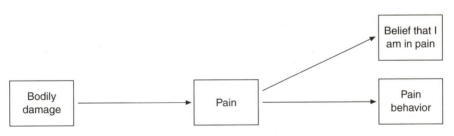

Figure 7.2 A functionalist account of pain.

2 Theory-theory and its opponents

In response to such difficulties, many have urged that a better variant of functionalism is *theory-theory*, as we will see in section 2.1 below. This account was first introduced in the mid-1960s by David Lewis. While some or other version of theory-theory is now the dominant position in the philosophy of mind, this is not to say that there are no difficulties, and no dissenting voices. In sections 2.2 through 2.5 we will consider, and criticize, two such alternatives.

2.1 The theory-theory

According to this view, mental state concepts (like theoretical concepts in science) get part of their life and sense from their position in a substantive *theory* of the causal structure and functioning of the mind. (The other part of their meaning they get from the relations which they bear to the things which they are *about*.) On this view, to know what a belief is (to grasp the concept of belief) is to know sufficiently much of the theory of mind within which that concept is embedded. All the benefits of analytic functionalism are preserved. But there need be no commitment to the viability of an analytic/synthetic distinction. We don't have to insist that some of our beliefs about beliefs are true purely in virtue of meaning whereas others are substantive. Rather, we can regard all of them as contributing (more or less) to our grasp of the belief-concept.

What of the point that some mental states can be conceptualized purely or primarily in terms of feel? A theory-theorist can allow that we have *recognitional capacities* for some of the theoretical entities characterized by the theory. But it can be claimed that the concepts employed in such capacities are also partly characterized by their place in the theory – these are *recognitional* applications of *theoretical* concepts. (Compare the diagnostician who can recognize a cancer – immediately and without inference – in the blur of an X-ray photograph.) Moreover, once someone possesses a recognitional concept, there can be nothing to stop them prizing it apart from its surrounding beliefs and theories, to form a concept which is *barely* recognitional. Our hypothesis can be that this is what takes place when people say that it is conceptually possible that there should be pains with quite different causal roles.

Theory-theory should thus adopt a "divide and conquer"

approach to explaining the *certainty thesis* which we defended in Chapter 1:4 when we were attempting to motivate the Cartesian conception of the meaning of mental state terms. Our certainty about our own current acts of thinking and reasoning should be handled in the way that the analytic functionalist did. We can postulate that such acts are apt to cause, reliably and as part of their normal functional role, higher-order beliefs in their own occurrence. So the act of thinking to myself, "Today is Tuesday" is apt to cause in me (reliably and immediately, without inference) the belief that I am thinking that today is Tuesday.

Our certainty about our own current experiences, in contrast, can be said to derive from the availability of those experiences to a set of recognitional concepts which can be applied to them. Some of these concepts can be broadly theoretical ones, specifying the type of experience by its place in the theory; but ones which nevertheless admit of recognitional applications. Others of these concepts can be *purely* recognitional, formed by prizing apart the recognitional from the theoretical component. It can be postulated that this is especially likely to occur when we take some special interest in the feelings being recognized, as in the case of pain. But either way, since the concepts are recognitional, applied on the basis of immediate awareness of the feelings recognized, there seems to be no room for error in our present-tensed judgments employing them. So the apparent certainty of those judgments is explained. (We will return to this issue at greater length in Chapter 8.)

2.2 The interpretationalist challenge

One alternative to theory-theory has been defended, in somewhat different versions, by the American philosophers Donald Davidson and Daniel Dennett (their differences needn't concern us here). Their position – generally referred to as "interpretationalism" – contains two key elements. First, they reject theory-theory's deep theoretical commitments (namely, to a set of discrete structured causally effective states). Secondly, they regard so-called "norms of rationality" as constitutive of mental state attribution. I shall elaborate on these points in turn.

According to theory-theory, we ordinary folk are up to our necks in theoretical commitments concerning the components and causal structure of the mind. We are supposed to believe that there are discrete states and events of various distinct kinds, which interact causally with one another in certain specified patterns to produce other such states and behavior (see Figure 7.1 above). Accordingly, we are wide open to empirical refutation, it seems. For it might turn out that either the postulated kinds of state, or their supposed patterns of causal interaction, don't really exist. So it would seem that we should stand ready to accept that there are no such things as minds, given the theory-theory construal of what it takes to have a mind. Indeed, one prominent theory-theorist (Paul Churchland) has maintained that we can already see that our theory of the mind is false, and that minds should be *eliminated*, now, from our scientific world picture. (This view is generally referred to as "eliminative materialism".)

Since this has seemed obviously unacceptable to many people – since we aren't really in the market of discovering that there are no such things as minds – there is some reason to accept a shallower, less deeply theoretical, account of our common-sense attitude towards ourselves and others. This is just what interpretationalism purports to provide. As the name suggests, our common-sense psychology is supposed to amount to a mere *scheme for interpreting behavior*, without any commitment to the nature of the events and processes which underlie the causation of that behavior. (As will be obvious from this, interpretationalism is a close descendent of holistic behaviorism.)

This brings us to the other key element of the approach, which is that the basic principles of interpretation are supposed to involve norms (or rules) of *rationality*. It is by assuming that people are rational, and by figuring out what they would think and want and do if they *were* rational, that we are supposed to arrive at our interpretations. But making this assumption isn't supposed to carry any commitments which might potentially turn out false. Rather, it is just a matter of whether or not it proves *useful*. Indeed, Dennett talks of "the intentional *stance*" here, and thinks that we can legitimately adopt that stance in relation to chess-playing computers, and indeed thermostats, if we find it useful to do so. (We can predict what the thermostat will do by assuming that it *wants* to keep the temperature above 70 degrees Fahrenheit, and *believes* that the temperature has just fallen to 66.) The only difference between thermostats and humans, on this account, is that our behavior is much more complex, and so the intentional stance is correspondingly much more useful to adopt.

Granted, we aren't ready to give up believing in minds and mental states. But how powerful a consideration is this against the truth of theory-theory? Not very, in fact – for two distinct, but mutually compatible, reasons. First, we mightn't be ready to give up our theory of the mind because that theory is just *obviously true*. Compare our attitude towards physical objects and their main properties and interactions. We believe that physical objects occupy discrete regions of space, and can be moved or changed by the operation of various physical forces, such as pushing and pulling. This is, undeniably, a theory. But we aren't prepared to give it up, because it is so obviously true (in general and on the whole). It is a theory which works wonderfully well, providing myriad successful predictions and explanations every day. Admittedly, some elements of this theory not only might, but have, turned out to be false. Thus we ordinary folk tend to think (following Aristotle) that an object won't continue moving unless a force continues to be applied to it; whereas the truth, as discovered by Newton, is that moving objects will continue moving *unless* a force is applied against them. But our attitude is sensible and pragmatic: we incorporate this correction into our theory of physical objects, rather than rejecting that theory altogether.

Similarly, then, in respect of our theory of mind. This, too, works wonderfully well in our daily lives, providing innumerable successful predictions and explanations. Here, as well, we are perfectly prepared to accept correction in part. Thus ordinary folk tend to think of *memory* as a single kind of state. But scientific psychologists now routinely distinguish between a number of different kinds of memory, each of which can be damaged while leaving the others intact. These include *semantic* memory (or memory of facts), *episodic* memory (or personal memory of events in one's own life), and *procedural* memory (or memory of skills and of how to do things); as well as *working* memory, *iconic* memory, and a variety of others. We can easily accept these corrections while leaving our belief in the character of the mind essentially unchanged.

The second reason why we might find it so hard to take seriously the thought of giving up our theory of mind, despite its substantive commitments, is that we might be literally incapable of doing so. As we will see in section 3 below, there is some reason to think that our theory of mind is *innate*, forming part of the fixed cognitive endowment of all normal human beings. If this is so, then our reluctance to countenance any thought of giving up our theory of mind provides no reason for denying that the theory makes deep empirical commitments, just as theory-theory supposes.

2.3 Against interpretationalism

On reflection, it is hard to deny that common-sense psychology is committed to the existence of a set of discrete causally effective mental events. Consider a case where someone reaches a conclusion, but could in fact have done so by means of either one of two distinct routes. Suppose I reach the conclusion that my daughter is lying when she tells me that she spent the evening at a neighbor's house watching TV. But two distinct items of knowledge might have enabled me to reach this conclusion: I called the houses of all of her neighborhood friends, and she wasn't there; and there was a local black-out last evening which took out all the television programs. Don't we believe that there must have been some determinate sequence of thoughts tokened, in virtue of which it is true that I reached my conclusion in one (or both) of these ways rather than the other? From the perspective of interpretationalism, in contrast, there may be nothing to choose between the two hypotheses – each might provide an equally good rational reconstruction of the reasons for my belief.

A similar conclusion can be reached by reflection on the so-called "Imitation Game", proposed by the English philosopher and logician Alan Turing, whose work was partially responsible for the computer revolution in the 20th century. Turing proposed a test for genuine intelligence in computers. He argued that if a computer could be programmed to successfully imitate a man or a woman in a free-wheeling open-ended conversation, then that would settle a positive answer. This is, in effect, the interpretationalist position: if a computer is richly *interpretable as* thinking, then the computer *is* thinking; there is no further question to be answered. Whereas we surely think that it matters a great deal exactly *how* the computer goes about generating its responses.

In order to demonstrate this point, the New Zealand philosopher Jack Copeland constructed the following imaginary example of a computer which passes the Turing test by mere pattern-matching. There are a finite number of possible English conversations consisting of less than, say, 1,000 sentences, each of which consists of less than 100 words. Then imagine a computer in which all of these conversations are listed in a vast look-up table. The computer operates by matching a given input against its lists, and selecting one possible continuation at random. Such a computer may well be dependent on computer technology far in advance of ours, but it does seem to be possible in principle. And it does seem plain that it would pass the Turing test in connection with any experimenter who doesn't actually know or suspect the details of its program. For we may suppose that no normal human conversation consists of more than 1,000 sentences, and that no normal human sentence consists of more than 100 words. But it is plain, is it not, that we would withhold mentality from the computer as soon as we *did* learn that it operates by pattern-matching? Learning the details of its internal operations, we would no longer seriously suppose that the computer believes what it says, or that its words are expressive of genuine thought – contrary to what an interpretationalist must claim.

(Admittedly, this conclusion only follows if there are possible computers – with appropriate internal organization – to which we *would* be prepared to attribute genuine thought. If our reaction to Copeland's example turns merely on the fact that what engages in the imitation game is a computer, made of metal and silicon rather than flesh and blood, then of course nothing follows about our commitments to internal organization. I shall return to this issue in the final chapter.)

Let us turn now to the assumption of *rationality*, which lies at the heart of the interpretationalist position. It is by assuming that people are rational – forming the beliefs which they *should* given their circumstances, and the desires which they *should* given their beliefs and needs, and the decisions which they *should* given their beliefs and desires – that we are supposed to go about predicting and explaining their behavior. It is, however, notoriously hard to say what rationality *is*, and there are a good many competing theories on the market. Are we to suppose that ordinary folk are committed to one such theory, using it in their interpretations of themselves and others, without having the capacity to articulate that theory explicitly? Possible, perhaps; but hard to believe. (Indeed, this provides one of the motives behind the simulationist proposal to be considered in the next section. This holds that we *use* our own rational thought processes in simulating others, without needing to have a theory of what rationality is.)

A further embarrassment for interpretationalism is the widespread evidence of human *ir*rationality gathered by psychologists over the last couple of decades. There are many, many circumstances in which people routinely reason in ways contrary to what our best theories of rationality say that they should. While these results are surprising – sometimes shocking – they don't interfere at all with our capacity to treat the people involved as minded agents. But an interpretationalist is committed to saying that, to the extent that people are irrational, to that extent they are uninterpretable in psychological terms. For the rationality assumption is said to be at the very heart of our conception of the mind. To have a mind at all is to behave and be disposed to behave as rationality dictates, according to the interpretationalist.

One doesn't really need to appeal to scientific evidence of irrationality to mount essentially this criticism, indeed. Suppose that while walking down the street one day you see someone bending over the open hood of their car, obviously doing something to the engine inside. As you get closer he suddenly leaps up with a look of fury on his face, and starts kicking the car's tires and beating its wings with his fists. You immediately know what is going on here: he has lost his temper, and is now angry with the car. But are we supposed to assume that this is rational? I surely don't ascribe a state of anger to the man because he is behaving as it would be *reasonable* to behave when angry! Nor is it because anger is the emotion which it is *rational* to feel when you can't fix your car! Contrary to what an interpretationalist would say, then, it looks like we routinely make attributions of mental states to other people without relying on any sort of rationality-assumption.

Note, finally, that the focus of interpretationalism is entirely on that aspect of the mind which deals with propositional attitudes – beliefs, desires, intentions, and so on – where the question of rationality makes good sense. It is hard to see how to extend the approach to account for the way in which we understand bodily sensations, experiences, and perceptual states generally. It looks as if something quite different will have to be said about our understanding of what pain is, for example, and of the way that pain feels. In contrast, it is one of the advantages of theory-theory that it can accord the same theoretical treatment to both experiences and propositional attitudes – all are characterized by their place in the causal theory (although some are states for which we also possess recognitional capacities).

2.4 *The simulationist challenge*

The other main alternative to theory-theory has again been defended by two American philosophers, and once more in two somewhat different versions: Alvin Goldman and Robert Gordon. In both versions, we come to understand the minds of others by *simulating* them. We do this by taking our own reasoning and decision-making processes "off-line" and using our own minds as a model for those of others – much as an engineer might use the behavior of a model airplane in a wind-tunnel to simulate the behavior of real airplanes. The two versions differ, though, in how they think this process gets started. (Note, however, that both versions are committed to denying that mental states are initially conceptualized theoretically, prior to input into the simulation process; for this would just give us a variety of theory-theory.) Goldman maintains that simulation begins with our primitive awareness of the feels of our own mental states, initially unconceptualized by causal role. Gordon maintains that it is by learning to *express* our own mental states in language that we begin to bootstrap our way into an understanding of them (for example, by initially learning a little "ascent routine" which permits me to assert, "I believe that P" whenever I find myself disposed to assert "P").

The debate between theory-theory and simulation theory has been fruitful. Almost all theory-theorists now accept that simulation plays an important *part* in enabling us to explain and predict the mental lives of others, as the work of the American philosophers Shaun Nichols and Stephen Stich illustrates. For example, suppose that I want to predict how many weekdays you think that there are to go before Christmas, knowing that you believe that there are seven weeks remaining before Christmas. If I were do to this entirely on the basis of *theory*, I should have to have, among other things, a theory of arithmetic reasoning – I should have to know that if someone thinks that there are seven sets of five, then they think that there are thirty-five items altogether; and so on for all arithmetic relations, and for all possible patterns of reasoning. I should have to have, in effect, a complete theory of human reasoning! It is doubtful whether the idea is even so much as coherent. What I actually do, of course, is *calculate* in my own right – multiplying seven by five on my own behalf, and then attributing the answer ("thirty-five") to the target person.

Everyone should now accept that simulation has a role to play when we predict or explain another, especially when we have to predict how another person will *reason*. The difference between theory-theory and simulation theory concerns our basic conception of what mental states *are*. Relatedly, it concerns how the whole business of predicting and explaining others gets started. A theory-theorist will say that our mentalistic concepts are theory-dependent from the start; and predicting and explaining, too, uses theoretical considerations from the outset, as we shall see more fully in section 3 below. But what of simulation theory? This is where the differences between the two different versions of the approach start to matter.

2.5 Against simulationism

Goldman will say that simulation needs to begin from our pre-theoretical awareness of the distinctive *feels* of our own mental states. The claim is, in effect, that our mentalistic concepts are, at the outset, just as the Cartesian conception describes – they consist in bare recognitional capacities for states of the various kinds, deployed in introspection. But this is now the position we examined, and found wanting, in section 1 above. It is very hard to believe that young children could get from such a meager basis to the rich causal understanding of the mind which older children and adults manifestly possess.

Gordon will say, on the other hand, that our simulation abilities depend upon language. For in his account, it is by first learning to express our own mental states in language that we acquire access to them. While essentially facing the same problem as Goldman's account, this version of simulationism faces difficulties of its own. Specifically, while there is evidence that mentalizing ability in children *correlates* with language abilities (as does almost every other aspect of cognition), there is no reason to believe that it is dependent upon it; and there is some reason to think that it isn't.

Most theories of the evolution of language assume that mentalizing abilities were presupposed at the outset of the process. The idea is that would-be communicators would need to have had beliefs about what others do and don't believe, and beliefs about what those others would be likely to come to believe as a result of a variety of communicative efforts, in order for the first halting efforts at communication to begin. A similar point can be made from studies of deaf children who grow up without exposure to sign languages. It is now well-established that such children invent a primitive system of "home-sign" of their own, for communicating with the hearing people around them. It is hard to make sense of what such a deaf child would be doing with these signs – especially on their first occasion of use – without supposing that the child has beliefs about the others' beliefs, and about the likely effects on those beliefs of the use of the sign in this context.

In conclusion, it should be noted that both forms of simulation theory also face one of the same problems as interpretationalism: neither is at all plausible in explaining how we come to understand and attribute experiences as opposed to thoughts. I can come to know what someone believes by simulating their reasoning processes; but how would simulation play a role in enabling me to know what another is *experiencing* in a given set of circumstances? Merely imagining myself to be *in* those circumstances (which is what simulationists will generally appeal to here) won't help, unless I already know a good deal about how experiences are caused, and about how their causation varies with circumstances. Granted, I can generally form some sort of mental image of what it is that the other is experiencing, which makes it sound as if some sort of simulation might be at work. (In *imagining* what the other is experiencing I am *simulating* their experience, you might say.) But this is a case in which imagination has to be theory-driven, surely. Background theoretical knowledge seems necessary to guide the process of image-construction.

3   Developing the theory: theorizing versus innateness

I shall assume, then, that our understanding of the mind is, at bottom, a theoretical one; and that the concepts in question get much of their life and sense from their position within the theory. In this section we turn to the question of how this theory develops in childhood. There are two alternatives to consider: that it develops through a process of *theorizing*, akin to scientific theorizing; and that it develops through a process of biological maturation, the theory in question being substantially innate. Let us take these in turn.

3.1   Theorizing theory

Much useful work has been done by the American developmental psychologist Henry Wellman and others, charting the development of children's understanding of the minds and mental states of themselves and others, and of the different stages that they pass through in the first few years of life. (See Figure 7.3 for a summary.) But the

Age	Abilities	Theory
Birth	Copying facial expressions – a capacity to map between a perception of an action and what it feels like to produce that action	Cross-modal mapping
1 year old	Pointing Shared attention, understanding of attention Understanding of goals Understanding of ignorance Pretend play Learning words; inventing new words	Goal/perception psychology
3–4 years old	Intentional lying and/or deceit Understanding of false belief Understanding of subjectivity	Belief/desire psychology

Figure 7.3 The development of common-sense psychology.

fact that children appear to be working with a succession of increasingly sophisticated theories doesn't show that those theories are constructed through a process akin to scientific theorizing, of course. It is equally compatible with the maturation of an innate theory of mind faculty (see section 3.2 below), with the different developmental stages perhaps corresponding to different stages in the evolution of that faculty. The theorizing-theory approach has been developed and defended most explicitly by Alison Gopnik and Andrew Melzoff, and it is on their account that I shall focus my critique.

The main difficulty for a theorizing-theory account is that it ignores the extent to which scientific activity needs to be supported by external resources. Scientists do not, and never have, worked alone, but constantly engage in discussion, co-operation, and mutual criticism with peers. If there is one thing which we have learned over the last thirty years of historically-oriented studies of science, it is that the romantic image of the lone scientist, gathering all data and constructing and testing hypotheses by him- or her-self, is a highly misleading abstraction.

Scientists such as Galileo and Newton engaged in extensive correspondence and discussion with other investigators at the time when they were developing their theories; and scientists in the 20th century, of course, have generally worked as members of research teams. Moreover, scientists cannot operate without the external prop of the written word (including written records of data, annotated diagrams and graphs, written calculations, written accounts of reasoning, and so on). Why should it be so different in childhood, if the cognitive processes involved are essentially the same?

I should emphasize that this point doesn't depend upon any sort of "social constructivist" account of science, of the sort that Gopnik and Melzoff find so rebarbative (and rightly so, in my view). It is highly controversial that scientific change is to be explained, to any significant extent, by the operation of wider social and political forces, in the way that some have claimed. But it is, now, utterly truistic that science is a social process in at least the minimal sense that it progresses through the varied social interactions of scientists themselves – co-operating, communicating, criticizing – and through their reliance on a variety of external socially-provided props and aids, such as books, paper, writing instruments, a variety of different kinds of scientific apparatus, and (now) calculators, computers and the internet. This truism is sufficient to cause a real problem for the "child as scientist" account of development.

One sort of response would be to claim that children don't *need* external props, because they have vastly better memories than adult scientists. But this is simply not credible, of course; for it isn't true that children's event-memories are better than those of adults. In any case it isn't true that science depends upon external factors *only* because of limitations of memory. On the contrary, individual limitations of rationality, insight and creativity all play an equally important part. For scientific discussion is often needed to point out the fallacies in an individual scientist's thinking; to show how well-known data can be explained by a familiar theory in ways that the originators hadn't realized; and to generate new theoretical ideas and proposals.

Nor can these differences between children and adults plausibly be explained in terms of differences of attention, motivation, or time, in the way that Gopnik and Melzoff try to argue. For adult scientists certainly attend very closely to the relevant phenomena, they may be highly motivated to succeed in developing a successful theory, and they may be able to devote themselves full-time to doing so. But still they cannot manage without a whole variety of external resources, both social and non-social. And still *radical* (conceptually-innovative) theory change in science (of the sort which Gopnik and Melzoff acknowledge occurs a number of times over within the first few years of a child's life) is generally spread out over a very lengthy time-scale (often as much as a hundred years or more).

Gopnik and Melzoff also claim that a significant difference between childhood theorizers and adult scientists lies in the extent and ease of availability of relevant data. In scientific enquiry, the relevant data are often hard to come by, and elaborate and expensive experiments and other information-gathering exercises may be needed to get it; perforce making scientific enquiry essentially social. But in childhood there are ample quantities of data easily available. Young children have plenty of opportunities to experiment with physical substances and their properties – knocking objects together, dropping or throwing them, pouring liquids, and mixing materials – when developing their naïve physics; and they have plenty of opportunity to observe and probe other agents when developing their naïve psychology as well. Moreover, since infants come into the world with a set of simple innate domain-specific theories, on Gopnik and Melzoff's account, they already possess theoretical frameworks which constrain possible hypotheses, determine relevant evidence, and so on.

This point, although valid as far as it goes, does not begin to address the real issue. If anything, the extent of the data available to the child is a further *problem* for the "child as scientist" view, given the lack of external aids to memory, and the lack of any public process for sorting through and discussing the significance of the evidence. That plenty of data is *available* to an enquirer is irrelevant, unless that data can be recalled, organized and surveyed at the moment of need – namely, during theory-testing or theory-development.

Gopnik and Melzoff also make the point that much relevant data is actually *presented to* children by adults, in the form of linguistic utterances of one sort or another. Now, their idea isn't that adults *teach* the theories in question to children, thus putting the latter into the position of little science *students* rather than little scientists. For such a claim would be highly implausible – there is no real evidence that any such teaching actually takes place (and quite a bit of evidence that it doesn't). Their point is rather that adults make a range of new sorts of evidence available to the child in the form of their linguistic utterances, since those utterances are embedded in semantic frameworks which contain the target theories. Adult utter-

ances may then provide crucial data for children, as they simultaneously elaborate their theories and struggle to learn the language of
their parents.

This proposal does at least have the virtue of providing a social
dimension to childhood development, hence in one sense narrowing
the gap between children and adult scientists. But actually this
social process is quite unlike any that an adult scientist will normally engage in, since scientists (as opposed to science students) are
rarely in the position of hearing or engaging in discussions with
those who have already mastered the theories which they themselves are still trying to develop. In any case the proposal does
nothing to address the fundamental problems of insufficient
memory, bounded rationality, and limited creativity which children
and adults both face, and which the social and technological dimensions of science are largely designed to overcome.

Might it be that the scientific problems facing adults are very
much more complex than those facing young children, and that this
is the reason why children, but not adult scientists, can operate
without much in the way of external support? This suggestion is
hardly very plausible, either. For folk psychology of the sort
attained by most normal four-year-old children has a deep structure
rivaling that of many scientific theories, involving the postulation of
a range of different kinds of causally-effective internal states,
together with a set of nomic principles (or "laws") concerning the
complex patterns of causation in which those states figure. There is
no reason at all to think that this theory should be easily arrived at.
Indeed, it is a theory which many adult scientific psychologists have
denied (especially around the middle part of the 20th century) –
namely, those who were behaviorists. It took a variety of sophisticated arguments, and the provision of a range of different kinds of
data, to convince most people that behaviorism should be rejected
in favor of cognitivism.

So why is it that *no* children (excepting perhaps those who are
autistic – see section 3.2 below) ever pass through a stage in which
they endorse some form of behaviorism? If cognitivism were really
such an easy theory to frame and establish, then the puzzle would
be that adult scientific psychologists had such difficulty in converg-
ing on it. Given that it is *not* so easy, the puzzle is that all normal
children *do* converge on it in the first four years of development (at
least if they are supposed to get there by means of processes structurally similar to those which operate in science). Not only do they

all get there, but they all do so within similar time-frame (give or take a year or so), and irrespective of wide variations in intelligence, life experiences, and so on. The natural conclusion to draw, at this point, is that folk psychology is both theoretically difficult and *not* arrived at by a process of theorizing, but rather through some sort of modular and innately channeled development.

3.2   *The innateness of our theory of mind*

If our theory of mind isn't acquired by a process of theorizing, and it isn't acquired through simulation, then what other alternatives are there? One possibility is that it is *taught*. Perhaps theory of mind is learned much as chemistry is learned – not through theorizing, but through instruction by older children and adults. There is not a shred of evidence that any such instruction takes place, however; and quite a bit of evidence that it doesn't. The idea that theory of mind is taught to children is a complete non-starter, in fact. Which leaves biological maturation (innateness) as the only remaining alternative.

On this nativist view, a theory of mind needn't be present at birth, of course – any more than pubic hair, or breasts in women, are present at birth. Rather, the theory would be genetically determined (or better: genetically *channeled*) to make its appearance at a certain stage in normal development. This is not to say that experience would have no input, however. On the contrary, one might expect that the richness of the social environment (including the linguistic environment) would have an impact of the pace of theory of mind acquisition. (An analogy: think of the theory of mind faculty as a bit like a muscle, which grows and develops through *use*. If used more intensely it will grow bigger and faster.) But the learning process would be guided by biologically-provided constraints and principles.

One independent line of reasoning in support of this proposal is that precursors (at least) of theory of mind ability appear to be present in our nearest cousins, the great apes (especially chimpanzees). Indeed, one important hypothesis for the evolution of characteristic human intelligence is the so-called "Machiavellian intelligence" hypothesis proposed and elaborated by the British primatologists Richard Byrne and Andrew Whiten. Among highly social creatures, such as our ancestors plainly were, there would have been intense selection pressures for the capacity to maneuver successfully in the social world – making friends, building alliances, seducing potential mates, forestalling enemies, and so forth; all of which requires reasoning about the mental states of other people, if it is to be done with subtlety and sophistication.

Even stronger evidence of the innateness of our theory of mind is provided by autism. This is a developmental condition which is known to have a substantial genetic basis, and which is known to involve a kind of "mind-blindness", as the English psychologist Simon Baron-Cohen has shown. For exactly what one would predict if theory of mind were a distinct genetically channeled mental faculty, would be that there should be cases involving genetic damage in which theory of mind fails to develop at all, or only very haltingly and slowly. This is, indeed, what we find in the case of autism, which is significantly heritable. Autistic children treat other people like *objects*, and fail to interact normally with care-givers during infancy. They fail to display normal attention getting behaviors. For example, they don't point to attract a care-giver's attention to what they want, rather they will lead the adult by the hand, and then push that hand in the direction of the desired object – as if they had learned that a hand is a useful instrument, but without knowing that it is guided by a mind. Moreover, on a whole battery of tests of theory of mind ability developed by psychologists for use with normal children, autistic children perform very badly indeed.

It is important to note that many autistic children are of otherwise normal intelligence, and can cope quite successfully with non-social tests and tasks. In contrast, there are groups of children, such as Down's syndrome children, whose intelligence is decidedly not normal, but whose theory of mind abilities appear undamaged. Down's children can be highly social and communicative, and when tested alongside autistic children on theory of mind tests they perform much better; indeed, at levels approaching that of normal children. This, too, supports the suggestion that theory of mind is an isolable and innately channeled system of the mind – a "module" – which can be present and intact when other systems are damaged (Down's), or damaged when other systems are intact (autism).

4   The problem of other minds revisited

We return, now, to the problem of other minds. Since all the ground-work necessary for a solution has already been laid in previous sections, this one can be brisk.

4.1 Putting nativist theory-theory to work

As we saw in Chapter 5:2, physicalism can help to underpin our knowledge that other people undergo mental states *in general*, but can't deliver knowledge of the specific states they undergo on particular occasions. What we now have on the table to help us approach a final solution are first, the claim that our concepts of the different kinds of mental states are embedded in a substantive causal theory of the operations of the mind; and secondly, that this theory is largely innate or innately channeled. Let us now put these claims to work.

Recall the form of the argument which gave rise to the problem of other minds: we cannot have immediate introspective awareness of the minds of other people, and we cannot perceive their mental states; so our knowledge must be by inference from what we do perceive, namely their circumstances and behavior. But such an inference cannot be deductively valid (unless behaviorism is true; which it isn't), and it cannot be inductively sound either, because it is based upon one case only (my own). We can now claim, however, that our knowledge of other people's mental states isn't based upon a (weak) enumerative induction, but rather on an inference to the best explanation. Our knowledge of the mental states of other people is just like our knowledge of the occurrence of any other theoretical entity: it is knowledge warranted by the theory's capacity to explain and predict the observable data (in this case, behavior in observable circumstances).

In our initial discussion of this proposal in Chapter 1:2, we raised a couple of objections. One was that our knowledge of our own mental states doesn't appear to be theoretical. I don't have to *postulate* the existence of my own mental states, in the way that I do for other people, because I am *aware of* them. But our discussion of theory-theory in section 2 above has made it clear how this objection can be answered. For our application of mentalistic concepts to our own case can involve *recognitional* applications of *theoretical* concepts (or recognitional applications of concepts which are parasitic upon their theoretical counterparts, having been "carved off" from them). There is nothing especially unusual about this idea. It is common in science for theoretical concepts – such as *cancer*, *stamen*, *cell-wall*, and even *electron* – to admit to recognitional applications. Given a background of theory one can see, just by looking, that the theoretical entity in question is present. The prac-

260

ticed theoretician will be able to see this "straight off", without having to make any inferences or consult any postulates of the theory.

Our other objection to the proposal that knowledge of other minds is knowledge by inference to the best theoretical explanation, was that our attitude to the mental states of others isn't tentative and indefinitely revisable in the way that our attitude towards a scientific theory usually is. Our discussion of the probable innateness of our theory of mind has now put us in position to give a decisive response to this objection, too. If our theory of mind is innate, then it is only to be expected that it should feel to us like a "given" aspect of reality, just like the three-dimensionality of space. This is especially so if most of the postulates of the theory aren't available to consciousness, and if most of the work of mentalistic theorizing takes place below the level of conscious awareness, internal to the operations of a distinct theory of mind faculty. For then exactly what one would expect is that we should find ourselves just "knowing", intuitively, what someone is thinking or feeling on many occasions, without being aware of the source of our own knowledge, or of its reliance on theory.

The innateness hypothesis provides us with an especially *satisfying* solution to the problem of other minds, indeed. For it can explain, not only why it should seem so obvious to us that we *do* have knowledge of other people's mental states, but also why we should have such difficulty in articulating the sources of that knowledge.

4.2 How the alternatives fare

Let us now briefly consider how well the alternatives to nativist theory-theory fare in relation to the problem of other minds.

Interpretationalism makes it hard to see why the problem of other minds should ever have been able to get such a grip on us in the first place. If all that we are doing, when we ascribe mental states to other people, is to interpret their behavior in the light of a rationality assumption, then how could it have seemed so difficult for us to know another person's thoughts? For to ascribe a thought to them is to say no more than that their behavior is well-interpretable in the light of that thought. There is no more depth to thought-ascription than that – having a given thought just *is* behaving in a way which is best interpretable in the light of that thought.

261

Admittedly, interpretationalism can be used to construct a close analogue of the problem of other minds. For the ultimate subject of interpretation, on this account, is the agent's *total* behavior over an entire life-time. An interpretation provided at any one time is just a provisional snap-shot, which can be over-turned as further interpretable behavior is provided. So at any given time it will be possible to doubt one's knowledge of the thoughts attributed to the other. For further behavior might yet emerge which would lead one to revise that initial interpretation, which looks like a kind of skeptical worry.

I have two problems with this suggestion. The first is that the original problem of other minds didn't *seem* to be focused on the future, in the way that these interpretationalist worries now are. Secondly, and more importantly, it looks like interpretationalists now have, by this maneuver, undercut their capacity to provide us with a *solution* to the problem of other minds at all. On the contrary, it looks like we now have to say that we cannot really know the thoughts of another person until all the behavioral evidence is in and we have constructed the best overall interpretation of it.

It is doubtful whether simulationism can provide a satisfying solution to the problem of knowledge of other minds, either (or at least not in its own right). Admittedly, given a reliabilist conception of knowledge, and given that simulation is in fact a reliable process, it can be claimed that simulation-based beliefs are reliably acquired, and hence known. But as we emphasized in Chapter 1:1, the problem of other minds is really a problem about *justification* – about the reasons for belief which we have available to us – and not a problem about truth or knowledge (understood in reliabilist terms) as such. What justification do I have for my beliefs about the mental states of others, on a simulationist account?

Well, if we knew that our beliefs about other minds were arrived at through a process of simulation, and we had good reason to think that simulation was a reliable process, then we would have good reason to think that our beliefs about others' beliefs are (largely) true. But this can hardly be the source of our everyday confidence in our beliefs in other minds. For how are we supposed to know that simulation *is* reliable? What independent access are we supposed to have to the minds of other people which would enable us to check on its reliability?

Most simulationists actually accept that we gradually build up a body of theoretical beliefs about the operations of the mind, as a result of engaging in the process of simulation. These beliefs, together with the predictions and explanations which they generate on specific occasions, can be justified in the manner that theories are generally justified: by predictive and explanatory success. So the simulationist can provide essentially the same solution to the problem of other minds as the theory-theorist. But it will not be *qua* simulationist that the solution is provided. On the contrary, it will only be by utilizing the resources of theory-theory that the account works. Simulationism *per se* is bereft of solutions.

Finally, then, what of the view that our theory of mind results from a process of theorizing in infancy, rather than being innately channeled? Plainly, as a form of theory-theory, just the same solution to the problem of other minds can be provided on this account, having the same form as the one sketched in the previous section. Our beliefs about other people's mental states will be justified because generated by a good explanatory theory – a theory whose warrant derives from its myriad successes in generating predictions and explanations in other cases.

But can this theorizing account give such a satisfying explanation for why the problem of other minds should initially have got such a firm grip on us? For if our theory of mind were explicitly constructed through a process of theorizing, then you would expect that we might have a good grasp of its theoretical status. Then when confronted with the question how we know of the mental states of others, the theory-theory response should immediately have sprung to mind. It remains puzzling that it did not. On the contrasting nativist proposal this can be explained: it is because the theory in question is formed and operates largely below the surface of awareness, internal to the operations of an innately built theory of mind faculty.

A theorizing-theorist might claim that by the time we reach adulthood the theory in question is so familiar and "over-learned" that it generally operates unconsciously, without us being aware any longer of what it is that we are doing. (Compare the way in which skills like car driving or chess can become over-learned, to the point where it becomes hard to describe to others how it is that one performs them.) This is a fair point. But the theorizing-theorist should at least make the prediction that young children take the theory-theory solution to the problem of other minds to be obvious, since the process of theory construction will still be fresh in their minds. This is an empirical question; and I know of no systematic evidence. But anecdotally I can report that my own children got gripped by the problem of other minds when it was presented to them in simple terms, even when they were still quite young.

None of these points has been at all decisive, of course. But we appear to have found at least some independent corroboration of the nativist form of theory-theory. This is the approach which can most smoothly explain both the *source* of our justification for our beliefs about other minds (it is the justification which derives from deployment of a well-warranted explanatory theory) *and* why this solution to the problem was by no means an obvious one (it is because the explanatory theory in question is largely unconscious, being embodied in the operations of an innately channeled theory of mind faculty).

Conclusion

In this chapter I have argued that a version of theory-theory provides the best account of how we conceive of mental states, both of ourselves and others; and also that it gives the best account of how we have knowledge of the specific mental states of other people on particular occasions.

Questions for discussion

1. How plausible is it that our concept of each different type of mental state is, at bottom, a bare recognitional capacity for the way such states feel to us when we have them?
2. Could there be a race of super-Spartans who feel pain but never exhibit any pain-behavior?
3. Is it possible that scientists might one day discover that there are really no such things as pains and mental images?
4. If a creature behaves in a way which we can sensibly *interpret* as intelligent, then does that mean that it *is* intelligent?
5. Might human infants be just like little scientists, developing a theory of the existence of the mind and how it works?
6. Does the supposition that our common-sense psychology is *innate* (and largely true) solve the problem of other minds for us?

Further reading

Armstrong, D. (1968) *A Materialist Theory of the Mind*, London: Rout-ledge.

Baron-Cohen, S. (1995) *Mindblindness*, Massachusetts: MIT Press.

Botterill, G. and Carruthers, P. (1999) *The Philosophy of Psychology*, Cambridge. Cambridge University Press, Chapters 2–5.

Byrne, R. and Whiten, A. (eds.) (1988), *Machiavellian Intelligence*, Oxford: Oxford University Press.

Churchland, P. (1979) *Scientific Realism and the Plasticity of Mind*, Cambridge: Cambridge University Press.

Copeland, J. (1993) *Artificial Intelligence*, Oxford: Blackwell.

Davidson, D. (1970) "Mental events", in Foster, L. and Swanson, J. (eds.), *Experience and Theory*, London: Duckworth. Reprinted in Block, N. (ed.) (1980), *Readings in the Philosophy of Psychology*, vol. 1, London: Methuen and in Davidson, D. (ed.) (1980) *Actions and Events*, Oxford: Oxford University Press.

Davidson, D. (1997) "Radical interpretation", *Dialectica*, vol. 27. Reprinted in Davidson, D. (ed.) (1980) *Actions and Events*, Oxford: Oxford University Press.

Dennett, D. (1971) "Intentional systems", *Journal of Philosophy*, vol. 68. Reprinted in Dennett, D. (ed.) (1978) *Brainstorms*, Brighton: Harvester Press.

Goldman, A. (1989) "Interpretation psychologized", *Mind and Language*, vol. 4. Reprinted in Davies, M. and Stone, T. (eds.) (1995), *Folk Psychology*, Oxford: Blackwell.

Gopnik, A. and Melzoff, A. (1997) *Words, Thoughts and Theories*, Massachusetts: MIT Press.

Gordon, R. (1986) "Folk psychology as simulation", *Mind and Language*, vol. 1. Reprinted in Davies, M. and Stone, T. (eds.) (1995), *Folk Psychology*, Oxford: Blackwell.

Lewis, D. (1966) "An argument for the identity theory", *Journal of Philosophy* vol. 63. Reprinted in Lewis, D. (ed.) (1983) *Philosophical Papers* volume 1, Cambridge: Cambridge University Press.

Nichols, S. and Stich, S. (2003) *Mindreading*, Oxford: Oxford University Press.

Putnam, H. (1963) "Brains and behavior" in Butler, R. (ed.), *Analytical Philosophy*, second series, Oxford: Blackwell. Reprinted in Putnam, H. (ed.) (1975) *Mind, Language and Reality*, Cambridge: Cambridge University Press.

Putnam, H. (1967) "The nature of mental states", in Capitan, W. and Merrill, D. (eds.), *Art, Mind and Religion*, Pittsburgh: Pittsburgh University Press. Reprinted in Block, N. (ed.) (1980), *Readings in the Philosophy of Psychology*, vol. 1, London: Methuen; in Putnam's (1975)

Mind, Language and Reality, Cambridge: Cambridge University Press; and in Rosenthal, D. (ed.), (1979) *Materialism and the Mind-Body Problem*, Harlow: Prentice Hall.

Quine, W. V. (1951) "Two dogmas of empiricism", *Philosophical Review*, vol. 60. Reprinted with additions in Quine, W. V. (ed.) (1953) *From a Logical Point of View*, Cambridge, MA: Harvard University Press.

Ryle, G. (1949) *The Concept of Mind*, London: Hutchinson.

Turing, A. "Computing machinery and intelligence", *Mind*, vol. 59. Reprinted in Hofstadter, D. and Dennett, D. (eds.) (1981), *The Mind's I*, Brighton: Harvester Press.

Wellman, H. (1990) *The Child's Theory of the Mind*, Massachusetts: MIT Press.

Wittgenstein, L. (1953) *Philosophical Investigations*. Oxford: Blackwell.

8

⋘∗⋙

Problems and prospects

All the main topics to be covered in this book are now complete. We have examined the various arguments (both Rationalist and Empiricist) in support of the existence of a non-physical soul, and have found them wanting. We have provided a variety of broadly-empirical arguments in support of the claim that both selves and their mental states are physical in nature, and have responded successfully to a range of objections to his idea. We have shown how physicalism is nevertheless consistent with the possibility of life after death, thus showing how it can be reconciled with many forms of religious faith. We have also explored the traditional problem of other minds, and the assumptions on which it is based; finally endorsing a solution to that problem which is grounded in a theory-theory view of the significance of our mental state concepts.

What remain are some unsolved problems for a physicalist approach to the mind, if physicalism is to be fully successful as a worked-out theory of ourselves. Some have been raised and responded to briefly in earlier chapters, where I may have said just enough to indicate that the problems do have a solution; others have only been mentioned. Here we have the opportunity to say just a little more, and to provide pointers towards more advanced work in the subject. This chapter can perhaps, then, be regarded as a "taster" for more advanced courses in philosophy of mind. I shall discuss the four problems, taken in roughly increasing order of seriousness and difficulty (at any rate, the first two problems strike me as much less hard than the last two).

1 Artificial minds

Both functionalism and theory-theory present us with a picture of

267

the human mind as a special sort of causal system, with many inter-acting parts as well as characteristic causal processes involved in perceiving, reasoning, and deciding. In both views, it is supposed to be a contingent matter that this system turns out to be realized in the human brain, or indeed in anything physical at all. On the con-trary, it was always a conceptual possibility that the mind should have been realized in some sort of non-physical soul-stuff. Given that this is so, then there ought to be no barriers, in principle, to the creation of an artificial mind. It ought to be possible to realize the very same kind of causal system in wires and electricity and silicon, rather than in flesh and blood and nerve-cells.

Indeed, we might surely wonder whether there can really be any fundamental difference between a computer and a human being, on a physicalist approach. For are not humans merely biological com-puters? Do we not have a basic "program" laid down in our genes, which is modified and developed by up-bringing and training, and which then has the capacity to modify itself, to some degree, in the light of further experience? (Some computers, too, can be pro-grammed to modify their own programs in the light of later inputs.) One of the themes of this chapter will be to explore (or rather, to begin exploring) the extent to which it is appropriate to think of the human brain as a kind of computer, running the special sort of soft-ware which is the human mind.

It seems unlikely that there are, as yet, any artificially intelligent systems in the fullest sense – that is, it seems unlikely that there are currently any artificial minds. I doubt whether any computer yet built is sophisticated enough to count as a believing, desiring, plan-ning agent. But is it logically possible that there might one day be computers who are minded? Could a thing made out of metal and silicon, which had been created by human beings, ever have a mind? I shall discuss a number of different aspects of this idea, including (in section 2) an objection based on the claim that a person, in order to count as such, must have free will.

Note, that if computers really can have minds, then we have dis-covered yet another possible form of life after death (at least in principle). For if personal survival consists in psychological connect-edness (as we argued in Chapter 6 that it does), and if computers can have psychological states, then I myself might survive as a com-puter. It might one day be possible for all of my beliefs, desires, interests and ties of affection to be programmed into an appropri-ately organized computer, enabling me to survive normal biological death. It would also follow, if it is true that all people have the right to life, that the destruction of such a computer would be murder. So the issues before us in this section may one day turn out to have considerable practical as well as theoretical importance.

1.1 Language and perception

Already there exist computers with which (with whom?) one can hold a limited conversation, e.g., relating to airline timetables. It is sometimes said that the ultimate test of genuine intelligence in a computer would be if it were indistinguishable in its conversational abilities from a normal person. So imagine that scientists have managed to build a computer which you can talk to down a phone-line for as long as you like without ever knowing that you are talking to a machine. Would this show that the computer possesses genuine intelligence, and thus counts as having a mind?

This is the so-called "Turing test" which we discussed in Chapter 7:2. I argued, there, that conversational expertise couldn't be suffi-cient for mindedness without the right kind of internal causal organization. A computer which just churned through a vast look-up table wouldn't count as thinking, no matter how closely its resulting conversation matched that of a normal human. But there is another reason, too, for doubting that a *merely* talking computer should count as minded. For there would, surely, be no reason to think that the computer understands what you say to it, nor that it means anything by its own replies.

A conversation-making computer would only need to be pro-vided with a system of rules for constructing appropriate spoken replies to any given verbal stimulus, as the American philosopher John Searle has pointed out. This system of rules would have to be immensely subtle and complicated, of course. But the important thing to notice is that it would only have to deal with linguistic signs (sounds) and not with their meanings. Thus one simple rule might take the form: *if you hear the sounds, "How are things with you?" respond with the sounds, "Good thanks; and yourself?"* A rule of this sort could be given to someone who understands no English, so long as they have the capacity to recognize and mimic the sounds of English sentences. Surely we think that to possess a set of rules for responding appropriately to any given verbal stimu-lus isn't necessarily to understand what is being said.

The most basic aspect of linguistic understanding is the capacity to apply linguistic signs to items in the world. A competent speaker must be able to recognize and identify the various types of thing for which the terms of their language stand. So in order to count as a genuine language-user, a computer would have to be capable of much more than engaging in agreeable conversation. At the very least it would have to be provided with sensors of various kinds to inform it about its surrounding environment. It could then make simple recognition-statements, such as, "This is a dagger that I see before me".

Even this would not be enough, however. For in order to mean something by an utterance it isn't sufficient that you emit sounds which other speakers can understand, and which generally represent accurately (if so interpreted) some feature of the world. Otherwise we should have to say that a chiming clock speaks a (simple) language, and that by chiming eight times it says that the hour is eight o'clock. You must also *intend* that the sounds you utter should accurately represent some aspect of the world. So a genuine language-using computer would need to be capable of having intentions, and would thus somehow have to be provided with desires.

1.2 Computer desire

A similar conclusion can also be reached from another direction. If computers are ever to possess minds, then they must be given desires, irrespective of whether or not they are programmed to use language. For a minded agent is a being which does things for reasons. To do things for reasons means doing them either because you want to, or because you believe that they may secure you something which you want. So a minded agent is also a desiring agent.

Now there is no logical difficulty about programming a computer to do things, in the sense of causing certain changes to take place in the world. But can it be programmed to *want* those changes to take place? Of course it can be programmed with states which cause it to move in certain directions, but these will only count as desires if there is such a thing as "the good" for that machine. Only entities which have a good can have desires: there must be things which are literally good *for* it (in a non-derivative sense). It may be said that only biological entities can have a good: things which are said to be "good for" a computer (such as dust-free conditions) are in reality only good for the person who makes or uses that machine.

It is hard to believe that this objection is really insurmountable.

To make the case as strong as possible, suppose that we have created an android. This is a computer housed in a physical structure similar to the human body, with similar possibilities of movement. It has sensors of various kinds, corresponding to eyes, ears, etc., to inform it about the states of the surrounding environment. It also has various internal sensors to inform it about some of its own states, especially those related to the continued functioning of the whole machine. For example, it requires a source of electricity in order to work, and has a sensor to inform it when its batteries are running low. It also has a sensor to measure the lubrication in its joints, and so on. Moreover, it has been programmed to respond appropriately to this internal information: seeking new batteries when the old are running low, looking for a shot of oil when its joints aren't sufficiently lubricated.

I see no reason why we shouldn't say that the android sometimes desires new batteries, or more oil. For it needs these things to function properly, and is itself often aware of these needs. Moreover, it is now capable of acting autonomously (without human direction) on the basis of information received from its internal and external sensors; indeed it has a "life" of its own. So full batteries are good for it, not just in the derivative sense that they are good for us who made it, but also in the sense that they are necessary for it to continue its own autonomous pattern of activity.

Someone might concede that a computer could have desires of the sort which a cat or a mouse does. That is to say: it could have behavior-directing states which are related in some way to its own continued functioning. But could it have the sort of self-conscious desires which are characteristic of humans? I can see no reason why not. Suppose that, besides having representations of both external and internal states, our android also has representations of some of its own internal representations. So it can represent, in one part of its program, the various informational and behavior-directing states which currently exist in other parts. These can then be compared with various programmed hierarchies of importance, to yield decisions as to which of the current behavior-directing states should, in this instance, be acted upon.

For example: the sensors report that both batteries and lubrication-oil are running low. These reports are themselves reported elsewhere, where they are compared with a hierarchy giving greater importance to a source of power than to the requirements of smooth motion. But there is also a report that there is a source of oil close at hand, and the android calculates that it would be more efficient to replenish that first. So it moves off in the direction of the oil, deferring the satisfaction of its more important desire until later. I can see no essential difference between this, and some of the kinds of reasoning about practical matters which a human being might go through.

1.3   Freedom and feel

Thus far the situation would seem to be just as theory-theory predicts: there are no conceptual barriers in the way of artificial minds. Provided that computers can be hooked up to the world in the right kind of way (through perception), and provided that they can sense and respond appropriately to their own needs – and provided, too, that their internal operations are organized in the right kinds of ways for thinking and reasoning, as specified by our theory of mind – then computers can be minded agents too. A pair of worries remain, however, to be pursued in later sections.

One concerns the characteristic *feel* of our conscious perceptual states, bodily sensations, and emotional feelings. (This is generally now referred to as "phenomenal consciousness"; sometimes the language of "qualia" is used as well.) Some people might concede that a computer could possess intentional/representational states of perception, belief and desire; and they might concede that computers could engage in processes of reasoning, deciding and acting; but they might deny that the states of a computer would ever possess the sort of phenomenal *feel* characteristic of human consciousness. Note that this position is left open by the theory-theory account we endorsed in Chapter 7:2. For there it was conceded that we can conceive of the feels of our experiences purely recognitionally, carved off from their normal causal roles. In which case, for all we know, no causal roles (of the sort which a computer might enter into) are sufficient for them. Perhaps it requires something *in addition to* causal roles and intentional states in order for a being to be phenomenally conscious.

We saw in Chapter 5:3 that there aren't any good arguments for saying that this "something in addition" is something non-physical; and that there are good reasons for saying that it isn't. So physicalism isn't under threat here. But it might be said that the "something in addition" is something peculiarly *biological*, and hence that only a living flesh-and-blood creature could ever be phenomenally conscious. Indeed, some people maintain that conscious feelings, as a type, are identical with states of the biological human/mammalian/ animal brain (just how widespread phenomenal consciousness is in the animal kingdom can be left open); and hence they claim that no computer could ever possess such feelings.

This is a very large and controversial issue indeed, to which we will return briefly in section 4 below. There I shall sketch out the prospects for explaining phenomenal consciousness in causal and intentional terms. If any such account can be made to work (and this is a big "if"), and if causal and intentional notions are "biology free", as we have suggested, then there will, after all, be no obstacle of principle in the way of creating a phenomenally conscious computer.

The other remaining worry concerns *freedom*. It might be objected that one crucial element in the rationality of humans is missing from the android example above: genuine freedom, or free will. It may be said that a computer can only do what its programmer has instructed it to do. So it doesn't really act autonomously ("for itself"), but merely carries out the instructions written into its program. If human beings, on the other hand, really are free agents, with the capacity to act for themselves, then it will follow that no computer can be minded in the fullest sense. This is the argument from freedom, which will occupy us through part of the next section.

2   Free will

Most people believe that human beings have free will, in some sense or other. Now theory-theory pictures the human mind as a sort of causal system, in many respects like the causal systems (e.g., weather systems) described by scientific theories. It is therefore natural to wonder whether (and if so, how) the existence of free will can be factored into this picture. If it turns out that it can't, then that will be an objection to theory-theory, and also an objection to the idea that a mere causal system like a computer could ever be minded in the fullest sense. This topic will be pursued in the first two of the three sub-sections below.

Moreover, many people have believed that the physical world is *deterministic* in character. They have believed, that is, that given the complete state of the physical universe at any one time, and given the laws of nature, then the complete state at the next (and all succeeding) times is fully determined. If this were true, it would be natural to wonder what place would be left for human freedom of action, unless the source of our freedom is somehow outside of the nexus of physical causality. Many have thus thought that the existence of human free will is inconsistent with physicalism, and that it requires us to opt for at least a weak form of dualism instead. Even now, when many believe that the physical universe is, at bottom, genuinely *chancy* and *un*determined, it is possible to wonder how human freedom can fit into such a system. These issues will be broached in the third of the sub-sections below.

2.1 *Artificial freedom*

Let us try to discover what lies behind the argument from freedom, when used as an argument against the idea of artificial mentality. In what sense is it true that we are free agents? Is it also true that no computer could be free in that sense?

First of all, consider some uninteresting senses of "free", in which the fact that (some) humans are free raises absolutely no difficulty for the idea of artificial minds. For instance, a human can be free rather than in chains. Here "free" means something like, "lacks any humanly imposed obstacles to action". Or someone can do something freely rather than with a gun in his back. Here "free" means something like, "lacks any humanly imposed threat which makes it irrational to act otherwise". Then so long as it is possible for computers to act, and to have motives, it will be possible for them to be free in both of these senses.

More interestingly, it may be said that persons are free in the sense of being radically *unpredictable*. It might be claimed that human beings (or at least those human beings who are minded in the fullest sense) are essentially unpredictable creatures, in a way that no computer ever could be. But in fact this unpredictability may have a number of different sources, none of which raises any difficulty for the idea of computer minds.

First: sheer complexity. Human beings are immensely complex creatures, and the human brain alone contains many millions of different nerve cells. But the differences between humans and computers, here, are merely a matter of degree. Although no computer yet built approaches anywhere near the complexity of the human brain, there is no logical objection to the idea that we may one day build one just as complicated, and so just as difficult to predict.

A second source of unpredictability in human beings has already been mentioned. It is that we are constantly being modified in various subtle ways by the impact of the environment. It will therefore be impossible to make accurate predictions unless you know exactly what that impact has been; but as a matter of empirical fact we can never possess such knowledge. This may be true of computers too, however. The state of a computer can depend, not just upon its original program, but also on the information which has since been fed into it. It may also have been programmed to modify itself in various ways in the light of later inputs. Then no computer programmers, no matter how clever, will be able to make accurate predictions unless they know all of the input which has occurred since the computer was turned on. But in the case of a free-moving android, which is constantly receiving new information about the environment through which it moves, such knowledge will in practice be impossible to obtain.

Thirdly, people can be bloody-minded. Once a human being has become aware of your prediction of their behavior, they can straight away set about falsifying it by doing something else instead. If you try to allow for this by predicting how the person will react to the knowledge of your original prediction, they can set about falsifying that in turn, and so on. But I can see no reason why it is supposed to be impossible, in principle, to build a bloody-minded computer. In any case the moral of the story merely is: if you want to make accurate predictions of the behavior of intelligent agents, then keep your predictions to yourself.

It may be said that there is a fourth, and much more radical, sense in which people's behavior is essentially unpredictable. It may be said that even given complete knowledge of all the laws of nature, together with complete knowledge of all current physical states of a human being, as well as complete knowledge of all future sensory stimulations, it would still be impossible to make accurate predictions of what the human will do. Now I have not the faintest idea how it is supposed to be possible for us to know that this is the case. We certainly have no evidence of it at the moment. But even if it were the case, nothing in principle would stand in the way of creating a computer which is unpredictable in precisely this radical sense.

All we should need, would be a computer with a randomizer in its decision process: a radiation source, for example. We could fix up the program in such a way that certain decisions only get made

if an alpha-particle is given off by a uranium source within a specified time-period. Then since such emissions are random, the resulting behavior of the machine would be essentially unpredictable,
even given complete knowledge of prior physical facts.

A free decision isn't the same thing as a random one, of course. A
free decision is one which is made on the basis of reasons. So it
might be said that persons are free agents in the following sense:
*they take decisions which aren't determined by the laws of nature
together with all prior physical facts, but where those decisions are
taken for reasons rather than randomly.* Now I agree that it is difficult, if not impossible, to see how any computer could be free in
this sense. But again I ask how we are supposed to be able to know
that any human beings are free in this sense either.

Indeed, it is doubtful whether this sense of "free" can even be
made coherent. For to make a decision on the basis of reasons is for
that decision to be explicable in the light of your beliefs and desires.
("Why did you decide to do it?" – "Because I believed this and
wanted that".) Yet if the decision isn't itself caused by the beliefs
and desires which explain it, then it is problematical – to say the
least – quite what the relationship between them is supposed to be.
How do reasons underlie or explain the making of decisions, if not
by causing them? What is it to take a decision for a reason, if that
reason did not (together with the thoughts, etc., surrounding it)
cause the decision? Myself, I can see no answers to these questions.

2.2 Higher-order decision making

Perhaps the most interesting sense of "free" arises out of our possession of second-order beliefs and desires, as the American philosopher Harry Frankfurt has pointed out. (A second-order belief is a
belief *about* another belief or desire; a second-order desire is a
desire *that* a certain belief should or shouldn't be possessed, or *that*
a certain desire should or shouldn't be possessed or acted upon.)
Since we have the capacity to act upon our second-order preferences
(together with our second-order beliefs about the reliability of our
other beliefs), we aren't slaves to our first-order desires. On the contrary, we are normally free to choose which of our first-order
desires (whether present or future) we should try to satisfy. So here
"free" means something like, "action in accordance with second-
order desires and preferences".

Our capacity to act on second-order preferences is intimately connected with our status as rational agents. For rational agents will generally have many long-term desires and intentions, only some of which will be present to consciousness at any given time as a *felt* desire. Rational agents have the capacity to weigh up the competing claims of desires which they currently feel against the desires which they think that they *will* feel on the morrow, as well as those that they know, in an abstract way, that they do really possess even though they don't presently feel their urgency. They are capable of acting on their second-order preference for the satisfaction of tomorrow's desire (or for the satisfaction of the desire they know themselves to have but don't currently feel) ignoring the claims of the desire which they feel at the moment.

This is certainly a large part of our sense of our own freedom. In so far as there is an argument from introspection for the existence of free will, then this is what it establishes. We know that we aren't normally driven to act by the desires we happen to feel at the time. We know that we aren't at the mercy of our own desires. On the contrary, we know that we have the capacity to stand back and reflect, forming preferences over the desires we feel as well as the desires we believe that we will or should feel, and assessing the reliability of the beliefs on which our various plans are based. We also know that we are capable of acting on our considered judgment, based upon these second-order beliefs and preferences.

(Indeed, this is why we find such things as weakness of will – as well as more extreme phenomena like kleptomania and drug addiction – so disturbing. For they threaten our status as rational agents. In such cases we find ourselves acting in accordance with a presently-felt desire against our own considered judgment.)

Thus we aren't in general slaves to our passions, but have the capacity – deriving from our possession of second-order beliefs and desires – to choose between them. (Most if not all animals, in contrast, are *wantons*. They are driven to act by whichever of their desires is currently strongest.) But I can see no objection in principle to the construction of a computer which is free in this sense. It need only be constructed so as to contain representations of its own representational states, with the part of the program which is concerned with these second-order representations being given ultimate control over the direction of the computer's behavior.

In conclusion, since all the various proposed senses of "free" are such that *either* there is no reason to believe that any people are free in that sense, *or* there is no objection to a computer being free in that sense, I conclude that there is no objection of principle to a computer possessing personal freedom.

2.3 Is determinism compatible with free will?

A number of philosophers have presented intuitively-compelling arguments that causal determinism and human free will are incompatible (notably the American writer Peter Van Inwagen). One such argument goes as follows.

(1)   If determinism is true, then what happens next (including which of the available actions I perform) is causally determined by the state of the universe long before I was born.

(2)   I am not free to alter the way the universe was long before I was born.

(C1) So (from (1) and (2)) if determinism is true, then I am not free to alter what happens next (including which action I perform).

(3)   If I am not free to alter which action I perform next, then I am not a free agent.

(C2) So (from (C1) and (3)) if determinism is true, then I am not a free agent.

Premise (1) of this argument seems just to spell out what determinism *is*. Premises (2) and (3) seem obviously true. The argument as a whole appears valid. Then if we believe in determinism while believing in our own status as free agents, we might *appear* to have a powerful motive for locating the source of our agency outside of the causal nexus of the world – that is to say, outside of the physical universe.

But actually, we just have to recall the arguments of Chapter 5:1 to realize that this won't help much. The most that dualism could get us is that we are free to alter our own *decisions*. But since our physical actions are presumably determined by physical causes (if determinism is true), we still won't have the power to alter those. This would be a "freedom" which wouldn't be worth very much. It looks like the truth of determinism either rules out human freedom altogether, or leaves it confined to the realm of the mental, divorced from any impact on the physical world.

To what extent is the argument above denuded of interest now that most people believe that determinism *isn't* true, in the light of the discoveries of modern physics? If we believe, as physicists tell us, that the physical universe is a fundamentally chancy place, then does that leave room for human freedom after all? It is hard to see how it would help, at least if we attempt to continue working within a physicalist framework. For as we saw in the previous sub-section, a *random* decision isn't at all the same as (nor sufficient for) a *free* decision. So the fact that some events within the physical world happen randomly doesn't appear to help us find a place for freedom within that world.

Matters might be otherwise, however, if we were to embrace dualism. If decisions can be freely made outside of the realm of the physical, and that physical realm isn't a deterministic one, but is partly a matter of chance, then there appears scope, here, for free decisions to make a difference. Perhaps our decisions can have an impact down at the sub-atomic level, resolving indeterminacies and raising or lowering chances of physical events. This is a suggestion which some philosophers have tried to exploit. It appears to hold out the possibility of reconciling genuine human freedom with inde-terministic physical causality.

Admittedly, large problems would remain. We should still have to make sense of the idea of a decision which is taken for reasons without being caused by them, and without being random either, which we discussed briefly in section 2.1 above. Otherwise a shift to a form of dualism won't help us – we should just have landed our-selves with the dilemma between determinism and random decision-making once again at the mental level. We should also have to bring ourselves to believe that our non-physical decisions can each have billions of distinct sub-atomic physical effects distributed across hundreds of thousands of cells and cellular connections in the brain at once, resolving enough indeterminacies at the sub-atomic level to make it the case that one set of brain-cells fires (causing one action) rather than another (causing another). This makes the relationship between mind and brain look *very* messy and complicated indeed.

What are our options? If, as it appears, we may be faced with a choice between giving up physicalism and giving up our belief in human freedom, which should we choose? It might be said that the practical effects of giving up belief in human freedom would be so disastrous that we really have no option here but to give up physi-calism. For isn't freedom necessary for us to hold people responsible for what they do (to praise or blame them)? Also, isn't freedom a pre-requisite of just punishment? (If people who cause harm couldn't have done otherwise, then we excuse them rather than punish them.) However, the discussion of the previous sub-sections should make us suspicious, at this point. If, as we saw, there are many different senses of the term "free", then the fact that we have to cease believing in human freedom in one of these senses doesn't mean that we have to give up on all of them. It will require a good deal of work to sort out which senses are in question, and which are required for which of our other beliefs and practical activities. I shall not attempt to pursue these questions here.

Another option is to return to examine the initial argument more closely. For there is some reason to think that, as presented, it commits a fallacy of equivocation (a shift of meaning). Specifically, the sense of "free to alter" in premise (2) would appear to be this: I am not free to alter something, in this sense, if that thing remains as it is independently of what I think or decide. This is what it means to say that I am not free to alter the remote past: no matter how much I think about it, or how many "decisions" I reach or how hard I try, those past facts will remain just as they are. But if this is what "free to alter" means in (C1), then (C1) isn't true. For which action I perform *isn't* independent of my thoughts and decisions – or at least, not if physicalism is true (as we saw in Chapter 5:1). On the contrary, we know that if I decide one thing, I generally do that thing; and if I decide on another, I generally do that other.

It looks like (C1) can only be true if "freedom to alter" is interpreted as meaning something like this: "I am not free to alter something if the *causes* of that thing, no matter how remote, are as they are independently of what I think or decide". But then this isn't the sense of "free" which figured in premise (2), so we have a fallacy of equivocation. It is, moreover, hugely controversial that this is the sense of "free" which should figure in premise (3). On the contrary, those who are so-called "compatibilists" (believing that human freedom and determinism are compatible with one another) have generally maintained that the sense in which we believe ourselves to be free agents is just that there are some things which depend upon *us* – our thoughts and decisions. On this view, to say that I am free to alter something means that it depends upon me and my mental states. It doesn't mean that I am free to alter all of those mental states and their causes in turn.

These are controversial and difficult waters, so I am content to leave them for further study. But I do want to emphasize that there are plenty of options here to be explored. It would be highly premature, in my view, to reject the powerful case for physicalism which we have been able to build up in previous chapters.

3 Intentionality

If physicalism is true, then all mental properties – including those involved in the *intentionality* of mental states, or in mental *representation* – have to be realized, somehow, in physical states and processes. A burgeoning research industry among philosophers in recent decades has been to try to explain in some detail how this can be so. Before sketching some of the main positions taken, however, I need to say a few words about the intellectual pressures driving their search.

Recall from Chapter 5:2.2 that physicalists needn't be reductionists – they needn't believe that mental properties can be reduced to, or replaced by, physical ones. But they must at least believe in the reductive *explicability* of all higher-level properties, including those involved in psychology. If physicalism is true, then it must be possible to explain how intentional properties are *realized in* properties of the brain, on at least some occasions (even if the same intentional property can be differently realized on different occasions). This has been the puzzle which has then motivated philosophical attempts to naturalize intentionality: if physicalism is to be defensible, then we need to be able to get some sort of handle on how intentional properties might be realized in physical processes in the brain.

3.1 *The language of thought hypothesis*

How, then, are propositional attitudes (beliefs, desires, and the rest) carried in cognition? How is intentional content represented? Recall that the theory-theorist's view is that propositional attitudes are discrete states which interact with one another causally to produce behavior, and in ways which respect their semantic contents. The belief that it is dark down in the cellar combines with the desire to see my way around down there, not randomly, but in such a way as to produce the intention to find some means of illumination. This in turn may combine with the belief that a flash-light is available, so as to cause me to carry that flash-light in my hand when I go down. How is this possible? How can propositional attitudes have causal powers which reflect their *relatedness to the world*, as well as their logical relations with one another, which is distinctive of their possessing an intentional content? There are really three different, but closely related, problems in need of solution here.

First, propositional attitudes are *systematic*, having contents which are related to one another systematically, in such a way that anyone capable of believing (or otherwise thinking) a given content will be capable of believing or thinking a number of closely related contents. Anyone capable of believing *that Jane loves John* will also be capable of the thought *that John loves Jane*. Why should this be so? How is this fact about propositional attitudes to be explained?

Secondly, propositional attitudes are *productive*, in the sense that anyone capable of thinking at all will be capable of entertaining unlimitedly many (or at least, a *very great* many) thoughts. If you can think that Jane has a mother, then you can think that Jane's mother has a mother, and that Jane's mother's mother has a mother, and so on (subject, of course, to limitations of memory and other cognitive space). There is no end to the new thoughts which thinkers are capable of entertaining. This fact, too, is in need of explanation.

Thirdly, propositional attitudes interact causally with one another in ways which respect their intentional contents and component concepts. This was the point which was closest to the surface in our initial statement of the problem three paragraphs back. Beliefs and desires interact to cause intentions, and beliefs interact with other beliefs to generate new beliefs, in ways which are closely responsive to the *contents* of those states, and by means of transitions which are generally rational ones. How can this happen? How can patterns of causality respect semantic relations of entailment and evidential support?

The classical solution to these three problems has been that beliefs are relations to internal sentences, or structured items in some sort of brain-code (generally referred to as "Mentalese"), as the American philosopher and cognitive scientist Jerry Fodor has forcefully argued. For sentences have contents which are systematically determined from the contents of their component words, together with rules of combination. If you understand the words, and know the rules of syntax, then you must be capable of understanding new combinations of those words, never before encountered. By the same token, of course, sentences are productive, in virtue of the fact that rules of syntax are recursive. So the sententialist hypothesis provides us with solutions to the problems of systematicity and productivity: thought is systematic and productive because there is *a language of thought* (LOT).

Moreover (and providing us with a solution to the third problem also) sentence tokens can have causal powers, by virtue of being physical particulars. If beliefs and desires consist of sentences, or sentence-like structures, encoded in some distinctive way in the brain, then there will be no difficulty in explaining how beliefs and desires can be causes. (By way of analogy, think of the manner in which sentences can be stored in magnetic patterns on an audio-tape. These sentence tokens then *cause* the sound-waves which result when the tape is played.) If we suppose, in addition, that the mind is arranged so as to effect computations on these sentences in ways which respect their syntax, then the causal roles of the sentences will respect their semantic properties. For semantics is, in part, a reflection of syntax. Then we shall have explained successfully how beliefs and desires can have causal roles which depend upon their intentional contents.

For example, a logical concept like *and* or *not* can be carried by a lexical item of some sort, distinguished by its capacity to enter into certain characteristic patterns of inference. Roughly, "&" means *and* provided that the computational system within which it belongs ensures that it is governed by the following forms of inference: *(P & Q) → P; (P & Q) → Q;* and *P, Q → (P & Q).* A concept such as *bus-stop*, too, can be constituted by some lexical item of Mentalese (BUS-STOP, as we will henceforward write items in brain-language), characterized both by its causal connections with worldly objects (bus-stops), and by the way in which it figures in distinctive patterns of inference (such as BUS-STOP → BUSES SHOULD STOP) involving yet other lexical items from other parts of the language of thought.

In fact the dominant paradigm in cognitive science for the last few decades has been that mental states and processes are realized *computationally*, and that the brain itself should be thought of as a sort of biological computer. Individual thoughts are carried by individual sentences in LOT, and patterns of thinking will be realized in computational processes defined over LOT representations. On this account, not only are thoughts carried by these Mentalese sentences, but the transitions among those sentences are *computational*, involving rule-governed causal sequences which serve to realize the intentional laws of common-sense and scientific psychology; and those sentences, and those computational transitions among sentences, are somehow realized in neural states of the brain.

(Before we move on, it should be noted that this now-classical computational picture of the mind–brain has been challenged by so-called "distributed connectionist" models of cognition. On this view, there are no internal symbols of Mentalese. Rather, representations are *smeared* or *distributed* across the activation levels in a vast inter-connected network of nodes in the brain. It would take us too far afield to pursue this dispute here. I merely note that connectionism appears inconsistent with the *discreteness* of cognitive states and processes which a theory-theory approach to the mind commits us to (as we saw in Chapter 7:2); and that those who have defended connectionism have, in fact, either been *interpretationalists* or *eliminative materialists* about the mind, of one sort or another. Moreover, connectionism seems increasingly to be inconsistent with emerging discoveries about localist – *non-distributed* – representation in the brain.)

I should stress that the Mentalese hypothesis *isn't* that the language of thought is English (or any other natural language). This is because most cognitive scientists believe that thought – or at any rate, most thought – is prior to and independent of natural language. Rather, the hypothesis is that thoughts are carried by discrete structured states, built up out of recombinable parts *somewhat like* natural language sentences. The easiest way to see the point, is to note that non-human animals, too, are capable of thought. Many of the same arguments for Mentalese can be run in connection with the thoughts of animals. For example, many animals can do *one-off learning* (which distributed connectionist systems can't do). Chimpanzees continually track the social relationships of the animals in their troupe, and adjust their expectations immediately as those relationships change. If a chimp can first believe something along the lines of, "Chico is in alliance with Zeno", and can then believe, "Chico is now in competition with Zeno", then it is very hard to see how this can be possible unless the chimp brain contains a structured state of some sort, with separate elements representing Chico and his relationships, so that the former can be held constant while the latter are varied.

3.2 Input-side semantics

One suggestion concerning how intentional contents are physically realized, then, is that such contents are carried by sentence-like structures in the human brain. But what is it about such structures which confers on them their intentional content? How do such sentences come to be *about* anything in the world?

Informational, causal co-variance, or pure input-side semantic theories claim that meaning is carried by the causal connections between the mind and the world. Roughly, the idea is that for a mental term "S" to mean S, is for tokenings of "S" to causally co-vary with Ss – that is, Ss, and only Ss, cause tokenings of "S". So for the term "mouse" (or its Mentalese equivalent, MOUSE) to mean *mouse*, is for tokenings of the term MOUSE in belief to be reliably caused by the presence of mice, and only by the presence of mice. Such an account is plainly physicalist, since the only terms which figure in it are "cause", together with terms referring to worldly properties on the one hand and physical word-tokens and sentence-tokens on the other.

Informational theories of mental content are modeled on the sense of "represent" which is appropriate whenever there are causal co-variance relations in the natural world, and so whenever one state of the world *carries information about* another. Thus we say, "Seven tree rings *mean* (represent) that the tree was seven years old", "Heavy clouds *mean* rain", "Those spots *mean* measles" (that is, "Spots of that type causally co-vary with the presence of measles"), and so on.

But why would anyone want to begin a *semantic* theory here? Since it is obvious that there is no real *intentionality*, or *aboutness*, present in these examples, why should we take them as our model? One line of attraction comes from noticing that this very same causal co-variance sense of "represent" is apparently employed by neuro-psychologists studying the brain. They will say, for example, "The firing of this cell *represents* the presence of an upright line in the visual field", on the grounds that the cell is caused to fire when, and only when, an upright line is present. The hope is then that we may be able to build up to a full-blown notion of mental representation from this simple starting point, just as the neuro-psychologist hopes to build up an account of the visual system from such simple materials.

The obvious problem that informational theories have to overcome, however, is to make room for the possibility of *misrepresentation*. For plainly it is possible – indeed, quite common – for our beliefs and thoughts to misrepresent the world. But it appears *im*possible for one state to carry *misinformation* about another, in the objective causal sense of information which is in question. Thus if heavy clouds don't just co-vary with rain, but also with strong winds, then heavy clouds which aren't followed by rain don't misrepresent the state of the weather (although *we*, as observers, may draw a false inference from them). Rather, what heavy clouds *really* represent (that is, causally co-vary with), is rain-or-strong-winds. Similarly, if the spots normally caused by measles can also be caused, say, by toxic metal poisoning, then the presence of those spots in the latter sort of case does *not* mean (that is, carry information about) measles (although they may lead a doctor into a misdiagnosis). Rather, what spots of that sort really mean is measles-or-toxic-metal-poisoning.

Applied to the case of mental states, then, the difficulty for informational theories is to avoid what is sometimes called "the disjunction problem". Suppose that I regularly mistake certain kinds of shrew for mice. That is, not only does the presence of a mouse in my environment reliably cause me to think MOUSE, but so too does the presence of a certain kind of shrew cause me to think MOUSE. What, then, does MOUSE represent, for me? If mental symbols mean what they reliably co-vary with, then it looks as if MOUSE must mean *shrew-or-mouse* rather than *mouse*. So I am not, after all, mistaken when I think MOUSE in the presence of a shrew. Indeed, if this problem generalizes, it looks as if, according to informational semantic theories, it is going to be impossible for *anyone, ever,* to be mistaken! And that, of course, is absurd.

The best-developed approach to this problem has been presented by Jerry Fodor, who formulates his theory in terms of *asymmetric causal dependence*. That is, he claims that a Mentalese term "S" will refer to Ss, and only Ss, provided that the causal connections between "S" and any other (non-S) objects which may happen to cause tokenings of "S" are asymmetrically causally dependent upon the causal connection between tokenings of "S" and Ss. So if any other types of object besides Ss cause tokenings of "S", they will only do so *because* Ss cause tokenings of "S". The account, then, is this (also represented pictorially in Figure 8.1):

MOUSE will mean *mouse* (and so shrews will be *mis*represented by MOUSE) if:

(i) mice cause tokenings of MOUSE, and
(ii) if mice had not caused tokenings of MOUSE, shrews would not have, and
(iii) if shrews had not caused tokenings of MOUSE, mice still would have.

Thus (i)-(iii) capture the idea that the *shrew*-to-MOUSE connection is

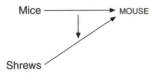

Figure 8.1 Asymmetric causal dependence.

asymmetrically causally dependent upon the *mouse*-to-MOUSE connection.

3.3 *Against pure input-side semantics*

Perhaps the biggest problem for any informational semantics, however, is this: where in the causal chain which leads to the tokening of a mental symbol do you stop, to fix on the meaning of the latter? Any mental symbol will always carry information about events further out, and events further in, from what we would intuitively take to be its referent. For example, any term which reliably co-varies with *mouse* will also reliably co-vary with *mouse-mating*, since the world is such that, whenever there is a mouse, there has also been a mating between mice in the past. So what shows as MOUSE means *mouse* and not *mouse-mating*?

It is doubtful whether an appeal to asymmetric causal dependence can help here. For it seems that we have a *symmetric* dependence between the *mouse*-to-MOUSE connection and the *mouse-mating*-to-MOUSE connection – that is, if mice had not caused me to think MOUSE, then nor would matings of mice; but if mouse-matings had not caused me to think MOUSE, then nor would mice. Examples of this sort provide powerful support for some form of teleological or functional-role semantics, in fact (see the sections below). Thus one might say that what makes MOUSE mean *mouse*, is that its *function* is to co-vary with mice and not mouse-matings – that is, the role of MOUSE in cognition is to focus our behavior differentially upon mice. Or one might say that what makes MOUSE mean *mouse*, is the kinds of *inference* which the subject is inclined to make – for example, from MOUSE to LIVING THING, and not from MOUSE to TEMPORAL EVENT.

A similar problem arises in respect of causal co-variance with events further in. Suppose that by electrically stimulating just the right spot in my cortex, an experimenter can make me think MOUSE.

Then what shows that MOUSE means *mouse* and not *immediate neural cause of MOUSE*? In this case we appear to have asymmetric dependence the wrong way round – if mice had not caused me to think MOUSE (for example, because the Mentalese term XYZ gets harnessed to do the job instead), then still the (actual) immediate neural cause of MOUSE would have caused me to think MOUSE (where MOUSE would now be harnessed to mean something else); and if the (actual) immediate neural cause of MOUSE had not caused me to think MOUSE (but some other neural event had), then nor would mice have caused me to think MOUSE (rather, MOUSE would have been harnessed to some other meaning). Here, too, the solution would appear to be to move to a form of teleological or functional-role semantics. At any rate, I predict that if there is any way of securing the asymmetric dependence of the *immediate-neural-cause-of-MOUSE-to-MOUSE* connection upon the *mouse-to-MOUSE* connection, it will have to make at least covert appeal to the *role* of the sign MOUSE in normal cognition.

3.4 *Varieties of consumer semantics*

The American philosopher Ruth Millikan draws an important distinction between the *producers* and *consumers* of mental representations in the course of developing her own form of teleo-semantics or function-semantics (see section 3.5 below). She claims that it is the consumers which are primary when it comes to determining intentional contents. In the case of a visual percept, for example, the producer system will be the visual module which constructs that representation out of the information striking the retina, whereas the consumer system will be the various practical reasoning and action-control systems which *use* (or can use) that percept in the course of their normal functioning. Now the teleological function of any given mental state lies in its evolved effects (the effects it is *supposed* to have) on the consumers of that state. So it is to the latter that we need to look in fixing the content of the state in question, according to Millikan.

There is an important point here, which is independent of teleological approaches as such, and which embodies a significant criticism of informational (or pure input-side) semantics. The point is that the meaning of a sign, *for a system*, can only be the meaning which it has for the processes within that system which consume, or make use of, that sign. It is no good a sign carrying information about some worldly state of affairs if, so to speak, the rest of the system doesn't know that it does! This now holds out some hope of making progress with the disjunction problem. If we ask why MOUSE doesn't mean *shrew-or-mouse* – given that I frequently mis-recognize shrews as mice, and so given that MOUSE often carries information about shrews – the answer can be that it is because the rest of the system only operates in ways appropriate to mice, and not to shrews-or-mice. Thus from MOUSE the system infers NOT SHREW, and also perhaps CAN BE AN INDOOR PEST. It will therefore lead me to answer "Yes" if asked whether there is a mouse and not a shrew nearby, and so on. So MOUSE representations have a variety of further effects, on inference and action, whose success requires the presence of a mouse, and not of a shrew. So if MOUSE is to have the effects which it is *supposed* to have, it needs to carry the information *mouse*, and not *shrew-or-mouse*. That, accordingly, can be said to be its meaning.

Many different varieties of consumer-semantics have been developed by philosophers over the years. But those accounts can be seen as falling into one of two broad classes – *teleo-semantics* or function-semantics (championed by Millikan) and *inferential-role semantics* or functional-role semantics (one of whose main propo-nents has been the American philosopher Ned Block). There is space here to say just a little by way of introduction of each.

3.5 *Teleo-semantics*

Consider teleo-semantics first. If we could say what it is for a state to have the content that *P* in terms of what that state is *supposed* to achieve in cognition, then we would have effected a naturalistic reduction, provided that the notion of *proper function* appealed to in the account is a genuinely scientific (physicalistically acceptable) one. Roughly, the idea will be that the content (truth-condition) of a belief is that state of the world which enables the belief to achieve those effects (namely, successful action) which it is *supposed* to achieve (that is, say, which it is its biological proper function to achieve).

One way of motivating this sort of teleological account is to notice that many naturally occurring signs employed by biological systems only rarely co-occur with the phenomena which (one wants to say) they represent. For an evolved feature doesn't have to be always or often successful in order to be selected for. It just has to confer *some* advantage on organisms which possess it (without incurring any significant disadvantage). For example, suppose that a particular species of ground-squirrel uses a series of alarm-calls to warn of potential predators (somewhat like the vervet monkey, only rather less discriminating) – one call for *eagle*, one for *snake*, and one for *big cat*. It is quite possible that the call which means *eagle* should mostly be a false alarm, triggered by any large bird flying overhead. For the costs to the squirrels of taking cover under a tree are small, whereas the gains, on those occasions when there *is* an eagle approaching, are very large. Better to hide unnecessarily many times, than to risk not hiding when you should, and be eaten. So in terms of *information carried* it looks like the alarm call would just mean "big bird". But when we consider the *function* of the alarm call in the lives of the squirrels, we see that it has been selected for in virtue of those occasions, and only those occasions, when it carries the information that an eagle is above. Then this, according to teleo-semantics (and in accordance with intuition) is what it means.

It is important to note that the concept of biological function at work here is an *evolutionary, selectionist,* one. On such an account, the functions of any property F are those effects of F which explain why the system in question has that property – that is, in terms of which we can explain how the property was selected for and/or has been sustained in systems of that type. So functions, on this account, are essentially historical. To know the function of a thing or property, it isn't enough to observe what it *presently* does. Rather, you must discover which effect, from among the things which it presently does (perhaps only rarely) explains why that thing or property exists. Thus, to know the function of the peacock's tail, you have to ask which of the effects of such tails in ancestral peacocks (presumably, in this case, attractiveness to female peacocks) explains why they were selected for and/or preserved.

Finally, let me note that although *one* natural home of such an historical notion of function is in biology, and in evolutionary theory in particular, it can also be used in connection with artifacts. The function of the brakes in my car, too, can be those of their effects which explain why cars have features of just this type, in this case selected by past designers, rather than by natural selection. So nothing in teleo-semantics, as such, rules out the possibility that computers might possess states with intentional content.

290

3.6   Functional-role semantics

The contrasting notion of function (*not* adopted by defenders of teleo-semantics) is an a-historical one. On this account, the functions of any property F are those effects of F which are beneficial to some wider system or process of which F forms a part, or which play a role in sustaining the capacities of that wider system. So on this account, whether or not a property has a function is entirely independent of the question of how that property came to be possessed in the first place. To ask, in this sense, about the function of the peacock's tail is to ask what the tail *does for* the peacock (what benefit it confers), in a way which just brackets off as irrelevant the question of how the peacock came to have such a tail. It is this a-historical notion of function which is put to work in inferential-role, or functional-role, semantics.

One argument in support of functional-role semantics is an argument from functionalism about mental states *in general*. As we saw in Chapter 7, the majority of philosophers now think that the way to avoid dualism about the mental, and to understand the relationship between mind and brain, is by accepting that mental states are individuated by their causal role, conceptualized at some level of abstraction from the physical mechanisms in the brain which instantiate those roles. Indeed, we have accepted that folk psychology embodies an implicit *theory* of the causal structure and functioning of the mind, in such a way that different mental state types can be individuated by their position within the theory. The argument then is, that when we extend this approach to states like *the belief that P* we get functional-role semantics.

A second argument for functional-role semantics is a kind of "what else?" argument from those working on the semantics of beliefs and statements. It is generally maintained that we cannot individuate contents purely in terms of reference, since this will slice them *too thick*. That is, it will fail to distinguish from one another thought-contents which are, intuitively, distinct. For example, Oedipus's belief *that Jocasta is more than 40 years'* old, differs in content from his belief *that Mother is more than 40 years' old*, even though Jocasta is, in fact, his mother. For, not knowing that Jocasta is his mother, it would be possible for him to have the one belief without the other. Yet if the reference is the same, what *else* can distinguish these beliefs *except* their differences of causal role? For example, Oedipus' belief that he is 30 years' old will tend to cause him to have the second of the above beliefs in the presence only of the belief that a girl of 10 cannot have a child, whereas the first of the above beliefs will only be caused if he *also* believes that Jocasta is his mother.

There are *many, many* issues and questions to be explored in relation to this and other attempts to provide a reductive explanation of intentional properties. Here I only want to claim two things. First, that we can make progress with the problem of intentionality if we suppose that propositional attitudes are realized in sentence-like structures of Mentalese, encoded in some distinctive way in the brain. Secondly, that it is at least *promising* that we might be able to explain how such sentences come to possess an intentional content by examining the causal relations into which they enter (either on the input side, or on the consumer side, or both), or by examining their evolutionary function. There is, I claim, good reason to hope that the intentional properties postulated by our folk-psychological theory can be integrated into a physicalist world-view through some-such means.

4   Consciousness

Just as our belief in physicalism puts pressure on us to explain how a physical system can have the property of intentionality, so it also puts pressure on us to explain how a physical system can be phenomenally conscious – that is, how it can have states which possess a subjective "feel" or *quale*. This, too, has provoked a lively and heated set of debates in recent decades, with some people declaring consciousness to be a mystery (claiming that it is one of the few remaining "final frontiers" for science to conquer, together with the mystery of the origin of the universe), while others have proposed a variety of reductive explanations. This concluding section will provide a brief introduction to some of the issues.

4.1   *Brute identities and the explanatory gap*

We saw in Chapter 5:3 that the existence of unanalyzable "feels" provides no real motive to reject physicalism. For we might have purely recognitional concepts for these properties of *feel*, and yet those properties might be none other than (might be strictly identical to) physical properties of the brain. So the truth of some or other version of an identity thesis (type or token) is not in question

292

here. What *is* in question, is whether the properties of *feel* involved in phenomenal consciousness can be given a reductive *explanation*. Can we show how and why just the right arrangements of physical properties should be, or should constitute or realize, some form of phenomenal consciousness?

Many philosophers have argued that there is an unbridgeable "explanatory gap" between all physical and functional properties, on the one hand, and the facts of phenomenal consciousness, on the other. They have said that we can see in advance that no matter how much information we acquire about the physical and causal facts involved in perception and sensation, we shall still not be able to understand *why* those physical facts should realize just those properties of *feel* which we are aware of in introspection. (Remember the case of color-deprived Mary from Chapter 5:3.)

Now, I deny that such an explanatory gap can be established in advance of enquiry, by thought alone. For the mere fact that we will always be capable of conjoining any physical story with the absence of phenomenal consciousness is only to be expected, if we have purely recognitional concepts for the properties involved in the latter. If I can form a concept *this* for some distinctive sort of feel, where that concept lacks any conceptual connections with any concepts of a physical or causal-role sort, then in connection with any proposed reductive account of that felt property I shall always be capable of thinking, "But all that might be true, and still *this* might be different or absent".

The availability of such thoughts isn't, itself, any real obstacle to providing a successful reductive explanation, I claim. Explanation is explanation of properties, not of concepts. So we might be able to explain the property *picked out by* our purely recognitional concept of feel, even if that explanation fails to "connect up with" the concept, by virtue of the recognitional character of the latter. But of course, saying that there are no obstacles *of principle* to reductive explanation is one thing, and actually *finding* such an explanation is quite another.

Other philosophers have said that if phenomenally conscious properties are identical with physical attributes of the human brain, then it is neither necessary nor appropriate to seek any further explanation of them. For identities aren't the kinds of facts which *admit* of further explanation. Consider the identity of water and H_2O, for example. If someone asks, "*Why* is water H_2O?", it looks like we can only reply (vacuously), "Because it is". You can't *explain* the identity of water and H_2O. Rather, identity facts are *brute* ones (not further explicable). Similarly, then, we can't ask, "*Why* is the feel of pain identical with such-and-such a brain process?" If the identity-claim is true, then it just has to be accepted as a brute fact about the world. It is a mistake to think that we either should, or could, seek any further explanation.

It is true that identities can't be explained, as such. But it is also true that, if the identity is to count as a successful reduction of the higher-level property involved, then it must be possible to deploy features of the property which figures on the reducing-side of the identity-claim in such a way as to explain the features distinctive of the property on the other side (the reduced property). Consider the identity of water and H_2O again. Don't we think that it must be possible to deploy facts about H_2O, as such, in order to explain the distinctive properties of water – why it is colorless and odorless; why it is liquid at room temperatures; why it boils at 100° Centigrade; and so forth?

Similarly, then, if we were to accept the identity between the feel of pain and some brain state, we would want to know how it is possible to use the latter in explaining the distinctive properties of the former – why it has a subjective aspect; how we can have a recognitional concept for it; why people are inclined to think of it as peculiarly private and "ineffable" (inexpressible); and so forth. But actually, it is very hard to see how any such identity claim could have the resources to provide such explanations, if the claim in question attempts to reduce phenomenal consciousness to properties of a neurological sort.

4.2   First-order representationalism

Many philosophers have recently come to think that the most promising avenue for seeking a reductive explanation of phenomenal consciousness is in terms of a distinctive kind of intentional content, figuring in a distinctive sort of way within the causal architecture of the mind. (Obviously this approach presupposes that intentional content can, in turn, be fully integrated into a physicalist framework, perhaps along one of the lines we investigated briefly in section 3 above. See Figure 8.2 for the resulting layered picture of the mind–brain.) Prominent defenders of this approach have been the two American philosophers Fred Dretske and Michael Tye.

On this view, phenomenally conscious states are a sub-class of

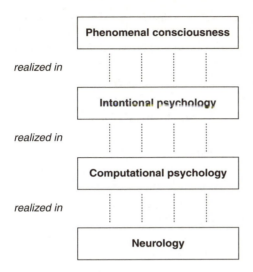

Figure 8.2 How psychology may be physically realized.

intentional, or representational, states. What is distinctive of the sort of intentional content possessed by phenomenally conscious states, however, is that it is *non-conceptual*, or at least *analog* ("fine-grained"), in character. Think of the way in which our visual system presents colors to us. The different hues and shades of color are represented in *immense* detail, which far outstrip our powers of description, categorization, and memory. We can discriminate different shades from one another where we couldn't begin to *describe* the differences, and where we not only lack distinct concepts for the shades of the different kinds, but couldn't even re-identify them after quite a short interval. Nor, it seems, do these color representations depend upon us possessing any concepts for colors of the various sorts. (The colors are discriminated just as well in cultures which lack any color concepts beyond "light" and "dark", for example.) What goes for colors, holds also for shapes, sounds, textures of surfaces, smells, tastes, and so on.

Our senses present us with an immensely rich and fine-grained set of intentional contents, or representations, then. Let us refer to such contents using a sub-scripted "a" for "analog". So vision generates states with the content red_a, which we classify using the comparatively coarse-grained concept *red*; touch generates states with the content $smooth_a$, which we classify using the concept *smooth*; and so on and so forth. But not *any* states with such contents will count as phenomenally conscious, on this approach. For example, there may be states internal to the visual system, at quite an early stage in processing, which carry the content red_a, but which are not thereby conscious. What is distinctive of consciousness, on Tye's account, is that the contents should be available to the processes of conceptual judgment and conceptual thought and reasoning which lead us to form beliefs and plans, and which guide our actions.

This sort of approach has a good many resources available to it for explaining the distinctive features of phenomenal consciousness. Consider *ineffability*, for example. Many people have wanted to say that the *feels* of our conscious states are ineffable, or peculiarly indescribable; and this has seemed to make those properties of *feel* especially mysterious. But representationalist theories have an easy explanation. For our experiences have a fineness of grain to their contents which must slip through the mesh of any conceptual net we attempt to impose on them. My experiences of color are more fine-grained than any color-concepts I possess. In which case I am aware of fine differences which I find myself incapable of describing, other than indexically ("It is the shade of *that* object there"). But there is nothing mysterious here: it is just the result of two distinct kinds of intentional content, one of which is fine-grained (perceptual), and the other of which is coarse-grained or "chunky" (judgment and belief).

Note that, so far, everything in this account is first-order. It is fine-grained representations *of the world* which get to be phenomenally conscious through their availability to thoughts *about the world* and planning directed *at the world*. Higher-order representations only enter the picture when it comes to explaining our capacity for recognizing these analog perceptual contents in ourselves, in introspection. For the concepts which we apply to these states (such as *this experience*) are higher-order ones: they are about the experience itself, rather than about the worldly property represented in the experience. But actually, herewith arises a problem. For if there aren't any higher-order analog contents involved, then all that exists to ground a purely-recognitional judgment of *this experience* [of red], is the analog intentional content red_a. This is a first-order intentional content, appropriate to ground a first-order judgment of *red*. How does it give rise to the higher-order judgment *this experience*?

The point is that our judgments of *this experience* [of red] seem related to the experience (which is, on the intentionalist hypothesis under consideration, none other than the first-order analog content red_a), in just the sort of manner that judgments of *red* are related to redness. That is, they are recognitional judgments grounded in some sort of non-judgmental analog awareness of their objects. When I make judgments about my own experiences, they seem to be presented to me in something like the way that redness is presented to me when I make judgments of color – I am aware of a fineness of grain in what I recognize which slips through the mesh of my conceptual net, for example. But the first-order analog content red_a isn't the right *sort* of content to ground an awareness of the experiential state itself. It can ground recognition of redness, but not experienced-redness. What I am aware of, by virtue of being in a state with the analog content red_a, is redness, not experienced-redness. All the fineness of grain in its content has to do with redness, not with the experience itself.

Another difficulty for first-order representationalist theories is that there is a range of scientific evidence of *non*-conscious perceptual states. (An excellent example is provided by the *two visual systems hypothesis* developed and defended by the psychologists David Milner and Mervyn Goodale, for those who wish to follow this up.) If there are some genuinely perceptual states which have the right sort of fine-grained content, and the right sort of functional role, to count as phenomenally conscious by Tye's account, but which are *not* conscious, then something must be missing from the story. It must be something *else* which explains why some of these perceptual states are phenomenally conscious and some are not.

4.3   Inner sense

The above problems can be overcome if we suppose that some (but only some) of our perceptual states are targeted by *higher-order experiences*, in virtue of which they are phenomenally conscious, and in virtue of which we can form recognitional concepts of them. This view is generally credited to John Locke; its reintroduction into contemporary philosophy is due to David Armstrong. These philosophers hypothesize that, in addition to our normal senses which generate analog representations of the environment and body, we also have an *inner sense*, which scans (some of) the outputs of our first-order senses to generate analog representations of those very states – namely, higher-order experiences, or experiences of experiences. The states which are so scanned will thereby be phenomenally conscious, those which are not will remain *non*-conscious, on this account.

An experience *as of* red, say, is a state with the first-order analog content *red$_a$*. A higher-order experience targeted on that very state, will be one with the second-order analog content *seems red$_a$* or *experience of red$_a$*. Such a higher-order experience can then serve to ground a higher-order recognitional concept. This can either be a recognitional application of the theoretically embedded concept *experience of red*, or it can be a concept which is purely-recognitional. A purely-recognitional concept of experience which is deployed in the presence of, and guided in its application by, a second-order analog content will be a recognition *of* a state of *experience of red$_a$*, but without conceptualizing *as* to what it is – an experience of red.

Inner-sense theory has a number of advantages, then. But one objection to it is this. If there really were such an organ of inner-sense, then it ought to be possible for it to malfunction, just as our first-order senses sometimes do. In that case, it ought to be possible for someone to have a first-order percept with the content *red$_a$* causing a higher-order percept with the content *seems orange$_a$*. Someone in this situation would be disposed to judge, "It is red", immediately and non-inferentially (i.e., not influenced by beliefs about the object's normal color or their own physical state), which would normally be sufficient grounds for us to say that the object seems red to them. But at the same time they would be disposed to judge, "It *seems* orange". Not only does this sort of thing never apparently occur, but the idea that it might do so conflicts with a powerful intuition. This is that our awareness of our own experiences is *immediate*, in such a way that to *believe* that you are undergoing an experience of a certain sort *is* to be undergoing an experience of that sort. But if inner-sense theory is correct, then it ought to be possible for someone to believe that they are in a state of *seeming-orange$_a$* when they are actually in a state of *seeming-red$_a$*.

Another objection to inner-sense theory is an evolutionary one. It is that, on the one hand, the computational demands placed on an organ of inner sense would surely be considerable (perceiving perceptions is going to be a task no easier than perceiving physical objects); and yet, on the other hand, there is no plausible story to be told about the powerful evolutionary pressures which would have been necessary to provide the incentive to build and maintain such an organ.

4.4 Higher-order contents and consumer-semantics

The present author has proposed a version of higher-order experience theory which, he claims, gets all of the benefits of inner-sense theory without any of the associated costs. The idea is to deploy some or other version of *consumer-semantics* to explain how perceptual contents can, by virtue of their availability to a theory of mind system capable of higher-order judgments of experience, come to have, at the same time, higher-order analog contents. On this account, the availability of our perceptual states to a "theory of mind" or "mind-reading" faculty is sufficient to transform the intentional contents of those states. Where before, in the absence of such a faculty, the states had merely first-order contents – containing analog representations of worldly color, texture, shape, and so on – now all of those states will have, at the same time, higher-order analog, experience-representing, contents. Each state which is an analog representation with the content *red*$_a$ is at the same time an analog representation with the content *experience of red*$_a$, in virtue of the fact that the theory of mind system contains concepts of experience which can be applied to those very states.

Here is how the story should go. We begin – both in evolutionary terms and in normal child development – with a set of first-order analog contents available to a variety of down-stream consumer systems. These systems may include a number of dedicated belief-forming faculties, as well as a practical reasoning faculty for figuring out what to do in the light of the perceived environment together with background beliefs and desires. One of these belief-forming systems will be a developing theory of mind system.

When our theory of mind faculty has reached the stage at which it confers on us an understanding of the subjective nature of experience, then we will easily – indeed, trivially – become capable of second-order recognitional judgments of experience, with these judgments riding piggy-back on our first-order recognitional concepts. So if subjects had a recognitional concept *red*, they will now acquire the concept *seems red*, or *experience of red*, knowing (a) that whenever a judgment of "red" is evoked by experience, a judgment of "seems red" is also appropriate on the very same grounds; and (b) that a judgment of "seems red" is still appropriate whenever a disposition to judge "red" has been blocked by considerations to do with abnormal lighting or whatever. Note that at this stage the higher-order concept in question is still a theoretically embedded one, with conceptual connections to worldly redness (it is, after all, a seeming *of red*). What one recognizes the state *as* is a state whose normal cause is worldly redness, and so on.

This change in the down-stream theory of mind consumer system is sufficient to transform all of the contents of experience, rendering them at the same time as higher-order ones. So our perceptual states will not only have the first order analog contents red_a, $green_a$, $loud_a$, $smooth_a$, and so on, but also and at the same time the higher-order analog contents *experience of red_a, experience of $green_a$, experience of $loudness_a$, experience of $smoothness_a$*, and so on. The subject will then be in a position to form recognitional concepts targeted via just these higher-order contents, free of any conceptual ties with worldly redness, greenness, loudness, and smoothness. Once possessed of such concepts, it is possible for the subject to wonder whether other people have experiences of *this* sort when they look at a ripe tomato, to conceive of worlds in which zombies perceive red without undergoing *this experience*, and so on.

Here we have an account of our purely recognitional concepts of experience which appeals to higher-order experiences, but without the need to postulate any sort of organ of inner-sense. So (in contrast with inner-sense theory) there should be no problem in telling some sort of evolutionary story concerning the emergence of higher-order experience. This now reduces to the problem of explaining the emergence of our "theory of mind" capacity, and some or other version of the "Machiavellian intelligence" hypothesis might suffice here (as mentioned in Chapter 7:3). Moreover, it should also be obvious why there can be no question of our higher-order analog contents getting out of line with their first-order counterparts, on this account – in such a way that one might be disposed to make recognitional judgments of *red* and *seems orange* at the same time, for example. This is because the content of the higher-order experience *seems red_a* is parasitic on the content of the first-order experience *red_a*, being formed from it by virtue of the latter's availability to a theory of mind system.

I have had space, here, to give just the very barest sketch of some of the theories which purport to provide a reductive explanation of phenomenal consciousness; and many issues and arguments remain unexplored. But enough has been said, I hope, to make it reasonable for us to believe that consciousness, as well as intentionality, might eventually be fitted smoothly into a physicalist framework.

Conclusion

Physicalism is not just a doctrine, but a thriving research program. Although there are strong reasons to join this program and to accept the physicalist assumption, as we saw in earlier chapters, much work remains to be done in working out the details. Some of this work is narrowly philosophical. But much of it is substantive (broadly empirical), and borders on work in the surrounding cognitive sciences (linguistics, cognitive and developmental psychology, evolutionary theory, artificial intelligence, and so on). For one of the major tasks facing physicalism is to show how mental properties can be integrated into a physicalist framework, and how the range of sciences which deal with human beings and various of their properties (anthropology, psychology, computer science, biology, and so on) can be unified. It is for this reason that much of the most vibrant work in contemporary philosophy of mind is highly interdisciplinary in character, drawing on discoveries and theoretical approaches in surrounding scientific fields. I hope this chapter has left the reader wanting to find out more.

Questions for discussion

1. Could a robot built of metal and silicon ever have a mind?
2. Can we make sense of the idea of reasons as uncaused causes of behavior?
3. Are thoughts structured states, built out of recombinable components? That is to say, is there a "language of thought"?
4. How much progress can we make in understanding how mental states have intentional content by looking at how such states are *caused*, or by looking at how they are *consumed* by other systems?
5. Is the "felt" aspect of phenomenal consciousness really just a matter of a certain sort of (analog) intentional content? And are the relevant contents of a first-order, or of a higher-order, variety?

Further reading

Armstrong, D. (1968) *A Materialist Theory of the Mind*, London: Routledge.

Block, N. (1986) "Advertisement for a semantics for psychology", *Midwest Studies in Philosophy*, vol. 10. Reprinted in Stich, S. and Warfield, T. (eds.) (1994), *Mental Representation*, Oxford: Blackwell.

Block, N. (1995) "A confusion about a function of consciousness", *Behavioral and Brain Sciences*, vol. 18.

Botterill, G. and Carruthers, P. (1999) *The Philosophy of Psychology*, Cambridge: Cambridge University Press, chapters 6–9.

Carruthers, P. (2000) *Phenomenal Consciousness: a naturalistic theory*, Cambridge: Cambridge University Press.

Chalmers, D. (1996) *The Conscious Mind*, Oxford: Oxford University Press.

Copeland, J. (1993) *Artificial Intelligence*, Oxford: Blackwell.

Dennett, D. (1985) *Elbow Room: the varieties of free will worth wanting*, Oxford: Blackwell.

Dennett, D. (1991) *Consciousness Explained*, London: Penguin Press.

Dretske, F. (1995) *Naturalizing the Mind*, Massachusetts: MIT Press.

Fodor, J. (1975) *The Language of Thought*, Brighton: Harvester Press.

Fodor, J. (1990) *A Theory of Content and Other Essays*, Massachusetts: MIT Press.

Frankfurt, H. (1971) "Freedom of the will and the concept of a person", *Journal of Philosophy*, vol. 68. Reprinted in Watson, G. (ed.) (1982), *Free Will*, Oxford: Oxford University Press.

Millikan, R. (1989) "Biosemantics", *Journal of Philosophy*, vol. 86. Reprinted Macdonald, C. and Macdonald, G. (eds.) (1995), *Philosophy of Psychology*, Oxford: Blackwell; in Millikan, R. (ed.) (1993) *White Queen Psychology and Other Essays for Alice*, Massachusetts: MIT Press; and in Stich, S. and Warfield, T. (eds.) (1994), *Mental Representation*, Oxford: Blackwell.

Milner, D. and Goodale, M. (1995) *The Visual Brain in Action*, Oxford: Oxford University Press.

Searle, J. (1980) "Minds, machines and programs", *Behavioral and Brain Sciences*, vol. 3. Reprinted in Hofstadter, D. and Dennett, D. (eds.) (1981) *The Mind's I*, Brighton: Harvester Press.

Turing, A. (1950) "Computing machinery and intelligence", *Mind*, vol. 59. Reprinted in Hofstadter, D. and Dennett, D. (eds.) (1981), *The Mind's I*, Brighton: Harvester Press.

Tye, M. (1995) *Ten Problems of Consciousness*, Massachusetts: MIT Press.

van Inwagen, P. (1983) *An Essay on Free Will*, Oxford: Oxford University Press.

Watson, G. (1975) "Free agency", *Journal of Philosophy*, vol. 72. Reprinted in Watson, G. (ed.) (1982), *Free Will*, Oxford: Oxford University Press.

Index

303